SHERIDAN'S THREE PLAYS

No. 203

R. B. SHERIDAN

From a pen-drawing by E. Heber Thompson

SHERIDAN'S
THREE PLAYS

THE RIVALS: THE SCHOOL FOR SCANDAL: THE CRITIC

Selected and Edited by
A. J. J. RATCLIFF M.A.

NELSON

THOMAS NELSON AND SONS LTD
36 Park Street London W1
Parkside Works Edinburgh 9
117 Latrobe Street Melbourne C1
10 Warehouse Road Apapa Lagos

THOMAS NELSON AND SONS (AFRICA) (Pty) LTD
P.O. Box 9881 Johannesburg

THOMAS NELSON AND SONS (CANADA) LTD
81 Curlew Drive Don Mills Ontario

THOMAS NELSON AND SONS
Copewood and Davis Streets Camden 3, N.J.

SOCIÉTÉ FRANÇAISE D'ÉDITIONS NELSON
97 rue Monge Paris 5

First published November 1937
Reprinted 1939, 1945, 1947, 1949, 1950
1951, 1956, 1959, 1960, 1964

CONTENTS

"'On my conscience,' Goldsmith writes, 'I believe we have all forgot to laugh in these days.' Outside Goldsmith and Sheridan the eighteenth century can show no comedy at which a man could conceivably laugh. It was not done; and it was not easy to persuade people that it should be done."—H. W. GARROD.

GENERAL INTRODUCTION

THE AUTHOR

His disposition.—Sheridan was not, like Sir Walter Scott and William Morris, of a schoolboyish disposition ; he was sophisticated, that is, worldly-wise. He liked brilliant society and brilliant repartee. He was a master of sarcasm and epigram. He knew people's faults and foibles, and was too well aware of them to go off into raptures about their virtues. He lived life as if acting in a polished play, and exercised a great actor's charm to cajole and persuade. He was a " fine gentleman," a man-about-town, a wit, a worldling. Generous, extravagant, undependable, on that side he was a " romantic " ; but on no other side. He had social sense too strongly to cultivate personal feelings, or to set much store on reality either. So that although his personages have none of the romance of Shakespeare's, they are just as far from the people we see every day as are Rosalind and Beatrice. Instead of direct poetry, they speak the inverted poetry of drawing-room wit. In fact, they are " modern " as Shakespeare's personages are not. They closely resemble the figures in Noel Coward's or Frederick Lonsdale's comedies.

Birth.—Richard Brinsley Sheridan was born in Dublin, 1751. He came of witty and talented stock. His clerical grandfather, friend of Dean Swift, had published *The Art of Punning*. His father, Thomas Sheridan, also a Dubliner, had acted Hamlet at Covent Garden, been manager of the Theatre Royal,

Dublin, and written a popular play, *Captain O'Blunder*. His mother, Frances, at fifteen had written a two-volume story, and later had had two comedies produced at Drury Lane, *The Discovery* and *The Dupe*.

School, and life in Bath.—At eleven, Richard Brinsley entered Harrow School, where he was popular through his confident air and wit. His mother died. His father settled in Bath. There Sheridan mixed with the " best people," and lived somewhat the life of Jack Absolute. He fell in love with a celebrated singer, Miss Linley, the Maid of Bath, who had had £3,000 settled on her by her former fiancé on the breaking of their engagement. Pestered by the attentions of a married man, Captain Matthews, Miss Linley was escorted for safety to a nunnery in France. It was young Sheridan who escorted her—and married her secretly on the way. In the *Bath Chronicle* the jealous captain inserted nasty insinuations about the departed pair. Sheridan, returning to England, responded by a challenge, and fought a duel with Matthews in Hyde Park. The duel was extremely unprofessional, but Sheridan cared little for that, as he managed at the point of the sword to extort an apology from his opponent. Matthews withdrew to his estate in Wales, where, however, the embers of his wrath were fanned by an Irishman of the O'Trigger type, and he issued a fresh challenge. Sheridan accepted, and fought his man in Bath. Tipsy at the time, he commandeered Matthews' chaise to drive to the duelling place, and fought violently, but was soon disarmed and ordered to beg for his life. " No, by God I won't," he declared ; and was saved by the intervention of the seconds. The affair was over.

When Miss Linley in her French nunnery heard the news of the duel, she let the cat out of the bag by exclaiming, " My husband ! My husband ! "

London.—Sheridan had no income. He spent

his wife's £3,000, however, on a fashionable London house and lavish entertainment. The money soon went ; and wishing to live henceforth by his own exertions, he looked round for a means of earning money. He found this in writing a play, *The Rivals*. He was twenty-three.

THE RIVALS

INTRODUCTION TO "THE RIVALS"

Presentation.—Talent without experience is useless on the stage. The first draft of *The Rivals* was clumsy and far too long. Nevertheless, it was produced at Covent Garden on January 17, 1775. The inevitable failure occurred. Sheridan withdrew the play, sought help of the manager, cut the text drastically, found a better actor for O'Trigger (a failure at the first show), and had the good fortune of a fresh presentation on the 28th. This time *The Rivals* was a success.

Kind of play.—It is a Comedy of Manners (or classical comedy) mixed with some farcical incidents and exaggerated character-types.[1] It deals with a very old subject, the conflict between father and son over the question of the son's choice of a wife ; and with very old situations like those of mistaken identity and family rows. The hero, Captain Absolute, is a schemer with a full share of self-assurance, but generous at heart, who loves Lydia Languish, a *poseuse* who has caught the prevailing sentimental fashion and decides to marry beneath her, for worth, not birth. As the complex plot is unfolding rapidly, the spectator is tickled with the sight of both young and old unconsciously working for the same end, and frustrating each other all the time through ludicrous misunderstandings. Other lovers of Lydia (the country coward Acres, the town gallant O'Trigger) come in at odd angles to the central plot, while a parallel interest (or contrast pattern) arises from the sensible Julia's troubles with her lover, the spoilt-

---

[1] This last feature goes back to the Comedy of Humours of Ben Jonson (1572-1637).

baby Faulkland. All the characters are stock types, but they are vastly amusing in the situations of the play.

The basis of society manners is observable not only in the incidental details of circulating library books, Mrs. Malaprop's efforts to talk like a blue-stocking, Acres's to swear like a gentleman, the servants' townish affectation (with David for contrast), and the daily routine of Bath in the season, but over all in the tone of the play, which sets up the gentlemanly ease of Captain Absolute as the ideal against freakish excitables like Sir Anthony, Faulkland, and Acres, and stamps its approval on polish and wit in conversation against affectation and dullness. The play is all for the " well-bred."

As for the Julia-Faulkland episodes, they seem out of keeping with the high spirits and detached caricature of the rest. They are, in fact, regarded differently by different critics : as either genuinely sentimental—sympathetic and a sop to the audience which was used to sentiment—or as mock-sentimental in an attack on the mode of the day. There is no final authority on the subject. But the relation of Sheridan to the dramatic fashion of the period may help the reader to make up his own mind.

Eighteenth-century Comedy

It is a far cry from Shakespeare's Romantic Comedy of Love (*e.g. As You Like It*) to the kind of comedy put on the boards after the reopening of the theatres in London at the Restoration, 1660. The court had known exile in France, and had grown to prefer French classical comedy, like Molière's—in prose, sarcastic, with few or no sympathetic personages, and worked up round the mockery of some folly of fashion or character (*e.g.* bluestockings or a miser).

Such comedy for some time flourished in England, and was polished, witty, and often licentious; its favourite topic adultery. It was comedy of the Smart Set only, and brilliant; and at the very time when actresses first took women's parts, it was comedy immodestly frank about sex.

In 1698 the Rev. Jeremy Collier attacked this laxity of moral tone in his *Short View of the Profaneness and Immorality of the English Stage*, and initiated a counter-movement. The pendulum gradually swung from the cynically aristocratic to the sentimentally middle-class, and from society intrigues to domestic themes.

One of the first playwrights to produce a sentimental comedy was Steele.[1] The "improving" tone was marked at every turn by a "sentiment," or unctuous moralizing remark. "If a man was to be hanged or married, out came a sentiment. If the butler was drunk or the chambermaid impudent, listen to a sentiment."[2] As the eighteenth century advanced the sentimental note grew stronger, till comedy tended to the tearful.

However, in 1773 Oliver Goldsmith tilted at the prevailing fashion in his boldly comic *She Stoops to Conquer*. He made a palpable hit. Sheridan followed him, in *The Rivals*, in a deliberate move towards high comedy; which seems to support the theory that the Julia-Faulkland scenes were written by Sheridan with his tongue in his cheek.

One last point. Because of the racy humour, it is possible to make a rustic noodle of Acres and an ill-bred nitwit of Mrs. Malaprop. But that would be a mistake. Sheridan is writing polished society comedy, not farce. Acres is, after all, a squire, and Mrs. Malaprop a woman of refinement; and the exaggeration should be discreet.

---

[1] *e.g. The Funeral* (1701).
[2] Parson Adams in Fielding's *Joseph Andrews*, a novel (1742).

INTRODUCTION TO "THE RIVALS"

SOURCES OF "THE RIVALS"

The prime source is obviously Sheridan's own experience of his circle in Bath. But he had many literary models and suggestions. There were Restoration and later plays with situations in this or that element resembling those in *The Rivals*. Similarly with dialogue, in which Goldsmith was an influence. For Mrs. Malaprop there were Shakespeare's Dogberry, Fielding's Mrs. Slipslop, and Sheridan's mother's Mrs. Tryfort (in *A Journey to Bath*, a novel). Acres and David go back to Goldsmith, Sir Lucius to Cumberland's O'Flaherty. Other characters go back as far as Latin comedy. But the sum total of *The Rivals* is unlike all the previous hints put together, or like any one else's play, and is characteristically Sheridan's own—lively, half-impudent, crisp, full of incident.

THE RIVALS

DRAMATIS PERSONÆ

(As originally acted at Covent Garden Theatre in 1775)

SIR ANTHONY ABSOLUTE . . .		Mr. Shuter
CAPTAIN ABSOLUTE		Mr. Woodward
FAULKLAND		Mr. Lewis
ACRES		Mr. Quick
SIR LUCIUS O'TRIGGER . . .		Mr. Lee
FAG		Mr. Lee Lewes
DAVID		Mr. Dunstal
COACHMAN (THOMAS) . . .		Mr. Fearon
MRS. MALAPROP		Mrs. Green
LYDIA LANGUISH		Miss Barsanti
JULIA		Mrs. Bulkley
LUCY		Mrs. Lessingham

Maid, Boy, Servants, etc.

SCENE.—Bath.
TIME OF ACTION.—Within one day.

THE RIVALS

ACT I

SCENE I. *A Street in Bath.*

(*Coachman* [*Thomas*] *crosses the stage. Enter Fag, looking after him.*)

Fag. What! Thomas!—sure 'tis he?—What! Thomas! Thomas!

Thomas. Hey!—Odd's life! Mr. Fag!—give us your hand, my old fellow-servant.

Fag. Excuse my glove, Thomas:—I'm devilish glad to see you, my lad. Why, my prince of charioteers, you look as hearty—but who the deuce thought of seeing you in Bath?

Thomas. Sure, master, Madam Julia, Harry, Mrs. Kate, and the postillion, be all come.

Fag. Indeed!

Thomas. Ay, master thought another fit of the gout was coming to make him a visit;—so he'd a mind to gi't the slip, and whip! we were all off at an hour's warning.

Fag. Ay, ay, hasty in everything, or it would not be Sir Anthony Absolute!

Thomas. But tell us, Mr. Fag, how does young master? Odd! Sir Anthony will stare to see the Captain here!

Fag. I do not serve Captain Absolute now.

Odd's life, For "God's life."
Postillion, Who rides the near-horse of the leading pair. (The coachman drives the rest.)

Thomas. Why sure !

Fag. At present I am employed by Ensign Beverley.

Thomas. I doubt, Mr. Fag, you ha'n't changed for the better.

Fag. I have not changed, Thomas.

Thomas. No ! Why, didn't you say you had left young master ?

Fag. No.—Well, honest Thomas, I must puzzle you no further :—briefly then—Captain Absolute and Ensign Beverley are one and the same person.

Thomas. The devil they are !

Fag. So it is indeed, Thomas ; and the *ensign* half of my master being on guard at present—the *captain* has nothing to do with me.

Thomas. So, so !—What, this is some freak, I warrant !—Do tell us, Mr. Fag, the meaning o't— you know I ha' trusted you.

Fag. You'll be secret, Thomas ?

Thomas. As a coach-horse.

Fag. Why then the cause of all this is—Love,— Love, Thomas, who (as you may get read to you) has been a masquerader ever since the days of Jupiter.

Thomas. Ay, ay ;—I guessed there was a lady in the case ;—but pray, why does your master pass only for *ensign* ? — Now if he had shammed *general* indeed——

Fag. Ah ! Thomas, there lies the mystery o' the matter. Hark'ee, Thomas, my master is in love with a lady of a very singular taste : a lady who likes him better as a *half-pay ensign* than if she knew he was son and heir to Sir Anthony Absolute, a baronet of three thousand a year.

Thomas. That is an odd taste indeed !—But has she got the stuff, Mr. Fag ? Is she rich, hey ?

Fag. Rich !—Why, I believe she owns half the

Ensign, Now Second Lieutenant.

stocks! Zounds! Thomas, she could pay the national debt as easily as I could my washerwoman! She has a lapdog that eats out of gold,—she feeds her parrot with small pearls,—and all her thread-papers are made of banknotes.

Thomas. Bravo, faith!—Odd! I warrant she has a set of thousands at least:—but does she draw kindly with the captain?

Fag. As fond as pigeons.

Thomas. May one hear her name?

Fag. Miss Lydia Languish.—But there is an old tough aunt in the way; though, by-the-bye, she has never seen my master—for we got acquainted with miss while on a visit in Gloucestershire.

Thomas. Well—I wish they were once harnessed together in matrimony.—But pray, Mr. Fag, what kind of a place is this Bath?—I ha' heard a deal of it—here's a mort o' merry-making, hey?

Fag. Pretty well, Thomas, pretty well—'tis a good lounge; in the morning we go to the pump-room (though neither my master nor I drink the waters); after breakfast we saunter on the parades, or play a game at billiards; at night we dance; but damn the place, I'm tired of it: their regular hours stupefy me—not a fiddle nor a card after eleven!—However, Mr. Faulkland's gentleman and I keep it up a little in private parties;—I'll introduce you there, Thomas —you'll like him much.

Thomas. Sure I know Mr. Du Peigne—you know his master is to marry Madam Julia.

Fag. I had forgot.—But, Thomas, you must polish a little—indeed you must.—Here now—this wig!— What the devil do you do with a *wig*, Thomas?— None of the London whips of any degree of *ton* wear *wigs now*.

Thread-paper, A scrap of paper to wrap up a skein of thread.
A set of thousands, A team of six horses, worth thousands.
Ton, Fashion, style.

Thomas. More's the pity ! more's the pity, I say.
—Odd's life ! when I heard how the lawyers and
doctors had took to their own hair, I thought how
'twould go next:—odd rabbit it ! when the fashion
had got foot on the bar, I guessed 'twould mount to
the box !—but 'tis all out of character, believe me,
Mr. Fag : and look'ee, I'll never gi' up mine—the
lawyers and doctors may do as they will.

Fag. Well, Thomas, we'll not quarrel about that.

Thomas. Why, bless you, the gentlemen of the
professions ben't all of a mind—for in our village
now, thoff Jack Gauge, the exciseman, has ta'en to
his carrots, there's little Dick the farrier swears he'll
never forsake his bob, though all the college should
appear with their own heads !

Fag. Indeed ! well said, Dick !—But hold—mark !
mark, Thomas !

Thomas. Zooks ! 'tis the captain.—Is that the lady
with him ?

Fag. No, no, that is Madam Lucy, my master's
mistress's maid. They lodge at that house—but I
must after him to tell him the news.

Thomas. Odd ! he's giving her money !—Well, Mr.
Fag——

Fag. Good-bye, Thomas. I have an appointment
in Gyde's Porch this evening at eight ; meet me
there, and we'll make a little party.

(*Exeunt severally.*)

Rabbit, Confound (Fr. Rabattre).
Bar, For climbing up to the *box*-seat.
Thoff, Though.
A gauger was an official who measured the contents of casks for
  assessment of duty. The *exciseman* was the inspector.
College, Viz., of Veterinary Surgeons.
Zooks, Gadzooks, God's hooks (the nails in Christ's hands and feet).
Gyde's Porch, Assembly rooms with a large card-room.

SCENE II. *A Dressing-room in Mrs. Malaprop's Lodgings.*

(*Lydia sitting on a sofa, with a book in her hand. Lucy has just returned from a message.*)

Lucy. Indeed, ma'am, I traversed half the town in search of it : I don't believe there's a circulating library in Bath I ha'n't been at.

Lydia. And could not you get *The Reward of Constancy* ?

Lucy. No, indeed, ma'am.

Lydia. Nor *The Fatal Connexion* ?

Lucy. No, indeed, ma'am.

Lydia. Nor *The Mistakes of the Heart* ?

Lucy. Ma'am, as ill luck would have it, Mr. Bull said Miss Sukey Saunter had just fetched it away.

Lydia. Heigh-ho !—Did you inquire for *The Delicate Distress* ?

Lucy. Or, *The Memoirs of Lady Woodford* ? Yes, indeed, ma'am. I asked everywhere for it ; and I might have brought it from Mr. Frederick's, but Lady Slattern Lounger, who had just sent it home, had so soiled and dog's-eared it, it wa'n't fit for a Christian to read.

Lydia. Heigh-ho !—Yes, I always know when Lady Slattern has been before me. She has a most observing thumb ; and, I believe, cherishes her nails for the convenience of making marginal notes.—Well, child, what *have* you brought me ?

Lucy. Oh ! here, ma'am.—(*Taking books from under her cloak, and from her pockets.*) This is *The Gordian Knot*,—and this *Peregrine Pickle*. Here are *The Tears of Sensibility*, and *Humphrey Clinker*. This is *The Memoirs of a Lady of Quality, written by herself*, and here the second volume of *The Sentimental Journey*.

23

Lydia. Heigh-ho !—What are those books by the glass ?

Lucy. The great one is only *The Whole Duty of Man*, where I press a few blonds, ma'am.

Lydia. Very well—give me the *sal volatile*.

Lucy. Is it in a blue cover, ma'am ?

Lydia. My smelling-bottle, you simpleton !

Lucy. Oh, the drops !—here, ma'am.

Lydia. Hold !—here's some one coming—quick, see who it is.—(*Exit Lucy.*) Surely I heard my cousin Julia's voice.

(*Re-enter Lucy.*)

Lucy. Lud ! ma'am, here is Miss Melville.

Lydia. Is it possible !—   (*Exit Lucy.*)

(*Enter Julia.*)

Lydia. My dearest Julia, how delighted am I !—(*Embrace.*) How unexpected was this happiness !

Julia. True, Lydia—and our pleasure is the greater.—But what has been the matter ?—you were denied to me at first !

Lydia. Ah, Julia, I have a thousand things to tell you !—But first inform me what has conjured you to Bath ?—Is Sir Anthony here ?

Julia. He is—we are arrived within this hour !—and I suppose he will be here to wait on Mrs. Malaprop as soon as he is dressed.

Lydia. Then before we are interrupted, let me impart to you some of my distress !—I know your gentle nature will sympathize with me, though your prudence may condemn me ! My letters have informed you of my whole connection with Beverley ; but I have lost him, Julia ! My aunt has discovered our intercourse by a note she intercepted, and has confined me ever since ! Yet, would you believe it ? she has fallen absolutely in love with a tall Irish baronet she met one night since we have been here, at Lady Macshuffle's rout.

Julia. You jest, Lydia !

24

Lydia. No, upon my word.—She really carries on a kind of correspondence with him, under a feigned name though, till she chooses to be known to him ;—but it is a Delia or a Celia, I assure you.

Julia. Then, surely, she is now more indulgent to her niece.

Lydia. Quite the contrary. Since she has discovered her own frailty, she is become more suspicious of mine ! Then I must inform you of another plague !—That odious Acres is to be in Bath to-day ; so that I protest I shall be teased out of all spirits !

Julia. Come, come, Lydia, hope for the best—Sir Anthony shall use his interest with Mrs. Malaprop.

Lydia. But you have not heard the worst. Unfortunately I had quarrelled with my poor Beverley, just before my aunt made the discovery, and I have not seen him since, to make it up.

Julia. What was his offence ?

Lydia. Nothing at all !—But, I don't know how it was, as often as we had been together, we had never had a quarrel, and, somehow, I was afraid he would never give me an opportunity. So, last Thursday, I wrote a letter to myself, to inform myself that Beverley was at that time paying his addresses to another woman. I signed it *your Friend unknown*, showed it to Beverley, charged him with his falsehood, put myself in a violent passion, and vowed I'd never see him more.

Julia. And you let him depart so, and have not seen him since ?

Lydia. 'Twas the next day my aunt found the matter out. I intended only to have teased him three days and a half, and now I've lost him for ever.

Julia. If he is as deserving and sincere as you have represented him to me, he will never give you up so. Yet consider, Lydia, you tell me he is but an ensign, and you have thirty thousand pounds.

Lydia. But you know I lose most of my fortune if

I marry without my aunt's consent, till of age; and that is what I have determined to do, ever since I knew the penalty. Nor could I love the man who would wish to wait a day for the alternative.

Julia. Nay, this is caprice!

Lydia. What, does Julia tax me with caprice?—I thought her lover Faulkland had inured her to it.

Julia. I do not love even *his* faults.

Lydia. But apropos—you have sent to him, I suppose?

Julia. Not yet, upon my word—nor has he the least idea of my being in Bath. Sir Anthony's resolution was so sudden, I could not inform him of it.

Lydia. Well, Julia, you are your own mistress (though under the protection of Sir Anthony), yet have you, for this long year, been a slave to the caprice, the whim, the jealousy of this ungrateful Faulkland, who will ever delay assuming the right of a husband, while you suffer him to be equally imperious as a lover.

Julia. Nay, you are wrong entirely. We were contracted before my father's death. That, and some consequent embarrassments, have delayed what I know to be my Faulkland's most ardent wish. He is too generous to trifle on such a point:—and for his character, you wrong him there too. No, Lydia, he is too proud, too noble to be jealous; if he is captious, 'tis without dissembling; if fretful, without rudeness. Unused to the fopperies of love, he is negligent of the little duties expected from a lover— but being unhackneyed in the passion, his affection is ardent and sincere: and as it engrosses his whole soul, he expects every thought and emotion of his mistress to move in unison with his. Yet, though his pride calls for this full return, his humility makes him undervalue those qualities in him which would entitle him to it; and not feeling why he should be loved to the degree he wishes, he still suspects that he is not loved enough. This temper, I must own, has cost me many unhappy hours ; but I have learned to think myself his debtor, for those imperfections which arise from the ardour of his attachment.

Lydia. Well, I cannot blame you for defending him. But tell me candidly, Julia, had he never saved your life, do you think you should have been attached to him as you are?—Believe me, the rude blast that overset your boat was a prosperous gale of love to him.

Julia. Gratitude may have strengthened my attachment to Mr. Faulkland, but I loved him before he had preserved me ; yet surely that alone were an obligation sufficient.

Lydia. Obligation ! why a water spaniel would have done as much !—Well, I should never think of giving my heart to a man because he could swim.

Julia. Come, Lydia, you are too inconsiderate.

Lydia. Nay, I do but jest. What's here ?
(*Enter Lucy in a hurry.*)

Lucy. O ma'am, here is Sir Anthony Absolute just come home with your aunt.

Lydia. They'll not come here.—Lucy, do you watch. (*Exit Lucy.*)

Julia. Yes, I must go. Sir Anthony does not know I am here, and if we meet, he'll detain me, to show me the town. I'll take another opportunity of paying my respects to Mrs. Malaprop, when she shall treat me, as long as she chooses, with her select words so ingeniously *misapplied*, without being *mispronounced*.
(*Re-enter Lucy.*)

Lucy. O Lud ! ma'am, they are both coming upstairs.

Lydia. Well, I'll not detain you, coz.—Adieu, my dear Julia, I'm sure you are in haste to send to Faulkland.—There—through my room you'll find another staircase.

Julia. Adieu ! (*Embrace. Exit Julia.*)

Lydia. Here, my dear Lucy, hide these books.

Quick, quick.—Fling *Peregrine Pickle* under the toilet—throw *Roderick Random* into the closet—thrust *Lord Aimworth* under the sofa—cram *Ovid* behind the bolster—there—put *The Man of Feeling* into your pocket—so, so—now lay *Mrs. Chapone* in sight, and leave *Fordyce's* Sermons open on the table.

Lucy. O burn it, ma'am ! the hairdresser has torn away as far as *Proper Pride.*

Lydia. Never mind—open at *Sobriety.*—Fling me *Lord Chesterfield's Letters.*—Now for 'em.

(Exit Lucy.)

(Enter Mrs. Malaprop and Sir Anthony Absolute.)

Mrs. Malaprop. There, Sir Anthony, there sits the deliberate simpleton who wants to disgrace her family, and lavish herself on a fellow not worth a shilling.

Lydia. Madam, I thought you once——

Mrs. Malaprop. You thought, miss ! I don't know any business you have to think at all—thought does not become a young woman. But the point we would request of you is, that you will promise to forget this fellow—to illiterate him, I say, quite from your memory.

Lydia. Ah, madam ! our memories are independent of our wills. It is not so easy to forget.

Mrs. Malaprop. But I say it is, miss ; there is nothing on earth so easy as to *forget*, if a person chooses to set about it. I'm sure I have as much forgot your poor dear uncle as if he had never existed—and I thought it my duty so to do ; and let me tell you, Lydia, these violent memories don't become a young woman.

Sir Anthony. Why sure she won't pretend to remember what she's ordered not !—ay, this comes of her reading !

Lydia. What crime, madam, have I committed, to be treated thus ?

Mrs. Chapone, Authoress of *Letters on the Improvement of the Mind.*

Mrs. Malaprop. Now don't attempt to extirpate yourself from the matter ; you know I have proof controvertible of it.—But tell me, will you promise to do as you're bid ? Will you take a husband of your friends' choosing ?

Lydia. Madam, I must tell you plainly, that had I no preference for any one else, the choice you have made would be my aversion.

Mrs. Malaprop. What business have you, miss, with *preference* and *aversion* ? They don't become a young woman ; and you ought to know, that as both always wear off, 'tis safest in matrimony to begin with a little *aversion.* I am sure I hated your poor dear uncle before marriage as if he had been a blacka-moor—and yet, miss, you are sensible what a wife I made !—and when it pleased Heaven to release me from him, 'tis unknown what tears I shed !—But suppose we were going to give you another choice, will you promise us to give up this Beverley ?

Lydia. Could I belie my thoughts so far as to give that promise, my actions would certainly as far belie my words.

Mrs. Malaprop. Take yourself to your room.— You are fit company for nothing but your own ill-humours.

Lydia. Willingly, ma'am—I cannot change for the worse.   (*Exit Lydia.*)

Mrs. Malaprop. There's a little intricate hussy for you.

Sir Anthony. It is not to be wondered at, ma'am, —all this is the natural consequence of teaching girls to read. Had I a thousand daughters, by Heaven ! I'd as soon have them taught the black art as their alphabet !

Mrs. Malaprop. Nay, nay, Sir Anthony, you are an absolute misanthropy.

Black art, Sorcery, magic.

29

Sir Anthony. In my way hither, Mrs. Malaprop, I observed your niece's maid coming forth from a circulating library !—She had a book in each hand— they were half-bound volumes, with marble covers ! —From that moment I guessed how full of duty I should see her mistress !

Mrs. Malaprop. Those are vile places, indeed !

Sir Anthony. Madam, a circulating library in a town is as an evergreen tree of diabolical knowledge ! It blossoms through the year !—And depend on it, Mrs. Malaprop, that they who are so fond of handling the leaves will long for the fruit at last.

Mrs. Malaprop. Fy, fy, Sir Anthony ! you surely speak laconically.

Sir Anthony. Why, Mrs. Malaprop, in moderation now, what would you have a woman know ?

Mrs. Malaprop. Observe me, Sir Anthony. I would by no means wish a daughter of mine to be a progeny of learning ; I don't think so much learning becomes a young woman ; for instance, I would never let her meddle with Greek, or Hebrew, or Algebra, or simony, or fluxions, or paradoxes, or such inflammatory branches of learning—neither would it be necessary for her to handle any of your mathematical, astronomical, diabolical instruments.—But, Sir Anthony, I would send her, at nine years old, to a boarding-school, in order to learn a little ingenuity and artifice. Then, sir, she should have a supercilious knowledge in accounts ;—and as she grew up, I would have her instructed in geometry that she might know something of the contagious countries ;—but above all, Sir Anthony, she should be mistress of orthodoxy, that she might not mis-spell, and mispronounce words so shamefully as girls usually do ; and likewise that she might reprehend the true meaning of what she

Simony, Obtaining good church posts by bribery. A wild guess at a word.
Fluxions, Perhaps for fractions.   *Inflammatory,* Informative.

is saying. This, Sir Anthony, is what I would have a woman know ;—and I don't think there is a superstitious article in it.

Sir Anthony. Well, well, Mrs. Malaprop, I will dispute the point no further with you ; though I must confess, that you are a truly moderate and polite arguer, for almost every third word you say is on my side of the question. But, Mrs. Malaprop, to the more important point in debate—you say you have no objection to my proposal ?

Mrs. Malaprop. None, I assure you. I am under no positive engagement with Mr. Acres, and as Lydia is so obstinate against him, perhaps your son may have better success.

Sir Anthony. Well, madam, I will write for the boy directly. He knows not a syllable of this yet, though I have for some time had the proposal in my head. He is at present with his regiment.

Mrs. Malaprop. We have never seen your son, Sir Anthony ; but I hope no objection on his side.

Sir Anthony. Objection !—let him object if he dare !—No, no, Mrs. Malaprop, Jack knows that the least demur puts me in a frenzy directly. My process was always very simple—in their younger days, 'twas " Jack, do this " ;—if he demurred, I knocked him down—and if he grumbled at that, I always sent him out of the room.

Mrs. Malaprop. Ay, and the properest way, o' my conscience !—nothing is so conciliating to young people as severity.—Well, Sir Anthony, I shall give Mr. Acres his discharge, and prepare Lydia to receive your son's invocations ;—and I hope you will represent *her* to the captain as an object not altogether illegible.

Sir Anthony. Madam, I will handle the subject prudently.—Well, I must leave you ; and let me beg you, Mrs. Malaprop, to enforce this matter roundly to the girl.—Take my advice—keep a tight hand : if she rejects this proposal, clap her under lock and key ; and if you were just to let the servants forget to bring her dinner for three or four days, you can't conceive how she'd come about.   (*Exit Sir Anthony Absolute.*)

Mrs. Malaprop. Well, at any rate I shall be glad to get her from under my intuition.   She has somehow discovered my partiality for Sir Lucius O'Trigger— sure, Lucy can't have betrayed me !—No, the girl is such a simpleton, I should have made her confess it.—Lucy !—Lucy !—(*Calls.*)   Had she been one of your artificial ones, I should never have trusted her.

(*Enter Lucy.*)

Lucy. Did you call, ma'am ?

Mrs. Malaprop. Yes, girl.—Did you see Sir Lucius while you was out ?

Lucy. No, indeed, ma'am, not a glimpse of him.

Mrs. Malaprop. You are sure, Lucy, that you never mentioned——

Lucy. Oh gemini !   I'd sooner cut my tongue out.

Mrs. Malaprop. Well, don't let your simplicity be imposed on.

Lucy. No, ma'am.

Mrs. Malaprop. So, come to me presently, and I'll give you another letter to Sir Lucius ; but mind, Lucy—if ever you betray what you are entrusted with (unless it be other people's secrets to me), you forfeit my malevolence for ever ; and your being a simpleton shall be no excuse for your locality.

(*Exit Mrs. Malaprop.*)

Lucy. Ha ! ha ! ha !—So, my dear *simplicity*, let me give you a little respite.—(*Altering her manner.*) Let girls in my station be as fond as they please of appearing expert and knowing in their trusts ; commend me to a mask of *silliness*, and a pair of sharp eyes for my own interest under it !—Let me see to what account have I turned my *simplicity* lately.—

Gemini, The twins, *i.e.* Castor and Pollux.

(*Looks at a paper.*) For *abetting Miss Lydia Languish in a design of running away with an ensign !—in money, sundry times, twelve pound twelve ; gowns, five ; hats, ruffles, caps, etc., etc., numberless !—From the said ensign, within this last month, six guineas and a half.*—About a quarter's pay !—Item, *from Mrs. Malaprop, for betraying the young people to her*—when I found matters were likely to be discovered !—*two guineas, and a black paduasoy.*—Item, *from Mr. Acres, for carrying divers letters*—which I never delivered—*two guineas, and a pair of buckles.*—Item, *from Sir Lucius O'Trigger, three crowns, two gold pocket-pieces, and a silver snuff-box !*—Well done, *simplicity !* Yet I was forced to make my Hibernian believe that he was corresponding, not with the *Aunt*, but with the *Niece* : for though not over rich, I found he had too much pride and delicacy to sacrifice the feelings of a gentleman to the necessities of his fortune. (*Exit.*)

Paduasoy, Rich silk coming originally from Padua.
Pocket-pieces, Pieces of money no longer current, but kept in the pocket for luck.

END OF THE FIRST ACT

ACT II

SCENE I. *Captain Absolute's Lodgings.*

(Captain Absolute and Fag.)

Fag. Sir, while I was there Sir Anthony came in : I told him you had sent me to inquire after his health, and to know if he was at leisure to see you.

Absolute. And what did he say on hearing I was at Bath ?

Fag. Sir, in my life, I never saw an elderly gentleman more astonished ! He started back two or three paces, rapped out a dozen interjectural oaths, and asked what the devil had brought you here.

Absolute. Well, sir, and what did you say ?

Fag. Oh, I lied, sir—I forget the precise lie ; but you may depend on't he got no truth from me. Yet, with submission, for fear of blunders in future, I should be glad to fix what *has* brought us to Bath ; in order that we may lie a little consistently. Sir Anthony's servants were curious, sir, very curious indeed.

Absolute. You have said nothing to them ?

Fag. Oh, not a word, sir,—not a word ! Mr. Thomas, indeed, the coachman (whom I take to be the discreetest of whips)——

Absolute. 'Sdeath !—you rascal ! you have not trusted him !

Fag. Oh, no, sir—no—no—not a syllable, upon my veracity !—He was, indeed, a little inquisitive ; but I was sly, sir—devilish sly ! My master (said I), honest Thomas (you know, sir, one says *honest* to one's inferiors), is come to Bath to *recruit*—Yes, sir, I said to *recruit*—and whether for men, money, or constitution, you know, sir, is nothing to him, nor anyone else.

Absolute. Well, *recruit* will do—let it be so.

Fag. Oh, sir, recruit will do surprisingly—indeed, to give the thing an air, I told Thomas that your honour had already enlisted five disbanded chairmen, seven minority waiters, and thirteen billiard-markers.

Absolute. You blockhead, never say more than is necessary.

Fag. I beg pardon, sir—I beg pardon—but, with submission, a lie is nothing unless one supports it. Sir, whenever I draw on my invention for a good current lie, I always forge indorsements as well as the bill.

Absolute. Well, take care you don't hurt your credit by offering too much security.—Is Mr. Faulkland returned?

Fag. He is above, sir, changing his dress.

Absolute. Can you tell whether he has been informed of Sir Anthony and Miss Melville's arrival?

Fag. I fancy not, sir; he has seen no one since he came in but his gentleman, who was with him at Bristol.—I think, sir, I hear Mr. Faulkland coming down——

Absolute. Go, tell him I am here.

Fag. Yes, sir.—(*Going.*) I beg pardon, sir, but should Sir Anthony call, you will do me the favour to remember that we are *recruiting*, if you please.

Absolute. Well, well.

Fag. And, in tenderness to my character, if your honour could bring in the chairmen and waiters, I shall esteem it as an obligation; for though I never scruple a lie to serve my master, yet it hurts one's conscience to be found out. (*Exit.*)

Minority waiters, Unemployed waiters; out of a job, like the minority party in Parliament.

Absolute. Now for my whimsical friend—if he does not know that his mistress is here, I'll tease him a little before I tell him——

(*Enter Faulkland.*)

Faulkland, you're welcome to Bath again; you are punctual in your return.

Faulkland. Yes; I had nothing to detain me, when I had finished the business I went on. Well, what news since I left you? how stand matters between you and Lydia?

Absolute. Faith, much as they were; I have not seen her since our quarrel; however, I expect to be recalled every hour.

Faulkland. Why don't you persuade her to go off with you at once?

Absolute. What, and lose two-thirds of her fortune? you forget that, my friend.—No, no, I could have brought her to that long ago.

Faulkland. Nay, then, you trifle too long—if you are sure of *her*, propose to the aunt *in your own character*, and write to Sir Anthony for his consent.

Absolute. Softly, softly; for though I am convinced my little Lydia would elope with me as Ensign Beverley, yet am I by no means certain that she would take me with the impediment of our friend's consent, a regular humdrum wedding, and the reversion of a good fortune on my side: no, no; I must prepare her gradually for the discovery, and make myself necessary to her, before I risk it.—Well, but, Faulkland, you'll dine with us to-day at the hotel?

Faulkland. Indeed I cannot; I am not in spirits to be of such a party.

Absolute. By heavens! I shall forswear your com-

Whimsical, Having queer ideas; in this case, sentimental. Faulkland is "a man of feeling," in the fashion of the period. He and Julia were the only characters liked by the original audiences of the play, the rest being considered too "daring."

pany. You are the most teasing, captious, incorrigible lover !—Do love like a man.

Faulkland. I own I am unfit for company.

Absolute. Am not *I* a lover ; ay, and a romantic one too ? Yet do I carry everywhere with me such a confounded farrago of doubts, fears, hopes, wishes, and all the flimsy furniture of a country miss's brain ?

Faulkland. Ah ! Jack, your heart and soul are not, like mine, fixed immutably on one only object. You throw for a large stake, but losing, you could stake and throw again :—but I have set my sum of happiness on this cast, and not to succeed were to be stripped of all.

Absolute. But, for Heaven's sake ! what grounds for apprehension can your whimsical brain conjure up at present ?

Faulkland. What grounds for apprehension, did you say ? Heavens ! are there not a thousand ! I fear for her spirits—her health—her life.—My absence may fret her ; her anxiety for my return, her fears for me may oppress her gentle temper : and for her health, does not every hour bring me cause to be alarmed ? If it rains, some shower may even then have chilled her delicate frame ! If the wind be keen, some rude blast may have affected her ! The heat of noon, the dews of the evening, may endanger the life of her, for whom only I value mine. O Jack ! when delicate and feeling souls are separated, there is not a feature in the sky, not a movement of the elements, not an aspiration of the breeze, but hints some cause for a lover's apprehension !

Absolute. Ay, but we may choose whether we will take the hint or not.—So, then, Faulkland, if you were convinced that Julia were well and in spirits, you would be entirely content ?

Faulkland. I should be happy beyond measure—I am anxious only for that.

Absolute. Then to cure your anxiety at once—

Miss Melville is in perfect health, and is at this moment in Bath.

Faulkland. Nay, Jack—don't trifle with me.

Absolute. She is arrived here with my father within this hour.

Faulkland. Can you be serious ?

Absolute. I thought you knew Sir Anthony better than to be surprised at a sudden whim of this kind.— Seriously, then, it is as I tell you—upon my honour.

Faulkland. My dear friend !—Hollo, Du Peigne ! my hat.—My dear Jack—now nothing on earth can give me a moment's uneasiness.

(Enter Fag.)

Fag. Sir, Mr. Acres, just arrived, is below.

Absolute. Stay, Faulkland, this Acres lives within a mile of Sir Anthony, and he shall tell you how your mistress has been ever since you left her.—Fag, show the gentleman up.   *(Exit Fag.)*

Faulkland. What, is he much acquainted in the family ?

Absolute. Oh, very intimate : I insist on your not going : besides, his character will divert you.

Faulkland. Well, I should like to ask him a few questions.

Absolute. He is likewise a rival of mine—that is, of my *other self's*, for he does not think his friend Captain Absolute ever saw the lady in question ; and it is ridiculous enough to hear him complain to me of *one Beverley*, a concealed skulking rival, who——

Faulkland. Hush !—he's here.

(Enter Acres.)

Acres. Ha ! my dear friend, noble captain, and honest Jack, how do'st thou ? just arrived, faith, as you see.—Sir, your humble servant.—Warm work on the roads, Jack !—Odds whips and wheels ! I've travelled like a comet, with a tail of dust all the way as long as the Mall.

The Mall, Running the length of St. James's Park.

Absolute. Ah! Bob, you are indeed an eccentric planet, but we know your attraction hither.—Give me leave to introduce Mr. *Faulkland* to you ; Mr. Faulkland, Mr. Acres.

Acres. Sir, I am most heartily glad to see you : sir, I solicit your connections.—Hey, Jack—what, this is Mr. Faulkland, who——

Absolute. Ay, Bob, Miss Melville's Mr. Faulkland.

Acres. Odso! she and your father can be but just arrived before me ;—I suppose you have seen them. Ah! Mr. Faulkland, you are indeed a happy man.

Faulkland. I have not seen Miss Melville yet, sir ; —I hope she enjoyed full health and spirits in Devonshire ?

Acres. Never knew her better in my life, sir,— never better. Odds blushes and blooms! she has been as healthy as the German Spa.

Faulkland. Indeed !—I did hear that she had been a little indisposed.

Acres. False, false, sir—only said to vex you : quite the reverse, I assure you.

Faulkland. There, Jack, you see she has the advantage of me ; I had almost fretted myself ill.

Absolute. Now are you angry with your mistress for not having been sick ?

Faulkland. No, no, you misunderstand me : yet surely a little trifling indisposition is not an unnatural consequence of absence from those we love.— Now confess—isn't there something unkind in this violent, robust, unfeeling health ?

Absolute. Oh, it was unkind of her to be well in your absence, to be sure !

Acres. Good apartments, Jack.

Faulkland. Well, sir, but you was saying that Miss Melville has been so *exceedingly* well—what, then, she has been merry and gay, I suppose ?—Always in spirits—hey ?

39

Acres. Merry, odds crickets! she has been the belle and spirit of the company wherever she has been—so lively and entertaining! so full of wit and humour!

Faulkland. There, Jack, there.—Oh, by my soul! there is an innate levity in woman that nothing can overcome.—What! happy, and I away!

Absolute. Have done.—How foolish this is! just now you were only apprehensive for your mistress's *spirits.*

Faulkland. Why, Jack, have I been the joy and spirit of the company?

Absolute. No indeed, you have not.

Faulkland. Have I been lively and entertaining?

Absolute. Oh, upon my word, I acquit you.

Faulkland. Have I been full of wit and humour?

Absolute. No, faith, to do you justice, you have been confoundedly stupid indeed.

Acres. What's the matter with the gentleman?

Absolute. He is only expressing his great satisfaction at hearing that Julia has been so well and happy—that's all—hey, Faulkland?

Faulkland. Oh! I am rejoiced to hear it—yes, yes, she has a *happy* disposition.

Acres. That she has indeed.—Then she is so accomplished—so sweet a voice—so expert at her harpsichord—such a mistress of flat and sharp, squallante, rumblante, and quiverante!—There was this time month—odds minums and crotchets! how she did chirrup at Mrs. Piano's concert!

Faulkland. There again, what say you to this? you see she has been all mirth and song—not a thought of me!

Absolute. Pho! man, is not music the food of love?

Faulkland, Well, well, it may be so.—Pray, Mr. ——, what's his damned name?—Do you remember what songs Miss Melville sung?

Acres. Not I indeed.

Absolute. Stay, now, they were some pretty melancholy purling-stream airs, I warrant ; perhaps you may recollect ;—did she sing, *When absent from my soul's delight ?*

Acres. No, that wa'n't it.

Absolute. Or, *Go, gentle gales !* (*Sings.*)

Acres. Oh, no ! nothing like it. Odds ! now I recollect one of them—*My heart's my own, my will is free.* (*Sings.*)

Faulkland. Fool ! fool that I am ! to fix all my happiness on such a trifler ! 'Sdeath ! to make herself the pipe and balladmonger of a circle ! to soothe her light heart with catches and glees !—What can you say to this, sir ?

Absolute. Why, that I should be glad to hear my mistress had been so merry, *sir.*

Faulkland. Nay, nay, nay—I'm not sorry that she has been happy—no, no, I am glad of that—I would not have had her sad or sick—yet surely a sympathetic heart would have shown itself even in the choice of a song—she might have been temperately healthy, and somehow, plaintively gay ;—but she has been dancing too, I doubt not !

Acres. What does the gentleman say about dancing ?

Absolute. He says the lady we speak of dances as well as she sings.

Acres. Ay, truly, does she—there was at our last race ball——

Faulkland. Hell and the devil ! There !—there—I told you so ! I told you so ! Oh ! she thrives in my absence !—Dancing ! but her whole feelings have been in opposition with mine ;—I have been anxious, silent, pensive, sedentary—my days have been hours of care, my nights of watchfulness.—She has been all health ! spirit ! laugh ! song ! dance !—Oh ! damned, damned levity !

Absolute. For Heaven's sake, Faulkland, don't expose yourself so !—Suppose she has danced, what

then ?—does not the ceremony of society often
oblige——

Faulkland. Well, well, I'll contain myself—perhaps
as you say—for form sake.—What, Mr. Acres, you
were praising Miss Melville's manner of dancing a
minuet—hey ?

Acres. Oh, I dare insure her for that—but what I
was going to speak of was her *country-dancing*. Odds
swimmings ! she has such an air with her !

Faulkland. Now disappointment on her !—Defend
this, Absolute ; why don't you defend this ?—
Country dances ! jigs and reels ! am I to blame now ?
A minuet I could have forgiven—I should not have
minded that—I say I should not have regarded a
minuet—but *country-dances !*—Zounds ! had she
made one in a *cotillon*—I believe I could have forgiven
even that—but to be monkey-led for a night !—to
run the gauntlet through a string of amorous palming
puppies !—to show paces like a managed filly !—Oh,
Jack, there never can be but *one* man in the world
whom a truly modest and delicate woman ought to
pair with in a *country-dance* ; and, even then, the rest
of the couples should be her great-uncles and aunts !

Absolute. Ay, to be sure !—grandfathers and grandmothers !

Faulkland. If there be but one vicious mind in the
set, 'twill spread like a contagion—the action of their
pulse beats to the movement of the jig—their quiver-
ing, warm-breathed sighs impregnate the very air—
the atmosphere becomes electrical to love, and each
amorous spark darts through every link of the chain !
—I must leave you—I own I am somewhat flurried
—and that confounded looby has perceived it.

(Going.)

Absolute. Nay, but stay, Faulkland, and thank
Mr. Acres for his good news.

Country-dancing, Like, for instance, the *Sir Roger de Coverley*.
Cotillon, A quick dance like a quadrille.   *Looby*, Lubber.

Faulkland. Damn his news !   (*Exit Faulkland*)

Absolute. Ha! ha! ha! poor Faulkland five minutes since—" nothing on earth could give him a moment's uneasiness ! "

Acres. The gentleman wa'n't angry at my praising his mistress, was he ?

Absolute. A little jealous, I believe, Bob.

Acres. You don't say so ? Ha! ha! jealous of me—that's a good joke.

Absolute. There's nothing strange in that, Bob ; let me tell you, that sprightly grace and insinuating manner of yours will do some mischief among the girls here.

Acres. Ah! you joke—ha! ha! mischief !—ha! ha! but you know I am not my own property, my dear Lydia has forestalled me. She could never abide me in the country, because I used to dress so badly— but odds frogs and tambours ! I shan't take matters so here, now ancient madam has no voice in it, I'll make my old clothes know who's master. I shall straightway cashier the hunting-frock, and render my leather breeches incapable. My hair has been in training some time.

Absolute. Indeed !

Acres. Ay—and thoff the side curls are a little restive, my hind-part takes it very kindly.

Absolute. Oh, you'll polish, I doubt not.

Acres. Absolutely I propose so—then if I can find out this Ensign Beverley, odds triggers and flints ! I'll make him know the difference o't.

Absolute. Spoke like a man ! But pray, Bob, I observe you have got an odd kind of a new method of swearing——

Acres. Ha! ha! you've taken notice of it—'tis genteel, isn't *it* !—I didn't invent it myself though ; but a commander in our militia, a great scholar, I

Frogs, Cloak buttons fastening into a loop.
Tambours, Circular frames on which to do embroidery.

assure you, says that there is no meaning in the common oaths, and that nothing but their antiquity makes them respectable ; —because, he says, the ancients would never stick to an oath or two, but would say, By Jove ! or By Bacchus ! or By Mars ! or By Venus ! or By Pallas ! according to the sentiment : so that to swear with propriety, says my little major, the " oath should be an echo to the sense " ; and this we call the *oath referential* or *sentimental swearing*—ha ! ha ! 'tis genteel, isn't it ?

Absolute. Very genteel, and very new, indeed !— and I daresay will supplant all other figures of imprecation.

Acres. Ay, ay, the best terms will grow obsolete— Damns have had their day.

(*Enter Fag.*)

Fag. Sir, there is a gentleman below desires to see you.—Shall I show him into the parlour ?

Absolute. Ay, you may.

Acres. Well, I must be gone——

Absolute. Stay ; who is it, Fag ?

Fag. Your father, sir.

Absolute. You puppy, why didn't you show him up directly ?   (*Exit Fag.*)

Acres. You have business with Sir Anthony.— I expect a message from Mrs. Malaprop at my lodgings. I have sent also to my dear friend Sir Lucius O'Trigger. Adieu, Jack ! we must meet at night, when you shall give me a dozen bumpers to little Lydia.

Absolute. That I will with all my heart.—

(*Exit Acres.*)

Now for a parental lecture—I hope he has heard nothing of the business that has brought me here— I wish the gout had held him fast in Devonshire, with all my soul !

Sentimental, Elevated, " highbrow."   *Genteel*, Stylish ; refined.

(Enter Sir Anthony.)

Absolute. Sir, I am delighted to see you here, looking so well! Your sudden arrival at Bath made me apprehensive for your health.

Sir Anthony. Very apprehensive, I daresay, Jack. —What, you are recruiting here, hey?

Absolute. Yes, sir, I am on duty.

Sir Anthony. Well, Jack, I am glad to see you, though I did not expect it, for I was going to write to you on a little matter of business.—Jack, I have been considering that I grow old and infirm, and shall probably not trouble you long.

Absolute. Pardon me, sir, I never saw you look more strong and hearty; and I pray frequently that you may continue so.

Sir Anthony. I hope your prayers may be heard, with all my heart. Well then, Jack, I have been considering that I am so strong and hearty I may continue to plague you a long time. Now, Jack, I am sensible that the income of your commission, and what I have hitherto allowed you, is but a small pittance for a lad of your spirit.

Absolute. Sir, you are very good.

Sir Anthony. And it is my wish, while yet I live, to have my boy make some figure in the world. I have resolved, therefore, to fix you at once in a noble independence.

Absolute. Sir, your kindness overpowers me—such generosity makes the gratitude of reason more lively than the sensations even of filial affection.

Sir Anthony. I am glad you are so sensible of my attention—and you shall be master of a large estate in a few weeks.

Absolute. Let my future life, sir, speak my gratitude; I cannot express the sense I have of your munificence.—Yet, sir, I presume you would not wish me to quit the army?

Sir Anthony. Oh, that shall be as your wife chooses.

Absolute. My wife, sir !

Sir Anthony. Ay, ay, settle that between you—settle that between you.

Absolute. A *wife*, sir, did you say ?

Sir Anthony. Ay, a wife—why, did not I mention her before ?

Absolute. Not a word of her, sir.

Sir Anthony. Odd so !—I mustn't forget *her* though.—Yes, Jack, the independence I was talking of is by a marriage—the fortune is saddled with a wife—but I suppose that makes no difference.

Absolute. Sir ! sir !—you amaze me !

Sir Anthony. Why, what the devil's the matter with the fool ? Just now you were all gratitude and duty.

Absolute. I was, sir—you talked to me of independence and a fortune, but not a word of a wife.

Sir Anthony. Why—what difference does that make ? Odds life, sir ! if you have the estate, you must take it with the live stock on it, as it stands.

Absolute. If my happiness is to be the price, I must beg leave to decline the purchase.—Pray, sir, who is the lady ?

Sir Anthony. What's that to you, sir ?—Come, give me your promise to love, and to marry her directly.

Absolute. Sure, sir, this is not very reasonable, to summon my affections for a lady I know nothing of !

Sir Anthony. I am sure, sir, 'tis more unreasonable in you to *object* to a lady you know nothing of.

Absolute. Then, sir, I must tell you plainly that my inclinations are fixed on another. Sir, my heart is engaged to an angel.

Sir Anthony. Then pray let it send an excuse. It is very sorry—but *business* prevents its waiting on her.

Absolute. But my vows are pledged to her.

Sir Anthony. Let her foreclose, Jack ; let her foreclose ; they are not worth redeeming ; besides, you have the angel's vows in exchange, I suppose; so there can be no loss there.

Absolute. You must excuse me, sir, if I tell you, once for all, that in this point I cannot obey you.

Sir Anthony. Hark'ee, Jack; I have heard you for some time with patience—I have been cool—quite cool; but take care—you know I am compliance itself—when I am not thwarted;—no one more easily led—when I have my own way;—but don't put me in a frenzy.

Absolute. Sir, I must repeat it—in this I cannot obey you.

Sir Anthony. Now damn me! if ever I call you *Jack* again while I live!

Absolute. Nay, sir, but hear me.

Sir Anthony. Sir, I won't hear a word—not a word! not one word! so give me your promise by a nod—and I'll tell you what, Jack—I mean, you dog —if you don't, by——

Absolute. What, sir, promise to link myself to some mass of ugliness! to——

Sir Anthony. Zounds! sirrah! the lady shall be as ugly as I choose: she shall have a lump on each shoulder; she shall be as crooked as the crescent; her one eye shall roll like the bull's in Cox's Museum; she shall have a skin like a mummy, and the beard of a Jew—she shall be all this, sirrah!—yet I will make you ogle her all day, and sit up all night to write sonnets on her beauty.

Absolute. This is reason and moderation indeed!

Sir Anthony. None of your sneering, puppy! no grinning, jackanapes!

Absolute. Indeed, sir, I never was in a worse humour for mirth in my life.

Sir Anthony. 'Tis false, sir, I know you are laughing in your sleeve; I know you'll grin when I am gone, sirrah!

Cox's Museum, In Bond Street, an exhibition of curiosities.

Absolute. Sir, I hope I know my duty better.

Sir Anthony. None of your passion, sir ! none of your violence, if you please !—It won't do with me, I promise you.

Absolute. Indeed, sir, I never was cooler in my life.

Sir Anthony. 'Tis a confounded lie !—I know you are in a passion in your heart ; I know you are, you hypocritical young dog ! but it won't do.

Absolute. Nay, sir, upon my word——

Sir Anthony. So you will fly out ! can't you be cool like me ! What the devil good can *passion* do ?— *Passion* is of no service, you impudent, insolent, over-bearing reprobate !—There, you sneer again ! don't provoke me !—but you rely upon the mildness of my temper—you do, you dog ! you play upon the meek-ness of my disposition !—You take care—the patience of a saint may be overcome at last !—but mark ! I give you six hours and a half to consider of this : if you then agree without any condition, to do every-thing on earth that I choose, why—confound you ! I may in time forgive you.—If not, zounds ! don't enter the same hemisphere with me ! don't dare to breathe the same air, or use the same light with me ; but get an atmosphere and a sun of your own ! I'll strip you of your commission ; I'll lodge a five-and-threepence in the hands of trustees, and you shall live on the interest.—I'll disown you, I'll disinherit you, I'll unget you ! and damn me ! if ever I call you Jack again !   (*Exit Sir Anthony.*)

(*Absolute solus.*)

Absolute. Mild, gentle, considerate father—I kiss your hands ! What a tender method of giving his opinion in these matters Sir Anthony has ! I dare not trust him with the truth.—I wonder what old wealthy hag it is that he wants to bestow on me !—Yet he married himself for love ! and was in his youth a bold intriguer, and a gay companion !

48

(Enter Fag.)

Fag. Assuredly, sir, your father is wrath to a degree;
he comes down stairs eight or ten steps at a time—
muttering, growling, and thumping the banisters all
the way: I and the cook's dog stand bowing at the
door—rap! he gives me a stroke on the head with his
cane; bids me carry that to my master; then kicking the poor turnspit into the area, damns us all, for
a puppy triumvirate!—Upon my credit, sir, were I
in your place, and found my father such very bad
company, I should certainly drop his acquaintance.

Absolute. Cease your impertinence, sir, at present.
—Did you come in for nothing more?—Stand out of
the way! *(Pushes him aside and exit.)*

(Fag solus.)

Fag. So! Sir Anthony trims my master: he is
afraid to reply to his father—then vents his spleen
on poor Fag! When one is vexed by one person, to
revenge one's self on another, who happens to come
in the way, is the vilest injustice! Ah! it shows the
worst temper—the basest——

(Enter Errand-boy.)

Boy. Mr. Fag; Mr. Fag! your master calls you.

Fag. Well, you little dirty puppy, you need not
bawl so!—The meanest disposition! the——

Boy. Quick, quick, Mr. Fag!

Fag. Quick! quick! you impudent jackanapes!
am I to be commanded by you too? you little impertinent, insolent, kitchen-bred——

(Exit kicking and beating him.)

Turnspit, Small, short-legged dog to work a treadmill wheel turning
a spit for roasting meat.
Trims, Rates, " ticks off."

SCENE II.　*The North Parade.*

(*Enter Lucy*)

Lucy. So—I shall have another rival to add to my mistress's list—Captain Absolute. However, I shall not enter his name till my purse has received notice in form. Poor Acres is dismissed!—Well, I have done him a last friendly office, in letting him know that Beverley was here before him.—Sir Lucius is generally more punctual when he expects to hear from his *dear Dalia*, as he calls her: I wonder he's not here!—I have a little scruple of conscience from this deceit; though I should not be paid so well, if my hero knew that *Delia* was near fifty, and her own mistress.

(*Enter Sir Lucius O'Trigger.*)

Sir Lucius. Ha! my little ambassadress—upon my conscience, I have been looking for you; I have been on the South Parade this half-hour.

Lucy (*speaking simply*). O gemini! and I have been waiting for your worship here on the North.

Sir Lucius. Faith!—maybe that was the reason we did not meet; and it is very comical too, how you could get out and I not see you—for I was only taking a nap at the Parade Coffee-house, and I chose the *window* on purpose that I might not miss you.

Lucy. My stars! Now I'd wager a sixpence I went by while you were asleep.

Sir Lucius. Sure enough it must have been so—and I never dreamt it was so late, till I waked. Well, but my little girl, have you got nothing for me?

Lucy. Yes, but I have—I've got a letter for you in my pocket.

Stage direction, The Parades (wide-paved walks) are near the Abbey Church. They were then the fashionable lounging places. The Coffee-house was in the North Parade.

Sir Lucius. O faith! I guessed you weren't come empty-handed.—Well—let me see what the dear creature says.

Lucy. There, Sir Lucius.   (*Gives him a letter.*)

Sir Lucius (*reads*). *Sir—there is often a sudden incentive impulse in love, that has a greater induction than years of domestic combination: such was the commotion I felt at the first superfluous view of Sir Lucius O'Trigger.*—Very pretty, upon my word.—*Female punctuation forbids me to say more, yet let me add, that it will give me joy infallible to find Sir Lucius worthy the last criterion of my affections.*   DELIA.

Upon my conscience! Lucy, your lady is a great mistress of language. Faith, she's quite the queen of the dictionary!—for the devil a word dare refuse coming at her call—though one would think it was quite out of hearing.

Lucy. Ay, sir, a lady of her experience——

Sir Lucius. Experience! what, at seventeen?

Lucy. O true, sir—but then she reads so—my stars! how she will read off hand!

Sir Lucius. Faith, she must be very deep read to write this way—though she is rather an arbitrary writer too—for here are a great many poor words pressed into the service of this note, that would get their *habeas corpus* from any court in Christendom.

Lucy. Ah! Sir Lucius, if you were to hear how she talks of you!

Sir Lucius. Oh, tell her I'll make her the best husband in the world, and Lady O'Trigger into the bargain.—But we must get the old gentlewoman's consent—and do everything fairly.

Lucy. Nay, Sir Lucius, I thought you wa'n't rich enough to be so nice!

Habeas Corpus, An Act of Charles II. providing for prompt **trial of** prisoners (L. Thou must have the body), and their discharge if there was no proper case against them. So Mrs. Malaprop's wrongly-used words would gain their discharge.

Nice, Particular.

Sir Lucius. Upon my word, young woman, you have hit it :—I am so poor, that I can't afford to do a dirty action.—If I did not want money, I'd steal your mistress and her fortune with a great deal of pleasure.—However, my pretty girl (*Gives her money*), here's a little something to buy you a riband ; and meet me in the evening, and I'll give you an answer to this. So, hussy, take a kiss beforehand to put you in mind.   (*Kisses her.*)

Lucy. O Lud ! Sir Lucius—I never see'd such a gemman ! My lady won't like you if you're so impudent.

Sir Lucius. Faith she will, Lucy !—That same— pho ! what's the name of it ?—*modesty*—is a quality in a lover more praised by the women than liked ; so, if your mistress asks you whether Sir Lucius ever gave you a kiss, tell her fifty—my dear.

Lucy. What, would you have me tell her a lie ?

Sir Lucius. Ah, then, you baggage ! I'll make it a truth presently.

Lucy. For shame now ! here is some one coming.

Sir Lucius. Oh, faith, I'll quiet your conscience !
                (*Sees Fag.   Exit, humming a tune.*)
                       (*Enter Fag.*)

Fag. So, so, ma'am ! I humbly beg pardon.

Lucy. O Lud ! now, Mr. Fag—you flurry one so.

Fag. Come, come, Lucy, here's no one by—so a little less simplicity, with a grain or two more sincerity, if you please.—You play false with us, madam —I saw you give the baronet a letter. My master shall know this—and if he don't call him out, I will.

Lucy. Ha ! ha ! ha ! you gentlemen's gentlemen are so hasty.—That letter was from Mrs. Malaprop, simpleton.—She is taken with Sir Lucius's address.

Fag. How ! what tastes some people have !—Why, I suppose I have walked by her window an hundred times.—But what says our young lady ? any message to my master ?

Lucy. Sad news, Mr. Fag.—A worse rival than Acres! Sir Anthony Absolute has proposed his son.

Fag. What, Captain Absolute?

Lucy. Even so—I overheard it all.

Fag. Ha! ha! ha! very good, faith. Good-bye, Lucy, I must away with this news.

Lucy. Well, you may laugh—but it is true, I assure you.—(*Going.*) But, Mr. Fag, tell your master not to be cast down by this.

Fag. Oh, he'll be disconsolate!

Lucy. And charge him not to think of quarrelling with young Absolute.

Fag. Never fear! never fear!

Lucy. Be sure—bid him keep up his spirits.

Fag. We will—we will.   (*Exeunt severally.*)

END OF THE SECOND ACT.

ACT III

SCENE I. *The North Parade.*

(*Enter Absolute.*)

[*Absolute*]. 'Tis just as Fag told me, indeed. Whimsical enough, faith ! My father wants to *force* me to marry the very girl I am plotting to run away with ! He must not know of my connection with her yet awhile. He has too summary a method of proceeding in these matters. However, I'll read my recantation instantly. My conversion is something sudden, indeed—but I can assure him it is very *sincere*. So, so—here he comes. He looks plaguy gruff.   (*Steps aside.*)

(*Enter Sir Anthony.*)

Sir Anthony. No—I'll die sooner than forgive him. *Die*, did I say ? I'll live these fifty years to plague him. At our last meeting, his impudence had almost put me out of temper. An obstinate, passionate, self-willed boy ! Who can he take after ? This is my return for getting him before all his brothers and sisters !—for putting him, at twelve years old, into a marching regiment, and allowing him fifty pounds a year, besides his pay, ever since ! But I have done with him ; he's anybody's son for me. I never will see him more, never—never—never.

Absolute (*aside, coming forward*). Now for a penitential face.

Sir Anthony. Fellow, get out of my way !

Absolute. Sir, you see a penitent before you.

Marching regiment, Regular army regiment—not either guards or volunteers.

Sir Anthony. I see an impudent scoundrel before me.

Absolute. A sincere penitent. I am come, sir, to acknowledge my error, and to submit entirely to your will.

Sir Anthony. What's that?

Absolute. I have been revolving, and reflecting, and considering on your past goodness, and kindness, and condescension to me.

Sir Anthony. Well, sir?

Absolute. I have been likewise weighing and balancing what you were pleased to mention concerning duty, and obedience, and authority.

Sir Anthony. Well, puppy?

Absolute. Why then, sir, the result of my reflections is—a resolution to sacrifice every inclination of my own to your satisfaction.

Sir Anthony. Why now you talk sense—absolute sense—I never heard anything more sensible in my life. Confound you! you shall be Jack again.

Absolute. I am happy in the appellation.

Sir Anthony. Why then, Jack, my dear Jack, I will now inform you who the lady really is. Nothing but your passion and violence, you silly fellow, prevented my telling you at first. Prepare, Jack, for wonder and rapture—prepare. What think you of Miss Lydia Languish?

Absolute. Languish! What, the Languishes of Worcestershire?

Sir Anthony. Worcestershire! No. Did you never meet Mrs. Malaprop and her niece, Miss Languish, who came into our country just before you were last ordered to your regiment!

Absolute. Malaprop! Languish! I don't remember ever to have heard the names before. Yet, stay—I think I do recollect something. *Languish! Languish!* She squints, don't she? A little red-haired girl?

Sir Anthony. Squints! A red-haired girl! Zounds! no.

Absolute. Then I must have forgot ; it can't be the same person.

Sir Anthony. Jack ! Jack ! what think you of blooming, love-breathing seventeen ?

Absolute. As to that, sir, I am quite indifferent. If I can please you in the matter, 'tis all I desire.

Sir Anthony. Nay, but, Jack, such eyes ! such eyes ! so innocently wild ! so bashfully irresolute ! not a glance but speaks and kindles some thought of love ! Then, Jack, her cheeks ! her cheeks, Jack ! so deeply blushing at the insinuations of her tell-tale eyes ! Then, Jack, her lips ! O Jack, lips smiling at their own discretion ; and if not smiling, more sweetly pouting ; more lovely in sullenness !

Absolute (*aside*). That's she indeed. Well done, old gentleman.

Sir Anthony. Then, Jack, her neck ! O Jack ! Jack !

Absolute. And which is to be mine, sir, the niece, or the aunt ?

Sir Anthony. Why, you unfeeling, insensible puppy, I despise you ! When I was of your age, such a description would have made me fly like a rocket ! The *aunt* indeed ! Odds life ! when I ran away with your mother, I would not have touched anything old or ugly to gain an empire.

Absolute. Not to please your father, sir ?

Sir Anthony. To please my father ! zounds ! not to please—Oh, my father—odd so !—yes—yes ; if my father indeed had desired—that's quite another matter. Though he wa'n't the indulgent father that I am, Jack.

Absolute. I dare say not, sir.

Sir Anthony. But, Jack, you are not sorry to find your mistress is so beautiful ?

Absolute. Sir, I repeat it—if I please you in this affair 'tis all I desire. Not that I think a woman the worse for being handsome ; but, sir, if you please to

recollect, you before hinted something about a hump
or two, one eye, and a few more graces of that kind
—now, without being very nice, I own I should rather
choose a wife of mine to have the usual number of
limbs, and a limited quantity of back; and though
one eye may be very agreeable, yet as the prejudice
has always run in favour of *two*, I would not wish
to affect a singularity in that article.

Sir Anthony. What a phlegmatic sot it is! Why,
sirrah, you're an anchorite!—a vile, insensible stock.
You a soldier!—you're a walking block, fit only to
dust the company's regimentals on! Odd's life! I
have a great mind to marry the girl myself.

Absolute. I am entirely at your disposal, sir : if
you should think of addressing Miss Languish yourself, I suppose you would have me marry the *aunt* ;
or if you should change your mind, and take the old
lady—'tis the same to me—I'll marry the *niece*.

Sir Anthony. Upon my word, Jack, thou'rt either
a very great hypocrite, or—but, come, I know your
indifference on such a subject must be all a lie—I'm
sure it must—come, now—damn your demure face!
—come, confess, Jack—you have been lying—ha'n't
you? You have been playing the hypocrite, hey !—
I'll never forgive you, if you ha'n't been lying and
playing the hypocrite.

Absolute. I'm sorry, sir, that the respect and duty
which I bear to you should be so mistaken.

Sir Anthony. Hang your respect and duty! But
come along with me, I'll write a note to Mrs. Malaprop, and you shall visit the lady directly. Her eyes
shall be the Promethean torch to you—come along,
I'll never forgive you, if you don't come back stark
mad with rapture and impatience—if you don't, egad,
I will marry the girl myself! (*Exeunt.*)

Promethean torch; The fire stolen from heaven by Prometheus
(*Gk.* " forethought ") to light into life a clay man he had made.
So, life-giving agent (for the " block," Captain Absolute).

SCENE II.   *Julia's Dressing-room.*

(Faulkland solus.)

Faulkland. They told me Julia would return directly ; I wonder she is not yet come ! How mean does this captious, unsatisfied temper of mine appear to my cooler judgment ! Yet I know not that I indulge it in any other point ; but on this one subject, and to this one subject, whom I think I love beyond my life, I am ever ungenerously fretful and madly capricious ! I am conscious of it—yet I cannot correct myself ! What tender honest joy sparkled in her eyes when we met ! how delicate was the warmth of her expressions ! I was ashamed to appear less happy—though I had come resolved to wear a face of coolness and upbraiding. Sir Anthony's presence prevented my proposed expostulations : Yet I must be satisfied that she has not been so *very* happy in my absence. She is coming ! Yes !—I know the nimbleness of her tread, when she thinks her impatient Faulkland counts the moments of her stay.

(Enter Julia.)

Julia. I had not hoped to see you again so soon.

Faulkland. Could I, Julia, be contented with my first welcome—restrained as we were by the presence of a third person ?

Julia. O Faulkland, when your kindness can make me thus happy, let me not think that I discovered something of coldness in your first salutation.

Faulkland. 'Twas but your fancy, Julia. I *was* rejoiced to see you—to see you in such health. Sure I had no cause for coldness ?

Julia. Nay, then, I see you have taken something ill. You must not conceal from me what it is.

Faulkland. Well, then—shall I own to you that

my joy at hearing of your health and arrival here, by your neighbour Acres, was somewhat damped by his dwelling much on the high spirits you had enjoyed in Devonshire—on your mirth—your singing—dancing—and I know not what ! For such is my temper, Julia, that I should regard every mirthful moment in your absence as a treason to constancy. The mutual tear that steals down the cheek of parting lovers is a compact, that no smile shall live there till they meet again.

Julia. Must I never cease to tax my Faulkland with this teasing minute caprice ? Can the idle reports of a silly boor weigh in your breast against my tried affection ?

Faulkland. They have no weight with me, Julia : No, no—I am happy if you have been so—yet only say, that you did not sing with *mirth*—say that you *thought* of Faulkland in the dance.

Julia. I never can be happy in your absence. If I wear a countenance of content, it is to show that my mind holds no doubt of my Faulkland's truth. If I seemed sad, it were to make malice triumph ; and say, that I had fixed my heart on one, who left me to lament his roving, and my own credulity. Believe me, Faulkland, I mean not to upbraid you, when I say, that I have often dressed sorrow in smiles, lest my friends should guess whose unkindness had caused my tears.

Faulkland. You were ever all goodness to me. Oh, I am a brute, when I but admit a doubt of your true constancy !

Julia. If ever without such cause from you, as I will not suppose possible, you find my affections veering but a point, may I become a proverbial scoff for levity and base ingratitude.

Faulkland. Ah ! Julia, that last word is grating to me. I would I had no title to your *gratitude !* Search your heart, Julia ; perhaps what you have mistaken for Love is but the warm effusion of a too thankful heart.

Julia. For what quality must I love you ?

Faulkland. For no quality ! To regard me for any quality of mind or understanding were only to *esteem* me. And for person—I have often wished myself deformed, to be convinced that I owed no obligation *there* for any part of your affection.

Julia. Where nature has bestowed a show of nice attention in the features of a man, he should laugh at it as misplaced. I have seen men, who in *this* vain article, perhaps, might rank above you ; but my heart has never asked my eyes if it were so or not.

Faulkland. Now this is not well from *you*, Julia— I despise person in a man—yet if you loved me as I wish, though I were an Æthiop, you'd think none so fair.

Julia. I see you are determined to be unkind ! The *contract* which my poor father bound us in gives you more than a lover's privilege.

Faulkland. Again, Julia, you raise ideas that feed and justify my doubts. I would not have been more free—no—I am proud of my restraint. Yet—yet— perhaps your high respect alone for this solemn compact has fettered your inclinations, which else had made a worthier choice. How shall I be sure, had you remained unbound in thought and promise, that I should still have been the object of your persevering love ?

Julia. Then try me now. Let us be free as strangers as to what is past : *my* heart will not feel more liberty.

Faulkland. There now ! so hasty, Julia ! so anxious to be free ! If your love for me were fixed and ardent, you would not lose your hold, even though I wished it !

Julia. Oh ! you torture me to the heart ! I cannot bear it.

Nice, Uncommon.

Faulkland. I do not mean to distress you. If I loved you less I should never give you an uneasy moment. But hear me. All my fretful doubts arise from this. Women are not used to weigh and separate the motives of their affections : the cold dictates of prudence, gratitude, or filial duty, may sometimes be mistaken for the pleadings of the heart. I would not boast—yet let me say, that I have neither age, person, nor character, to found dislike on ; my fortune such as few ladies could be charged with *indiscretion* in the match. O Julia ! when *love* receives such countenance from *prudence*, nice minds will be suspicious of its birth.

Julia. I know not whither your insinuations would tend :—but as they seem pressing to insult me, I will spare you the regret of having done so.—I have given you no cause for this ! (*Exit in tears.*)

Faulkland. In tears ! Stay, Julia ; stay but for a moment.—The door is fastened !—Julia !—my soul—but for one moment !—I hear her sobbing !—'Sdeath ! what a brute am I to use her thus ! Yet stay.—Ay—she is coming now :—how little resolution there is in woman !—how a few soft words can turn them !—No, faith !—she is not coming either.—Why, Julia—my love—say but that you forgive me—come but to tell me that—now this is being *too* resentful. Stay ! she is coming to—I thought she would—*no steadiness* in anything : her going must have been a mere trick then—she shan't see that I was hurt by it.—I'll affect indifference—(*Hums a tune : then listens.*) No—zounds ! she's *not* coming !—nor don't intend it, I suppose.—This is not *steadiness*, but *obstinacy* ! Yet I deserve it.—What, after so long an absence to quarrel with her tenderness !—'twas barbarous and unmanly !—I should be ashamed to see her now. I'll wait till her just resentment is abated—and when I

Nice, Critical, observant.

distress her so again, may I lose her for ever, and be linked instead to some antique virago, whose gnawing passions, and long hoarded spleen, shall make me curse my folly half the day and all the night !   (*Exit*.)

SCENE III.   *Mrs. Malaprop's Lodgings.*

(*Mrs. Malaprop, with a letter in her hand, and Captain Absolute.*)

Mrs. Malaprop. Your being Sir Anthony's son, captain, would itself be a sufficient accommodation ; but from the ingenuity of your appearance, I am convinced you deserve the character here given of you.

Absolute. Permit me to say, madam, that as I never yet have had the pleasure of seeing Miss Languish, my principal inducement in this affair at present is the honour of being allied to Mrs. Malaprop ; of whose intellectual accomplishments, elegant manners, and unaffected learning, no tongue is silent.

Mrs. Malaprop. Sir, you do me infinite honour ! I beg, captain, you'll be seated.—(*Sit.*) Ah ! few gentlemen, nowadays, know how to value the ineffectual qualities in a woman ! few think how a little knowledge becomes a gentlewoman !—Men have no sense now but for the worthless flower of beauty !

Absolute. It is but too true, indeed, ma'am :—yet I fear our ladies should share the blame—they think our admiration of *beauty* so great, that *knowledge* in *them* would be superfluous. Thus, like garden-trees, they seldom show fruit, till time has robbed them of the more specious blossom.—Few, like Mrs. Malaprop and the orange-tree, are rich in both at once.

Mrs. Malaprop. Sir, you overpower me with good-breeding.—He is the very pine-apple of politeness ! —You are not ignorant, captain, that this giddy girl has somehow contrived to fix her affections on a beggarly, strolling, eavesdropping Ensign, whom none of us have seen, and nobody knows anything of.

Absolute. Oh, I have heard the silly affair before. —I'm not at all prejudiced against her on *that* account.

Mrs. Malaprop. You are very good and very considerate, captain. I am sure I have done everything in my power since I exploded the affair ; long ago I laid my positive conjunctions on her, never to think on the fellow again ;—I have since laid Sir Anthony's preposition before her ; but, I am sorry to say, she seems resolved to decline every particle that I enjoin her.

Absolute. It must be very distressing, indeed, ma'am.

Mrs. Malaprop. Oh ! it gives me the hydrostatics to such a degree !—I thought she had persisted from corresponding with him ; but, behold, this very day, I have interceded another letter from the fellow ; I believe I have it in my pocket.

Absolute. Oh, the devil ! my last note. (*Aside.*)

Mrs. Malaprop. Ay, here it is.

Absolute. Ay, my note indeed ! O the little traitress Lucy. (*Aside.*)

Mrs. Malaprop. There, perhaps you may know the writing. (*Gives him the letter.*)

Absolute. I think I have seen the hand before— yes, I certainly must have seen this hand before——

Mrs. Malaprop. Nay, but read it, captain.

Absolute (reads). *My soul's idol, my adored Lydia !* —Very tender indeed !

Mrs. Malaprop. Tender ! ay, and profane too, o' my conscience.

Absolute (reads). *I am excessively alarmed at the intelligence you send me, the more so as my new rival——*

Mrs. Malaprop. That's you, sir.

Absolute (reads). —*has universally the character of being an accomplished gentleman and a man of honour.* Well, that's handsome enough.

Mrs. Malaprop. Oh, the fellow has some design in writing so.

Absolute. That he had, I'll answer for him, ma'am.

Mrs. Malaprop. But go on, sir — you'll see presently.

Absolute (reads). *As for the old weather-beaten she-dragon who guards you——* Who can he mean by that ?

Mrs. Malaprop. Me, sir !—*me* !—he means *me* there !—What do you think now ?—but go on a little further.

Absolute. Impudent scoundrel !—(Reads.)—*it shall go hard but I will elude her vigilance, as I am told that the same ridiculous vanity, which makes her dress up her coarse features, and deck her dull chat with hard words which she don't understand——*

Mrs. Malaprop. There, sir, an attack upon my language ! what do you think of that ?—an aspersion upon my parts of speech ! was ever such a brute ! Sure, if I reprehend anything in this world, it is the use of my oracular tongue, and a nice derangement of epitaphs !

Absolute. Hs deserves to be hanged and quartered ! let me see—(Reads)—*same ridiculous vanity——*

Mrs. Malaprop. You need not read it again, sir.

Absolute. I beg pardon, ma'am.—(Reads)—*does also lay her open to the grossest deceptions from flattery and pretended admiration*—an impudent coxcomb !—*so that I have a scheme to see you shortly with the old harridan's consent, and even to make her a go-between in our interviews.*—Was ever such assurance !

Mrs. Malaprop. Did you ever hear anything like it ?—he'll elude my vigilance, will he ?—yes, yes ! ha! ha ! he's very like to enter these doors ; we'll try who can plot best !

Absolute. So we will, ma'am—so we will ! Ha ! ha ! ha ! a conceited puppy, ha ! ha ! ha !—Well, but, Mrs. Malaprop, as the girl seems so infatuated by this fellow, suppose you were to wink at her corresponding with him for a little time—let her even plot an elopement with him—then do you connive at her escape—while I, just in the nick, will have the fellow laid by the heels, and fairly contrive to carry her off in his stead.

Mrs. Malaprop. I am delighted with the scheme; never was anything better perpetrated!

Absolute. But, pray, could not I see the lady for a few minutes now?—I should like to try her temper a little.

Mrs. Malaprop. Why, I don't know—I doubt she is not prepared for a visit of this kind. There is a decorum in these matters.

Absolute. O Lord! she won't mind *me*—only tell her Beverley——

Mrs. Malaprop. Sir!

Absolute. Gently, good tongue. (*Aside.*)

Mrs. Malaprop. What did you say of Beverley?

Absolute. Oh, I was going to propose that you should tell her, by way of jest, that it was Beverley who was below; she'd come down fast enough then —ha! ha! ha!

Mrs. Malaprop. 'Twould be a trick she well deserves; besides, you know the fellow tells her he'll get my consent to see her—ha! ha! Let him if he can, I say again. Lydia, come down here! (*Calling.*) —He'll make me a *go-between in their interviews*!— ha! ha! ha! Come down, I say, Lydia! I don't wonder at your laughing, ha! ha! ha! his impudence is truly ridiculous.

Absolute. 'Tis very ridiculous, upon my soul, ma'am, ha! ha! ha!

Mrs. Malaprop. The little hussy won't hear. Well, I'll go and tell her at once who it is—she shall know that Captain Absolute is come to wait on her. And I'll make her behave as becomes a young woman.

Absolute. As you please, ma'am.

Mrs. Malaprop. For the present, captain, your servant. Ah! you've not done laughing yet, I see—*elude my vigilance*; yes, yes; ha! ha! ha! (*Exit.*)

Absolute. Ha! ha! ha! one would think now that I might throw off all disguise at once, and seize my prize with security; but such is Lydia's caprice, that to undeceive were probably to lose her. I'll see whether she knows me.

(*Walks aside, and seems engaged in looking at the pictures.*)

(*Enter Lydia.*)

Lydia. What a scene am I now to go through! surely nothing can be more dreadful than to be obliged to listen to the loathsome addresses of a stranger to one's heart. I have heard of girls persecuted as I am, who have appealed in behalf of their favoured lover to the generosity of his rival; suppose I were to try it—there stands the hated rival—an officer too!—but oh, how unlike my Beverley! I wonder he don't begin—truly he seems a very negligent wooer!—quite at his ease, upon my word! —I'll speak first—Mr. Absolute.

Absolute. Ma'am.   (*Turns around.*)

Lydia. O heavens! Beverley!

Absolute. Hush!—hush, my life! softly! be not surprised!

Lydia. I am so astonished? and so terrified! and so overjoyed!—for Heaven's sake! how came you here?

Absolute. Briefly, I have deceived your aunt—I was informed that my new rival was to visit here this evening, and contriving to have him kept away, have passed myself on *her* for Captain Absolute.

Lydia. O charming! And she really takes you for young Absolute!

Absolute. Oh, she's convinced of it.

Lydia. Ha! ha! ha! I can't forbear laughing to think how her sagacity is overreached!

Absolute. But we trifle with our precious moments
—such another opportunity may not occur ; then let
me now conjure my kind, my condescending angel,
to fix the time when I may rescue her from unde-
serving persecution, and with a licensed warmth plead
for my reward.

Lydia. Will you then, Beverley, consent to forfeit
that portion of my paltry wealth ?—that burden on
the wings of love ?

Absolute. Oh, come to me—rich only thus—in
loveliness ! Bring no portion to me but thy love—
'twill be generous in you, Lydia—for well you know,
it is the only dower your poor Beverley can repay.

Lydia. How persuasive are his words !—how charming will poverty be with him ! (*Aside.*)

Absolute. Ah ! my soul, what a life will we then
live ! Love shall be our idol and support ! we will
worship him with a monastic strictness ; abjuring
all worldly toys, to centre every thought and action
there. Proud of calamity, we will enjoy the wreck
of wealth ; while the surrounding gloom of adversity
shall make the flame of our pure love show doubly
bright. By Heaven ! I would fling all goods of fortune from me with a prodigal hand, to enjoy the
scene where I might clasp my Lydia to my bosom,
and say, the world affords no smile to me but here—
(*Embracing her.*) If she holds out now, the devil is
in it ! (*Aside.*)

Lydia. Now could I fly with him to the antipodes !
but my persecution is not yet come to a crisis.

(*Re-enter Mrs. Malaprop, listening.*)

Mrs. Malaprop. I am impatient to know how the
little hussy deports herself. (*Aside.*)

Absolute. So pensive, Lydia !—is then your warmth
abated ?

Mrs. Malaprop. Warmth abated !—so !—she has
been in a passion, I suppose. (*Aside.*)

Lydia. No—nor ever can while I have life.

Mrs. Malaprop. An ill-tempered little devil ! She'll be in a passion all her life—will she ?   (*Aside.*)

Lydia. Think not the idle threats of my ridiculous aunt can ever have any weight with me.

Mrs. Malaprop. Very dutiful, upon my word !
          (*Aside.*)

Lydia. Let her choice be Captain *Absolute*, but Beverley is mine.

Mrs. Malaprop. I am astonished at her assurance ! —to his face—this is to his face !   (*Aside.*)

Absolute. Thus then let me enforce my suit.
          (*Kneeling.*)

Mrs. Malaprop (*aside*). Ay, poor young man !—down on his knees entreating for pity !—I can contain no longer.—(*Coming forward.*) Why, thou vixen !—I have overheard you.

Absolute. Oh, confound her vigilance !   (*Aside.*)

Mrs. Malaprop. Captain *Absolute*, I know not how to apologize for her shocking rudeness.

Absolute (*aside*). So all's safe, I find.—(*Aloud*) I have hopes, madam, that time will bring the young lady——

Mrs. Malaprop. Oh, there's nothing to be hoped for from her ! she's as headstrong as an allegory on the banks of the Nile.

Lydia. Nay, madam, what do you charge me with now ?

Mrs. Malaprop. Why, thou unblushing rebel—didn't you tell this gentleman to his face that you loved another better ?—didn't you say you never would be his ?

Lydia. No, madam—I did not.

Mrs. Malaprop. Good Heavens ! what assurance ! —Lydia, Lydia, you ought to know that lying don't become a young woman !—Didn't you boast that *Beverley*, that stroller *Beverley*, possessed your heart ? —Tell me that, I say.

Lydia. 'Tis true, ma'am, and none but *Beverley*——

68

Mrs. Malaprop. Hold !—hold, Assurance !—you shall not be so rude.

Absolute. Nay, pray, Mrs. Malaprop, don't stop the young lady's speech : she's very welcome to talk thus—it does not hurt *me* in the least, I assure you.

Mrs. Malaprop. You are *too* good, captain—*too* amiably patient—but come with me, miss.—Let us see you again soon, captain—remember what we have fixed.

Absolute. I shall, ma'am.

Mrs. Malaprop. Come, take a graceful leave of the gentleman.

Lydia. May every blessing wait on my *Beverley*, my loved *Bev*——

Mrs. Malaprop. Hussy ! I'll choke the word in your throat !—come along—come along.

(*Exeunt severally ; Beverley kissing his hand to Lydia—Mrs. Malaprop stopping her from speaking.*)

SCENE IV.   *Acres' Lodgings.*

(*Acres and David.   Acres, as just dressed.*)

Acres. Indeed, David—do you think I become it so ?

David. You are quite another creature, believe me, master, by the mass ! an we've any luck we shall see the Devon monkeyrony in all the print-shops in Bath !

Acres. Dress *does* make a difference, David.

David. 'Tis all in all, I think.—Difference ! why, an you were to go now to Clod Hall, I am certain the

Monkeyrony, David's version of *macaroni*, a dandy. (From " The Macaroni Club," a fashionable eighteenth-century club for introducing Continental freakish modes into England, *e.g.* monstrous wigs.)

old lady wouldn't know you : master Butler wouldn't believe his own eyes, and Mrs. Pickle would cry, Lard presarve me ! Our dairymaid would come giggling to the door, and I warrant Dolly Tester, your honour's favourite, would blush like my waistcoat. —Oons ! I'll hold a gallon, there an't a dog in the house but would bark, and I question whether *Phillis* would wag a hair of her tail !

Acres. Ay, David, there's nothing like polishing.

David. So I says of your honour's boots ; but the boy never heeds me !

Acres. But, David, has Mr. *De-la-grace* been here ? I must rub up my balancing, and chasing, and boring.

David. I'll call again, sir.

Acres. Do—and see if there are any letters for me at the post-office.

David. I will.—By the mass, I can't help looking at your head !—if I hadn't been by at the cooking, I wish I may die if I should have known the dish again myself !

(*Exit. Acres comes forward, practising a dancing step.*)

Acres. Sink, slide—coupee.—Confound the first inventors of cotillons ! say I—they are as bad as algebra to us country gentlemen—I can walk a minuet easy enough when I am forced !—and I have been accounted a good stick in a country-dance.—Odds jigs and tabors ! I never valued your cross-over to couple—figure in—right and left—and I'd foot it with e'er a captain in the county !—but these outlandish heathen allemandes and cotillons are quite beyond me !—I shall never prosper at 'em, that's sure—mine are true-born English legs—they don't understand their curst French lingo !—their *pas* this, and *pas*

Balancing, chasing, boring, Dancing terms meaning moving forward and retiring, quick walking, slow walking.
Coupee, Dancing step in which one foot is bent forward.
Cross-over to couple, etc., Dancing terms. *Cf.* in the Lancers.
Allemandes, A lively dance of a German type.

that, and *pas* t'other!—damn me! my feet don't like to be called paws! no, 'tis certain I have most Antigallican toes!

(*Enter Servant.*)

Servant. Here is Sir Lucius O'Trigger to wait on you, sir.

Acres. Show him in.   (*Exit Servant.*)

(*Enter Sir Lucius.*)

Sir Lucius. Mr. Acres, I am delighted to embrace you.

Acres. My dear Sir Lucius, I kiss your hands.

Sir Lucius. Pray, my friend, what has brought you so suddenly to Bath?

Acres. Faith! I have followed Cupid's Jack-a-lantern, and find myself in a quagmire at last.—In short, I have been very ill-used, Sir Lucius.—I don't choose to mention names, but look on me as on a very ill-used gentleman.

Sir Lucius. Pray what is the case?—I ask no names.

Acres. Mark me, Sir Lucius, I fall as deep as need be in love with a young lady—her friends take my part—I follow her to Bath—send word of my arrival; and receive answer, that the lady is to be otherwise disposed of.—This, Sir Lucius, I call being ill-used.

Sir Lucius. Very ill, upon my conscience.—Pray, can you divine the cause of it?

Acres. Why, there's the matter; she has another lover, one *Beverley*, who, I am told, is now in Bath.—Odds slanders and lies! he must be at the bottom of it.

Sir Lucius. A rival in the case, is there?—and you think he has supplanted you unfairly?

Acres. Unfairly! to be sure he has. He never could have done it fairly.

Sir Lucius. Then sure you know what is to be done!

Acres. Not I, upon my soul !

Sir Lucius. We wear no swords here, but you understand me.

Acres. What ! fight him !

Sir Lucius. Ay, to be sure : what can I mean else ?

Acres. But he has given me no provocation.

Sir Lucius. Now, I think he has given you the greatest provocation in the world. Can a man commit a more heinous offence against another than to fall in love with the same woman ? Oh, by my soul ! it is the most unpardonable breach of friendship.

Acres. Breach of friendship ! ay, ay ; but I have no acquaintance with this man. I never saw him in my life.

Sir Lucius. That's no argument at all—he has the less right then to take such a liberty.

Acres. Gad, that's true—I grow full of anger, Sir Lucius ?—I fire apace ! Odds hilts and blades ! I find a man may have a deal of valour in him, and not know it ! But couldn't I contrive to have a little right of my side ?

Sir Lucius. What the devil signifies *right*, when your *honour* is concerned ? Do you think, *Achilles* or my little *Alexander the Great*, ever inquired where the right lay ? No, by my soul, they drew their broadswords, and left the lazy sons of peace to settle the justice of it.

Acres. Your words are a grenadier's march to my heart ! I believe courage must be catching ! I certainly do feel a kind of valour rising as it were—a kind of courage, as I may say.—Odds flints, pans, and triggers ! I'll challenge him directly.

Sir Lucius. Ah, my little friend, if I had *Blunderbuss Hall* here, I could show you a range of ancestry, in the O'Trigger line, that would furnish the new

We wear no swords, Because forbidden (to prevent duelling).

room ; every one of whom had killed his man !—
For though the mansion-house and dirty acres have
slipped through my fingers, I thank heaven our honour
and the family-pictures are as fresh as ever.

Acres. O, Sir Lucius ! I have had ancestors too !—
every man of 'em colonel or captain in the militia !—
Odds balls and barrels ! say no more—I'm braced
for it. The thunder of your words has soured the
milk of human kindness in my breast ;—Zounds ! as
the man in the play says, *I could do such deeds* !

Sir Lucius. Come, come, there must be no passion
at all in the case—these things should always be done
civilly.

Acres. I must be in a passion, Sir Lucius—I must
be in a rage.—Dear Sir Lucius, let me be in a rage, if
you love me. Come, here's pen and paper.—(*Sits
down to write.*) I would the ink were red !—Indite,
I say indite !—How shall I begin ? Odds bullets and
blades ! I'll write a good bold hand, however.

Sir Lucius. Pray compose yourself.

Acres. Come—now, shall I begin with an oath ?
Do, Sir Lucius, let me begin with a damme.

Sir Lucius. Pho ! pho ! do the thing decently, and
like a Christian. Begin now—*Sir*——

Acres. That's too civil by half.

*Sir Lucius. To prevent the confusion that might
arise*——

Acres. Well——

*Sir Lucius. —from our both addressing the same
lady*——

Acres. Ay, there's the reason—*same lady*—well——

*Sir Lucius. —I shall expect the honour of your
company*——

Acres. Zounds ! I'm not asking him to dinner.

Sir Lucius. Pray be easy.

Acres. Well, then, *honour of your company*——

Sir Lucius. —to settle our pretensions——

Acres. Well.

73

Sir Lucius. Let me see, ay, King's-Mead-Fields will do—*in King's-Mead-Fields.*

Acres. So, that's done — Well, I'll fold it up presently ; my own crest—a hand and dagger shall be the seal.

Sir Lucius. You see now this little explanation will put a stop at once to all confusion or misunderstanding that might arise between you.

Acres. Ay, we fight to prevent any misunderstanding.

Sir Lucius. Now I'll leave you to fix your own time. Take my advice, and you'll decide it this evening if you can ; then let the worst come of it, 'twill be off your mind to-morrow.

Acres. Very true.

Sir Lucius. So I shall see nothing more of you, unless it be by letter, till the evening.—I would do myself the honour to carry your message ; but, to tell you a secret, I believe I shall have just such another affair on my own hands. There is a gay captain here, who put a jest on me lately, at the expense of my country, and I only want to fall in with the gentleman, to call him out.

Acres. By my valour, I should like to see you fight first ! Odds life ! I should like to see you kill him if it was only to get a little lesson.

Sir Lucius. I shall be very proud of instructing you.—Well, for the present—but remember now, when you meet your antagonist, do everything in a mild and agreeable manner.—Let your courage be as keen, but at the same time as polished, as your sword.

　　　　　　　　　　　　　　　(*Exeunt severally.*)

King's-Mead-Fields, Situated to the south-west of Bath.

END OF THE THIRD ACT.

ACT IV

SCENE I. *Acres' Lodgings.*

(Acres and David.)

David. Then, by the mass, sir ! I would do no such thing—ne'er a Sir Lucius O'Trigger in the kingdom should make me fight, when I wa'n't so minded. Oons ! what will the old lady say when she hears o't ?

Acres. Ah ! David, if you had heard Sir Lucius !— Odds sparks and flames ! he would have roused your valour.

David. Not he, indeed. I hate such bloodthirsty cormorants. Look'ee, master, if you'd wanted a bout at boxing, quarter-staff, or short-staff, I should never be the man to bid you cry off : but for your curst sharps and snaps, I never knew any good come of 'em.

Acres. But my honour, David, my honour ! I must be very careful of my honour.

David. Ay, by the mass ! and I would be very careful of it ; and I think in return my *honour* couldn't do less than to be very careful of *me*.

Acres. Odds blades ! David, no gentleman will ever risk the loss of his honour.

David. I say then, it would be but civil in *honour* never to risk the loss of a *gentleman*.—Look'ee, master, this *honour* seems to me to be a marvellous

Quarter-staff, A cudgel. It was held by one hand half-way along, the other a quarter.
Sharps and snaps, Sharpers and cheats.

75

false friend : ay, truly, a very courtier-like servant.—
Put the case, I was a gentleman (which, thank God, no
one can say of me) ; well—my honour makes me
quarrel with another gentleman of my acquaintance.
—So—we fight. (Pleasant enough that !) Boh ! I
kill him—(the more's my luck !) now, pray who gets
the profit of it ?—Why, my *honour*. But put the case
that he kills me !—by the mass ! I go to the worms,
and my honour whips over to my enemy.

Acres. No, David—in that case—Odds crowns and
laurels !—your honour follows you to the grave.

David. Now, that's just the place where I could
make a shift to do without it.

Acres. Zounds ! David, you are a coward !—It
doesn't become my valour to listen to you.—What,
shall I disgrace my ancestors ?—Think of that,
David—think what it would be to disgrace my
ancestors !

David. Under favour, the surest way of not dis-
gracing them is to keep as long as you can out of
their company. Look'ee now, master, to go to them
in such haste—with an ounce of lead in your brains—
I should think might as well be let alone. Our
ancestors are very good kind of folks ; but they are
the last people I should choose to have a visiting
acquaintance with.

Acres. But, David, now, you don't think there is
such very, very, *very* great danger, hey ?—Odds life !
people often fight without any mischief done !

David. By the mass, I think 'tis ten to one against
you !—Oons ! here to meet some lion-hearted fellow,
I warrant, with his damned double-barrelled swords,
and cut-and-thrust pistols !—Lord bless us ! it makes
me tremble to think o't—Those be such desperate
bloody-minded weapons ! Well, I never could abide
'em !—from a child I never could fancy 'em !—I
suppose there a'nt been so merciless a beast in the
world as your loaded pistol !

Acres. Zounds ! I *won't* be afraid !—Odds fire and fury ! you shan't make me afraid.—Here is the challenge, and I have sent for my dear friend Jack Absolute to carry it for me.

David. Ay, i' the name of mischief, let *him* be the messenger.—For my part, I wouldn't lend a hand to it for the best horse in your stable. By the mass ! it don't look like another letter. It is, as I may say, a designing and malicious-looking letter ; and I warrant smells of gunpowder like a soldier's pouch !—Oons ! I wouldn't swear it mayn't go off !

Acres. Out, you poltroon ! you ha'n't the valour of a grasshopper.

David. Well, I say no more—'twill be sad news, to be sure, at Clod Hall ! but I ha' done.—How Phillis will howl when she hears of it !—Ay, poor bitch, she little thinks what shooting her master's going after ! And I warrant old Crop, who has carried your honour, field and road, these ten years, will curse the hour he was born.   (*Whimpering.*)

Acres. It won't do, David—I am determined to fight—so get along, you coward, while I'm in the mind.

(*Enter Servant.*)

Servant. Captain Absolute, sir.

Acres. Oh ! show him up.   (*Exit Servant.*)

David. Well, Heaven send we be all alive this time to-morrow.

Acres. What's that ?—Don't provoke me, David !

David. Good-bye, master.   (*Whimpering.*)

Acres. Get along, you cowardly, dastardly, croaking raven !   (*Exit David.*)

(*Enter Absolute.*)

Absolute. What's the matter, Bob ?

Acres. A vile, sheep-hearted blockhead ! If I hadn't the valour of St. George and the dragon to boot——

Absolute. But what did you want with me, Bob ?

77

Acres. Oh !—There—— (*Gives him the challenge.*)

Absolute. To Ensign Beverley.—So what's going on now ! (*Aside.*)—Well, what's this ?

Acres. A challenge !

Absolute. Indeed ! Why, you won't fight him ; will you, Bob ?

Acres. Egad, but I will, Jack. Sir Lucius has wrought me to it. He has left me full of rage—and I'll fight this evening, that so much good passion mayn't be wasted.

Absolute. But what have I to do with this ?

Acres. Why, as I think you know something of this fellow, I want you to find him out for me, and give him this mortal defiance.

Absolute. Well, give it to me, and trust me he gets it.

Acres. Thank you, my dear friend, my dear Jack ; but it is giving you a great deal of trouble.

Absolute. Not in the least—I beg you won't mention it.—No trouble in the world I assure you.

Acres. You are very kind.—What it is to have a friend !—You couldn't be my second, could you, Jack ?

Absolute. Why no, Bob—not in *this* affair—it would not be quite so proper.

Acres. Well, then, I must get my friend Sir Lucius. I shall have your good wishes, however, Jack ?

Absolute. Whenever he meets you, believe me.

(*Enter Servant.*)

Servant. Sir Anthony Absolute is below, inquiring for the captain.

Absolute. I'll come instantly.—(*Exit Servant.*) Well, my little hero, success attend you. (*Going.*)

Acres. Stay—stay, Jack.—If Beverley should ask you what kind of a man your friend Acres is, do tell him I am a devil of a fellow—will you, Jack ?

Absolute. To be sure I shall. I'll say you are a determined dog—hey, Bob ?

Acres. Ay, do, do—and if that frightens him, egad, perhaps he mayn't come. So tell him I generally kill a man a week ; will you, Jack ?

Absolute. I will, I will ; I'll say you are called in the country *Fighting Bob.*

Acres. Right—right—'tis all to prevent mischief ; for I don't want to take his life if I clear my honour.

Absolute. No !—that's very kind of you.

Acres. Why, you don't wish me to kill him—do you, Jack ?

Absolute. No, upon my soul, I do not. But a devil of a fellow, hey ? (*Going.*)

Acres. True, true—but stay—stay, Jack—you may add, that you never saw me in such a rage before—a most devouring rage !

Absolute. I will, I will.

Acres. Remember, Jack—a determined dog.

Absolute. Ay, ay, *Fighting Bob* !

(*Exeunt severally.*)

SCENE II. *Mrs. Malaprop's Lodgings.*

(*Mrs. Malaprop and Lydia.*)

Mrs. Malaprop. Why, thou perverse one !—tell me what you can object to him ? Isn't he a handsome man ?—tell me that. A genteel man ? a pretty figure of a man ?

Lydia. She little thinks whom she is praising ! (*Aside.*)—So is Beverley, ma'am.

Mrs. Malaprop. No caparisons, miss, if you please. Caparisons don't become a young woman. No ! Captain Absolute is indeed a fine gentleman !

Lydia. Ay, the Captain Absolute *you* have seen. (*Aside.*)

Mrs. Malaprop. Then he's *so* well bred ;—*so* full of alacrity, and adulation !—and has *so much* to say for himself :—in such good language too ! His

physiognomy so grammatical! Then his presence is
so noble! I protest when I saw him, I thought of
what Hamlet says in the play :—

> " Hesperian curls—the front of *Job* himself !—
> An eye, like *March*, to threaten at command !
> A station, like Harry Mercury, new——"

Something about kissing—on a hill—however, the
similitude struck me directly.

Lydia. How enraged she'll be presently, when she
discovers her mistake !   (*Aside.*)

(*Enter Servant.*)

Servant. Sir Anthony and Captain Absolute are
below, ma'am.

Mrs. Malaprop. Show them up here. — (*Exit
Servant.*) Now, Lydia, I insist on your behaving as
becomes a young woman. Show your good breeding,
at least, though you have forgot your duty.

Lydia. Madam, I have told you my resolution !—
I shall not only give him no encouragement, but I
won't even speak to, or look at him.

(*Flings herself into a chair, with her face from the
door.*)

(*Enter Sir Anthony and Absolute.*)

Sir Anthony. Here we are, Mrs. Malaprop ; come
to mitigate the frowns of unrelenting beauty,—and
difficulty enough I had to bring this fellow.—I don't
know what's the matter ; but if I had not held him
by force, he'd have given me the slip.

Mrs. Malaprop. You have infinite trouble, Sir
Anthony, in the affair.—I am ashamed for the cause !—
(*Aside to her.*) Lydia, Lydia, rise, I beseech you !—
pay your respects.

Hesperian curls, etc., Hamlet, III. iv., 56–59 :
> " Hyperion's curls ; the front of Jove himself ;
> An eye, like Mars, to threaten or command ;
> A station, like the herald Mercury,
> New lighted on a heaven-kissing hill."

Sir Anthony. I hope, madam, that Miss Languish
has reflected on the worth of this gentleman, and the
regard due to her aunt's choice, and *my* alliance.—
(*Aside to him.*)   Now, Jack, speak to her.

Absolute (*aside*).   What the devil shall I do !—You
see, sir, she won't even look at me whilst you are
here.   I knew she wouldn't !   I told you so.   Let me
entreat you, sir, to leave us together !

(*Absolute seems to expostulate with his father.*)

Lydia (*aside*).   I wonder, I ha'n't heard my aunt
exclaim yet !   sure she can't have looked at him !—
perhaps their regimentals are alike, and she is something blind.

Sir Anthony. I say, sir, I won't stir a foot yet !

Mrs. Malaprop. I am sorry to say, Sir Anthony,
that my affluence over my niece is very small.—
(*Aside to her.*)   Turn round, Lydia : I blush for
you !

Sir Anthony. May I not flatter myself, that Miss
Languish will assign what cause of dislike she can
have to my son !—(*Aside to him.*)   Why don't you
begin, Jack ?—Speak, you puppy—speak !

Mrs. Malaprop. It is impossible, Sir Anthony, she
can have any.   She will not say she has.—(*Aside to
her.*)   Answer, hussy !   why don't you answer ?

Sir Anthony. Then, madam, I trust that a childish
and hasty predilection will be no bar to Jack's
happiness.—(*Aside to him.*)   Zounds !   sirrah !   why
don't you speak ?

Lydia (*aside*).   I think my lover seems as little inclined to conversation as myself.—How strangely
blind my aunt must be !

Absolute. Hem !   hem !   madam—hem !—(*Absolute
attempts to speak, then returns to Sir Anthony.*)   Faith !
sir, I am so confounded !—and—so—so—confused !—
I told you I should be so, sir—I knew it !—The—the—
tremor of my passion entirely takes away my presence
of mind.

Sir Anthony. But it don't take away your voice, fool, does it ?—Go up, and speak to her directly !

(*Absolute makes signs to Mrs. Malaprop to leave them together.*)

Mrs. Malaprop. Sir Anthony, shall we leave them together ?—(*Aside to her.*) Ah ! you stubborn little vixen !

Sir Anthony. Not yet, ma'am, not yet !—(*Aside to him.*) What the devil are you at ? unlock your jaws, sirrah, or——

Absolute (*aside*). Now Heaven send she may be too sullen to look round !—I must disguise my voice.—(*Draws near Lydia, and speaks in a low, hoarse tone.*) Will not Miss Languish lend an ear to the mild accents of true love ? Will not——

Sir Anthony. What the devil ails the fellow ? Why don't you speak out ?—not stand croaking like a frog in a quinsy !

Absolute. The—the—excess of my awe, and my—my—my modesty, quite choke me !

Sir Anthony. Ah ! your *modesty* again !—I'll tell you what, Jack ; if you don't speak out directly, and glibly too, I shall be in such a rage !—Mrs. Malaprop, I wish the lady would favour us with something more than a side-front.

(*Mrs. Malaprop seems to chide Lydia.*)

Absolute (*aside*). So all will out, I see !—(*Goes up to Lydia, speaks softly.*) Be not surprised, my Lydia, suppress all surprise at present.

Lydia (*aside*). Heavens ! 'tis Beverley's voice ! Sure he can't have imposed on Sir Anthony too !—(*Looks round by degrees, then starts up.*) Is this possible !—my Beverley !—how can this be ?—my Beverley ?

Absolute. Ah ! 'tis all over.   (*Aside.*)

Sir Anthony. Beverley !—the devil—Beverley !—What can the girl mean ?—This is my son, Jack Absolute.

Mrs. Malaprop. For shame, hussy! for shame! your head runs so on that fellow, that you have him always in your eyes!—beg Captain Absolute's pardon directly.

Lydia. I see no Captain Absolute, but my loved Beverley!

Sir Anthony. Zounds! the girl's mad!—her brain's turned by reading.

Mrs. Malaprop. O' my conscience, I believe so! —What do you mean by Beverley, hussy!—You saw Captain Absolute before to-day; there he is—your husband that shall be.

Lydia. With all my soul, ma'am—when I refuse my Beverley——

Sir Anthony. Oh! she's as mad as Bedlam!—or has this fellow been playing us a rogue's trick!— Come here, sirrah, who the devil are you?

Absolute. Faith, sir, I am not quite clear myself; but I'll endeavour to recollect.

Sir Anthony. Are you my son or not?—answer for your mother, you dog, if you won't for me.

Mrs. Malaprop. Ay, sir, who are you? O mercy! I begin to suspect!——

Absolute (aside). Ye powers of impudence, befriend me!—(*Aloud.*) Sir Anthony, most assuredly I am your wife's son, and that I sincerely believe myself to be *yours* also I hope my duty has always shown.—Mrs. Malaprop I am your most respectful admirer, and shall be proud to add affectionate nephew.—I need not tell my Lydia, that she sees her faithful *Beverley*, who, knowing the singular generosity of her temper, assumed that name and station, which has proved a test of the most disinterested love, which he now hopes to enjoy in a more elevated character.

Bedlam, Contracted form of Bethlehem, the name of the first London lunatic asylum, founded 1247, in the priory of the church of St. Mary of Bethlehem. In the eighteenth century the patients were exhibited as a sight, and were harshly treated.

Lydia. So !—there will be no elopement after all !
(*Sullenly.*)

Sir Anthony. Upon my soul, Jack, thou art a very impudent fellow ! to do you justice, I think I never saw a piece of more consummate assurance !

Absolute. Oh, you flatter me, sir—you compliment —'tis my *modesty* you know, sir,—my *modesty* that has stood in my way.

Sir Anthony. Well, I am glad you are not the dull, insensible varlet you pretended to be, however !— I'm glad you have made a fool of your father, you dog—I am. So this was your *penitence*, your *duty* and *obedience* !—I thought it was damned sudden !—You *never heard their names before*, not you !—*what*, the Languishes *of Worcestershire*, hey ?—*if you could please me in the affair 'twas all you desired !*—Ah ! you dissembling villain !—What !—(*pointing to Lydia*) *she squints, don't she ?—a little red-haired girl !*—hey ? —Why, you hypocritical young rascal !—I wonder you an't ashamed to hold up your head !

Absolute. 'Tis with difficulty, sir.—I *am* confused— very much confused, as you must perceive.

Mrs. Malaprop. O Lud ! Sir Anthony !—a new light breaks in upon me !—hey !—how ! what ! captain, did *you* write the letters then ?—What—am I to thank *you* for the elegant compilation of *an old weather-beaten she-dragon*—hey !—O mercy !—was it *you* that reflected on my parts of speech ?

Absolute. Dear sir ! my modesty will be over-powered at last, if you don't assist me—I shall certainly not be able to stand it !

Sir Anthony. Come, come, Mrs. Malaprop, we must forget and forgive ;—odds life ! matters have taken so clever a turn all of a sudden, that I could find in my heart to be so good-humoured ! and so gallant ! hey ! Mrs. Malaprop !

Mrs. Malaprop. Well, Sir Anthony, since *you* desire it, we will not anticipate the past !—so mind,

young people—our retrospection will be all to the
future.

Sir Anthony. Come, we must leave them together ;
Mrs. Malaprop, they long to fly into each other's
arms, I warrant !—Jack,—isn't the cheek as I said,
hey ?—and the eye, you rogue !—and the lip—hey ?
—Come, Mrs. Malaprop, we'll not disturb their
tenderness—theirs is the time of life for happiness !
—*Youth's the season made for joy*—(*Sings.*)—hey !—
Odds life ! I'm in such spirits,—I don't know what I
could not do !—Permit me, ma'am—(*Gives his hand
to Mrs. Malaprop. Sings.*) Tol-de-rol—gad, I should
like to have a little fooling myself—Tol-de-rol ! de-rol.
    (*Exit, singing and handing Mrs. Malaprop. Lydia
        sits sullenly in her chair.*)

Absolute (*aside*). So much thought bodes me no
good.—(*Aloud.*) So grave, Lydia !

Lydia. Sir !

Absolute (*aside*). So !—egad ! I thought as much !
—that damned monosyllable has froze me !—(*Aloud.*)
What, Lydia, now that we are as happy in our
friends' consent, as in our mutual vows——

Lydia. Friends' consent indeed !   (*Peevishly.*)

Absolute. Come, come, we must lay aside some of
our romance—a little *wealth* and *comfort* may be
endured after all. And for your fortune, the lawyers
shall make such settlements as——

Lydia. Lawyers ! I hate lawyers !

Absolute. Nay, then, we will not wait for their
lingering forms, but instantly procure the licence,
and——

Lydia. The *licence* !—I hate licence !

Absolute. Oh my love ! be not so unkind !—thus
let me entreat——   (*Kneeling.*)

Lydia. Pshaw !—what signifies kneeling, when you
know I *must* have you ?

Youth's the season made for joy, A song from Act II. Sc. vi. of Gay's
    Beggar's Opera, 1727.

Absolute (*rising*). Nay, madam, there shall be no constraint upon your inclinations, I promise you.— If I have lost your heart, I resign the rest.—(*Aside.*) 'Gad, I must try what a little *spirit* will do.

Lydia (*rising*). Then, sir, let me tell you, the interest you had there was acquired by a mean, unmanly imposition, and deserves the punishment of fraud. —What, you have been treating *me* like a child!— humouring my romance! and laughing, I suppose, at your success!

Absolute. You wrong me, Lydia, you wrong me— only hear——

Lydia. So, while *I* fondly imagined we were deceiving my relations, and flattered myself that I should outwit and incense them all—behold my hopes are to be crushed at once, by my aunt's consent and approbation—and *I* am myself the only dupe at last! —(*Walking about in a heat.*)　But here, sir, here is the picture—*Beverley's* picture! (*taking a miniature from her bosom*) which I have worn, night and day, in spite of threats and entreaties!—There, sir; (*flings it to him*) and be assured I throw the original from my heart as easily.

Absolute. Nay, nay, ma'am, we will not differ as to that.—Here (*taking out a picture*), here is Miss Lydia Languish.—What a difference!—ay, *there* is the heavenly assenting smile that first gave soul and spirit to my hopes!—those are the lips which sealed a vow, as yet scarce dry in Cupid's calendar! and there the half-resentful blush, that *would* have checked the ardour of my thanks!—Well, all that's past!— all over indeed!—There, madam—in beauty, that copy is not equal to you, but in my mind its merit over the original, in being still the same, is such—that —I cannot find in my heart to part with it.

(*Puts it up again.*)

Lydia (*softening*). 'Tis *your own* doing, sir—I—I—I suppose you are perfectly satisfied.

86

Absolute. O, most certainly—sure, now, this is much better than being in love !—ha ! ha ! ha !—there's some spirit in *this* !—What signifies breaking some scores of solemn promises :—all that's of no consequence, you know.—To be sure people will say, that miss don't know her own mind—but never mind that ! Or, perhaps, they may be ill-natured enough to hint, that the gentleman grew tired of the lady and forsook her—but don't let that fret you.

Lydia. There is no bearing his insolence.

(*Bursts into tears.*)

(*Enter Mrs. Malaprop and Sir Anthony.*)

Mrs. Malaprop (*entering*). Come, we must interrupt your billing and cooing awhile.

Lydia. This is worse than your treachery and deceit, you base ingrate ! (*Sobbing.*)

Sir Anthony. What the devil's the matter now !—Zounds ! Mrs. Malaprop, this is the *oddest billing* and *cooing* I ever heard !—but what the deuce is the meaning of it ?—I am quite astonished !

Absolute. Ask the lady, sir.

Mrs. Malaprop. Oh mercy !—I'm quite analysed, for my part !—Why, Lydia, what is the reason of this ?

Lydia. Ask the gentleman, ma'am.

Sir Anthony. Zounds ! I shall be in a frenzy !—Why, Jack, you are not come out to be any one else, are you ?

Mrs. Malaprop. Ay, sir, there's no more trick, is there ?—you are not like Cerberus, *three* gentlemen at once are you ?

Absolute. You'll not let me speak—I say the lady can account for this much better than I can.

Lydia. Ma'am, you once commanded me never to think of Beverley again—there is the man—I now obey you : for, from this moment, I renounce him for ever. (*Exit Lydia.*)

Mrs. Malaprop. O mercy ! and miracles ! what a

turn here is—why sure, captain, you haven't behaved disrespectfully to my niece !

Sir Anthony. Ha ! ha ! ha !—ha ! ha ! ha !—now I see it. Ha ! ha ! ha !—now I see it—you have been too lively, Jack.

Absolute. Nay, sir, upon my word——

Sir Anthony. Come, no lying, Jack—I'm sure 'twas so.

Mrs. Malaprop. O Lud ! Sir Anthony !—O fy, captain !

Absolute. Upon my soul, ma'am——

Sir Anthony. Come, no excuses, Jack ; why, your father, you rogue, was so before you :—the blood of the Absolutes was always impatient.—Ha ! ha ! ha ! poor little Lydia ! why, you've frightened her, you dog, you have.

Absolute. By all that's good, sir——

Sir Anthony. Zounds ! say no more, I tell you—Mrs. Malaprop shall make your peace.—You must make his peace, Mrs. Malaprop :—you must tell her 'tis Jack's way—tell her 'tis all our ways—it runs in the blood of our family !—Come away, Jack—Ha ! ha ! ha ! Mrs. Malaprop—a young villain !

(*Pushes him out.*)

Mrs. Malaprop. Oh ! Sir Anthony !—O fy, captain !   (*Exeunt severally.*)

SCENE III.   *The North Parade.*

(*Enter Sir Lucius O'Trigger.*)

Sir Lucius. I wonder where this Captain Absolute hides himself ! Upon my conscience ! these officers are always in one's way in love affairs :—I remember I might have married lady Dorothy Carmine, if it had not been for a little rogue of a major, who ran away with her before she could get a sight of me ! And I wonder too what it is the ladies can see in them to be so fond of them—unless it be a touch of the old serpent in 'em, that makes the little creatures be caught, like vipers, with a bit of red cloth. Ha ! isn't this the captain coming ?—faith it is !—There is a probability of succeeding about that fellow, that is mighty provoking ! Who the devil is he talking to ?

(Steps aside.)

(Enter Captain Absolute.)

Absolute. To what fine purpose I have been plotting ! a noble reward for all my schemes, upon my soul !—a little gipsy !—I did not think her romance could have made her so damned absurd either. 'Sdeath I never was in a worse humour in my life !—I could cut my own throat, or any other person's, with the greatest pleasure in the world !

Sir Lucius. Oh, faith ! I'm in the luck of it. I never could have found him in a sweeter temper for my purpose—to be sure I'm just come in the nick ! Now to enter into conversation with him, and so quarrel genteelly.—*(Sir Lucius goes up to Absolute.)* With regard to that matter, captain, I must beg leave to differ in opinion with you.

Absolute. Upon my word, then, you must be a very subtle disputant :—because, sir, I happened just then to be giving no opinion at all.

Sir Lucius. That's no reason. For give me leave to tell you, a man may *think* an untruth as well as *speak* one.

Absolute. Very true, sir ; but if a man never utters his thoughts, I should think they might stand a chance of escaping controversy.

Sir Lucius. Then, sir, you differ in opinion with me, which amounts to the same thing.

Absolute. Hark'ee, Sir Lucius ; if I had not before known you to be a gentleman, upon my soul, I should not have discovered it at this interview : for what you can drive at, unless you mean to quarrel with me, I cannot conceive !

Sir Lucius. I humbly thank you, sir, for the quickness of your apprehension.—(*Bowing.*)   You have named the very thing I would be at.

Absolute. Very well, sir ; I shall certainly not balk your inclinations.—But I should be glad you would please to explain your motives.

Sir Lucius. Pray, sir, be easy ; the quarrel is a very pretty quarrel as it stands ; we should only spoil it by trying to explain it.   However, your memory is very short, or you could not have forgot an affront you passed on me within this week.   So, no more, but name your time and place.

Absolute. Well, sir, since you are so bent on it, the sooner the better ; let it be this evening—here, by the Spring Gardens.   We shall scarcely be interrupted.

Sir Lucius. Faith ! that same interruption in affairs of this nature shows very great ill-breeding.   I don't know what's the reason but in England, if a thing of this kind gets wind, people make such a pother, that a gentleman can never fight in peace and quietness.   However, if it's the same to you, captain, I should take it as a particular kindness if you'd let us meet in King's-Mead-Fields, as a little business will call me there about six o'clock, and I may dispatch both matters at once.

Absolute. 'Tis the same to me exactly.   A little after six, then, we will discuss this matter more seriously.

Sir Lucius. If you please, sir ; there will be very pretty small-sword light, though it won't do for a long shot.   So that matter's settled, and my mind's at ease !   (*Exit Sir Lucius.*)

(*Enter Faulkland, meeting Absolute.*)

Absolute. Well met !   I was going to look for you.

Spring Gardens, Pleasure gardens, with places for refreshments, music, and dancing.   On the east side of the river.
Small-sword, A light sword (for thrusting with the point) worn by civilians earlier in the eighteenth century ; but, at the time of the play, used for fencing.

O Faulkland! all the demons of spite and disappointment have conspired against me! I'm so vexed, that if I had not the prospect of a resource in being knocked o' the head by-and-by, I should scarce have spirits to tell you the cause.

Faulkland. What can you mean?—Has Lydia changed her mind?—I should have thought her duty and inclination would now have pointed to the same object.

Absolute. Ay, just as the eyes do of a person who squints: when her love-eye was fixed on me, t'other, her eye of duty, was finely obliqued: but when duty bid her point that the same way, off t'other turned on a swivel, and secured its retreat with a frown!

Faulkland. But what's the resource you——

Absolute. Oh, to wind up the whole, a good-natured Irishman here has—(*mimicking Sir Lucius*)—begged leave to have the pleasure of cutting my throat; and I mean to indulge him—that's all.

Faulkland. Prithee, be serious!

Absolute. 'Tis fact, upon my soul! Sir Lucius O'Trigger—you know him by sight—for some affront which I am sure I never intended, has obliged me to meet him this evening at six o'clock: 'tis on that account I wished to see you; you must go with me.

Faulkland. Nay, there must be some mistake, sure. Sir Lucius shall explain himself, and I daresay matters may be accommodated. But this evening, did you say? I wish it had been any other time.

Absolute. Why? there will be light enough: there will (as Sir Lucius says) be very pretty small-sword light, though it will not do for a long shot. Confound his long shots!

Faulkland. But I am myself a good deal ruffled by a difference I have had with Julia. My vile torment-

Mimicking, e.g. saying " lave " for " leave."

ing temper has made me treat her so cruelly, that I shall not be myself till we are reconciled.

Absolute. By heavens! Faulkland, you don't deserve her!

(*Enter Servant, gives Faulkland a letter, and exit.*)

Faulkland. Oh, Jack! this is from Julia. I dread to open it! I fear it may be to take a last leave!—perhaps to bid me return her letters, and restore——Oh, how I suffer for my folly!

Absolute. Here, let me see.—(*Takes the letter and opens it.*) Ay, a final sentence, indeed!—'tis all over with you, faith!

Faulkland. Nay, Jack, don't keep me in suspense!

Absolute. Hear then.—*As I am convinced that my dear Faulkland's own reflections have already upbraided him for his last unkindness to me, I will not add a word on the subject. I wish to speak with you as soon as possible. Yours ever and truly,* JULIA. There's stubbornness and resentment for you!—(*Gives him the letter.*) Why, man, you don't seem one whit the happier at this!

Faulkland. O yes, I am; but—but——

Absolute. Confound your *buts*! you never hear anything that would make another man bless himself, but you immediately damn it with a but!

Faulkland. Now, Jack, as you are my friend, own honestly—don't you think there is something forward, something indelicate, in this haste to forgive? Women should never sue for reconciliation: that should always come from us. They should retain their coldness till *wooed* to kindness; and their *pardon*, like their *love*, should " not unsought be won."

Absolute. I have not patience to listen to you! thou'rt incorrigible! so say no more on the subject. I must go to settle a few matters. Let me see you before six, remember, at my lodgings. A poor industrious devil like me, who have toiled, and drudged, and plotted to gain my ends, and am at last disappointed by other people's folly, may in pity be allowed to swear and grumble a little ; but a captious sceptic in love, a slave to fretfulness and whim, who has no difficulties but of his own creating, is a subject more fit for ridicule than compassion ! *(Exit Absolute.)*

Faulkland. I feel his reproaches ; yet I would not change this too exquisite nicety for the gross content with which *he* tramples on the thorns of love ! His engaging me in this duel has started an idea in my head which I will instantly pursue. I'll use it as the touchstone of Julia's sincerity and disinterestedness. If her love prove pure and sterling ore, my name will rest on it with honour ; and once I've stamped it there, I lay aside my doubts for ever ! But if the dross of selfishness, the alloy of pride, predominate, 'twill be best to leave her as a toy for some less cautious fool to sigh for ! *(Exit Faulkland.)*

END OF THE FOURTH ACT.

ACT V

SCENE I. *Julia's Dressing-room.*

(*Julia* sola.)

Julia. How this message has alarmed me! what dreadful accident can he mean? why such charge to be alone?—O Faulkland!—how many unhappy moments—how many tears have you cost me.

(*Enter Faulkland.*)

Julia. What means this?—why this caution, Faulkland?

Faulkland. Alas! Julia, I am come to take a long farewell.

Julia. Heavens! what do you mean?

Faulkland. You see before you a wretch, whose life is forfeited. Nay, start not!—the infirmity of my temper has drawn all this misery on me. I left you fretful and passionate—an untoward accident drew me into a quarrel—the event is, that I must fly this kingdom instantly. O Julia, had I been so fortunate as to have called you mine entirely, before this mischance had fallen on me, I should not so deeply dread my banishment!

Julia. My soul is oppressed with sorrow at the nature of your misfortune: had these adverse circumstances arisen from a less fatal cause, I should have felt strong comfort in the thought that I could now chase from your bosom every doubt of the warm sincerity of my love. My heart has long known no other guardian—I now entrust my person to your honour—we will fly together. When safe from pursuit my father's will may be fulfilled—and I receive a legal

94

claim to be the partner of your sorrows, and tenderest comforter. Then on the bosom of your wedded Julia, you may lull your keen regret to slumbering ; while virtuous love, with a cherub's hand, shall smooth the brow of upbraiding thought, and pluck the thorn from compunction.

Faulkland. O Julia ! I am bankrupt in gratitude ! but the time is so pressing, it calls on you for so hasty a resolution !—Would you not wish some hours to weigh the advantages you forego, and what little compensation poor Faulkland can make you beside his solitary love ?

Julia. I ask not a moment. No, Faulkland, I have loved you for yourself ; and if I now, more than ever, prize the solemn engagement which so long has pledged us to each other, it is because it leaves no room for hard aspersions on my fame, and puts the seal of duty to an act of love. But let us not linger. Perhaps this delay——

Faulkland. 'Twill be better I should not venture out again till dark. Yet am I grieved to think what numberless distresses will press heavy on your gentle disposition !

Julia. Perhaps your fortune may be forfeited by this unhappy act. I know not whether 'tis so ; but sure that alone can never make us unhappy. The little I have will be sufficient to support us ; and exile never should be splendid.

Faulkland. Ay, but in such an abject state of life, my wounded pride perhaps may increase the natural fretfulness of my temper, till I become a rude, morose companion, beyond your patience to endure. Perhaps the recollection of a deed my conscience cannot justify may haunt me in such gloomy and unsocial fits, that I shall hate the tenderness that would relieve me, break from your arms, and quarrel with your fondness !

Julia. If your thoughts should assume so unhappy

a bent, you will the more want some mild and affectionate spirit to watch over and console you : one who, by bearing *your* infirmities with gentleness and resignation, may teach you so to bear the evils of your fortune.

Faulkland. Julia, I have proved you to the quick ! and with this useless device I throw away all my doubts. How shall I plead to be forgiven this last unworthy effect of my restless, unsatisfied disposition ?

Julia. Has no such disaster happened as you related ?

Faulkland. I am ashamed to own that it was all pretended ; yet in pity, Julia, do not kill me with resenting a fault which never can be repeated : but sealing, this once, my pardon, let me to-morrow, in the face of Heaven, receive my future guide and monitress, and expiate my past folly by years of tender adoration.

Julia. Hold, Faulkland !—that you are free from a crime, which I before feared to name, Heaven knows how sincerely I rejoice ! These are tears of thankfulness for that ! But that your cruel doubts should have urged you to an imposition that has wrung my heart, gives me now a pang more keen than I can express !

Faulkland. By Heaven ! Julia——

Julia. Yet hear me.—My father loved you, Faulkland ! and you preserved the life that tender parent gave me ; in his presence I pledged my hand—joyfully pledged it—where before I had given my heart. When, soon after, I lost that parent, it seemed to me that Providence had, in Faulkland, shown me whither to transfer, without a pause, my grateful duty as well as my affection : hence I have been content to bear from you what pride and delicacy would have forbid me from another. I will not upbraid you, by repeating how you have trifled with my sincerity——

Faulkland. I confess it all ! yet hear——

Julia. After such a year of trial, I might have flattered myself that I should not have been insulted with a new probation of my sincerity, as cruel as unnecessary ! I now see it is not in your nature to be content or confident in love. With this conviction— I never will be yours. While I had hopes that my persevering attention, and unreproaching kindness, might in time reform your temper, I should have been happy to have gained a dearer influence over you ; but I will not furnish you with a licensed power to keep alive an incorrigible fault, at the expense of one who never would contend with you.

Faulkland. Nay, but, Julia, by my soul and honour, if after this——

Julia. But one word more.—As my faith has once been given to you, I never will barter it with another. I shall pray for your happiness with the truest sincerity ; and the dearest blessing I can ask of Heaven to send you will be to charm you from that unhappy temper, which alone has prevented the performance of our solemn engagement. All I request of *you* is, that you will yourself reflect upon this infirmity, and when you number up the many true delights it has deprived you of, let it not be your *least* regret, that it lost you the love of one who would have followed you in beggary through the world ! *(Exit.)*

Faulkland. She's gone—for ever !—There was an awful resolution in her manner, that riveted me to my place.—O fool !—dolt !—barbarian ! Cursed as I am, with more imperfections than my fellow-wretches, kind Fortune sent a heaven-gifted cherub to my aid, and, like a ruffian, I have driven her from my side !— I must now haste to my appointment. Well, my mind is tuned for such a scene. I shall wish only to become a principal in it, and reverse the tale my cursed folly put me upon forging here.—O Love !—tormentor !

—fiend !—whose influence, like the moon's, acting on men of dull souls, makes idiots of them, but meeting subtler spirits, betrays their course, and urges sensibility to madness !   (*Exit.*)

(*Enter Maid and Lydia.*)

Maid. My mistress, ma'am, I know, was here just now—perhaps she is only in the next room.

(*Exit Maid.*)

Lydia. Heigh-ho ! Though he has used me so, this fellow runs strangely in my head. I believe one lecture from my grave cousin will make me recall him.

(*Enter Julia.*)

Lydia. O Julia, I am come to you with such an appetite for consolation.—Lud ! child, what's the matter with you ? You have been crying !—I'll be hanged if that Faulkland has not been tormenting you !

Julia. You mistake the cause of my uneasiness !—Something *has* flurried me a little. Nothing that you can guess at.—(*Aside.*) I would not accuse Faulkland to a sister !

Lydia. Ah ! whatever vexations you may have, I can assure you mine surpass them. You know who Beverley proves to be ?

Julia. I will now own to you, Lydia, that Mr. Faulkland had before informed me of the whole affair. Had young Absolute been the person you took him for, I should not have accepted your confidence on the subject, without a serious endeavour to counteract your caprice.

Lydia. So, then, I see I have been deceived by every one ! But I don't care—I'll never have him.

Julia. Nay, Lydia——

Lydia. Why, is it not provoking ? when I thought we were coming to the prettiest distress imaginable, to find myself made a mere Smithfield bargain of at

Smithfield bargain, A bad bargain—being cheated. (Originally a horse-market, Smithfield became a cattle market, and is still a meat market. Horse sales were notorious for cheating.)

last ! There had I projected one of the most sentimental elopements !—so becoming a disguise !—so
amiable a ladder of ropes !—conscious moon—four
horses—Scotch parson—with such surprise to Mrs.
Malaprop—and such paragraphs in the newspaper !
—Oh, I shall die with disappointment !

Julia. I don't wonder at it !

Lydia. Now—sad reverse !—what have I to expect
but, after a deal of flimsy preparation with a bishop's
licence, and my aunt's blessing, to go simpering up to
the altar ; or perhaps be cried three times in a country
church, and have an unmannerly fat clerk ask the
consent of every butcher in the parish to join John
Absolute and Lydia Languish, spinster ! Oh that I
should live to hear myself called spinster !

Julia. Melancholy indeed !

Lydia. How mortifying, to remember the dear
delicious shifts I used to be put to, to gain half a
minute's conversation with this fellow ! How often
have I stole forth, in the coldest night in January, and
found him in the garden, stuck like a dripping statue !
There would he kneel to me in the snow, and sneeze
and cough so pathetically ! he shivering with cold
and I with apprehension ! and while the freezing
blast numbed our joints, how warmly would he press
me to pity his flame, and glow with mutual ardour !—
Ah, Julia, that was something like being in love.

Julia. If I were in spirits, Lydia, I should chide
you only by laughing heartily at you ; but it suits
more the situation of my mind, at present, earnestly
to entreat you not to let a man, who loves you with
sincerity, suffer that unhappiness from your caprice,
which I know too well caprice can inflict.

Lydia. O Lud ! what has brought my aunt here ?

Scotch parson, A reference to Gretna Green marriages. At the time,
marriage celebration in Scotland required a witness merely (*e.g.*
the blacksmith at Gretna), and not a church or state official.

Spinster, An echo of Dogberry in *Much Ado.* Only Dogberry was
written down " an ass."

(*Enter Mrs. Malaprop, Fag, and David.*)

Mrs. Malaprop. So! so! here's fine work!—here's fine suicide, parricide, and simulation, going on in the fields! and Sir Anthony not to be found to prevent the antistrophe!

Julia. For Heaven's sake, madam, what's the meaning of this?

Mrs. Malaprop. That gentleman can tell you—'twas he enveloped the affair to me.

Lydia. Do, sir, will you, inform us?   (*To Fag.*)

Fag. Ma'am, I should hold myself very deficient in every requisite that forms the man of breeding, if I delayed a moment to give all the information in my power to a lady so deeply interested in the affair as you are.

Lydia. But quick! quick, sir!

Fag. True, ma'am, as you say, one should be quick in divulging matters of this nature; for should we be tedious, perhaps while we are flourishing on the subject, two or three lives may be lost!

Lydia. O patience!—Do, ma'am, for Heaven's sake! tell us what is the matter?

Mrs. Malaprop. Why, murder's the matter! slaughter's the matter! killing's the matter!—but he can tell you the perpendiculars.

Lydia. Then, prithee, sir, be brief.

Fag. Why then, ma'am, as to murder—I cannot take upon me to say—and as to slaughter, or man-slaughter, that will be as the jury finds it.

Lydia. But who, sir—who are engaged in this?

Fag. Faith, ma'am, one is a young gentleman whom I should be very sorry anything was to happen to—a very pretty behaved gentleman! We have lived much together, and always on terms.

Lydia. But who is this? who! who! who?

Fag. My master, ma'am—my master—I speak of my master.

Lydia. Heavens! What, Captain Absolute!

Mrs. Malaprop. Oh, to be sure, you are frightened now !

Julia. But who are with him, sir ?

Fag. As to the rest, ma'am, this gentleman can inform you better than I.

Julia. Do speak, friend. (*To David.*)

David. Look'ee, my lady—by the mass ! there's mischief going on. Folks don't use to meet for amusement with firearms, firelocks, fire-engines, fire-screens, fire-office, and the devil knows what other crackers beside !—This, my lady, I say, has an angry favour.

Julia. But who is there beside Captain Absolute, friend ?

David. My poor master—under favour for mentioning him first. You know me, my lady—I am David— and my master of course is, or *was*, Squire Acres. Then comes Squire Faulkland.

Julia. Do, ma'am, let us instantly endeavour to prevent mischief.

Mrs. Malaprop. O fy !—it would be very inelegant in us :—we should only participate things.

David. Ah ! do, Mrs. Aunt, save a few lives—they are desperately given, believe me.—Above all, there is that bloodthirsty Philistine, Sir Lucius O'Trigger.

Mrs. Malaprop. Sir Lucius O'Trigger ? O mercy ! have they drawn poor little dear Sir Lucius into the scrape ?—Why, how you stand, girl ! you have no more feeling than one of the Derbyshire putre-factions !

Lydia. What are we to do, madam ?

Mrs. Malaprop. Why, fly with the utmost felicity, to be sure, to prevent mischief !—Here, friend, you can show us the place ?

Putrefactions, Petrifactions. Probably refers to the oddly shaped stalactites and stalagmites in caverns like Poole's at Buxton. Names were given to prominent pieces, like *Lion's Head*, *Flitch of Bacon*. (See Charles Cotton's *The Wonders of the Peak*.)

Fag. If you please, ma'am, I will conduct you.—David, do you look for Sir Anthony.　(*Exit David.*)

Mrs. Malaprop. Come, girls! this gentleman will exhort us.—Come, sir, you're our envoy—lead the way, and we'll precede.

Fag. Not a step before the ladies for the world!

Mrs. Malaprop. You're sure you know the spot?

Fag. I think I can find it, ma'am; and one good thing is, we shall hear the report of the pistols as we draw near, so we can't well miss them;—never fear, ma'am, never fear.　　(*Exeunt, he talking.*)

SCENE II.　*The South Parade.*

(*Enter Absolute, putting his sword under his great-coat.*)

Absolute. A sword seen in the streets of Bath would raise as great an alarm as a mad dog.—How provoking this is in Faulkland!—never punctual! I shall be obliged to go without him at last.—Oh, the devil! here's Sir Anthony! how shall I escape him?

(*Muffles up his face, and takes a circle to go off.*)
(*Enter Sir Anthony.*)

Sir Anthony. How one may be deceived at a little distance! only that I see he don't know me, I could have sworn that was Jack!—Hey! Gad's life! it is.—Why, Jack, what are you afraid of? hey!—sure I'm right.—Why, Jack, Jack Absolute!

(*Goes up to him.*)

Absolute. Really, sir, you have the advantage of me:—I don't remember ever to have had the honour—my name is Saunderson, at your service.

Sir Anthony. Sir, I beg your pardon—I took you—hey?—why, zounds! it is—Stay-(*Looks up to his face.*) So, so—your humble servant, Mr. Saunderson! Why, you scoundrel, what tricks are you after now?

Absolute. Oh, a joke, sir, a joke! I came here on purpose to look for you, sir.

Sir Anthony. You did! well, I am glad you were so lucky;—but what are you muffled up so for?—what's this for?—hey!

Absolute. 'Tis cool, sir; isn't?—rather chilly somehow;—but I shall be late—I have a particular engagement.

Sir Anthony. Stay!—Why, I thought you were looking for me?—Pray, Jack, where is't you are going?

Absolute. Going, sir!

Sir Anthony. Ay, where are you going?

Absolute. Where am I going?

Sir Anthony. You unmannerly puppy!

Absolute. I was going, sir, to—to—to—to Lydia, sir, to Lydia—to make matters up if I could;—and I was looking for you, sir, to—to——

Sir Anthony. To go with you, I suppose.—Well, come along.

Absolute. Oh! zounds! no, sir, not for the world! —I wished to meet with you, sir,—to—to—to—— You find it cool, I'm sure, sir—you'd better not stay out.

Sir Anthony. Cool!—not at all.—Well, Jack—and what will you say to Lydia?

Absolute. Oh, sir, beg her pardon, humour her— promise and vow: but I detain you, sir—consider the cold air on your gout.

Sir Anthony. Oh, not at all!—not at all! I'm in no hurry.—Ah! Jack, you youngsters, when once you are wounded here (*putting his hand to Captain Absolute's breast*). Hey! what the deuce have you got here?

Absolute. Nothing, sir—nothing.

Sir Anthony. What's this?—here's something hard.

Absolute. Oh, trinkets, sir! trinkets!—a bauble for Lydia!

Sir Anthony. Nay, let me see your taste.—(*Pulls his coat open, the sword falls.*) Trinkets!—a bauble for Lydia!—Zounds! sirrah, you are not going to cut her throat, are you?

Absolute. Ha! ha! ha!—I thought it would divert you, sir, though I didn't mean to tell you till afterwards.

Sir Anthony. You didn't?—Yes, this is a very diverting trinket, truly!

Absolute. Sir, I'll explain to you.—You know, sir, Lydia is romantic, devilish romantic, and very absurd of course: now, sir, I intend, if she refuses to forgive me, to unsheath this sword, and swear I'll fall upon its point, and expire at her feet!

Sir Anthony. Fall upon a fiddlestick's end!—why, I suppose it is the very thing that would please her.—Get along, you fool.

Absolute. Well, sir, you shall hear of my success— you shall hear—" O Lydia!—forgive me, or this pointed steel "—says I.

Sir Anthony. " Oh, Booby! stab away and welcome " — says she. — Get along! and damn your trinkets!   (*Exit Aboslute.*)

(*Enter David, running.*)

David. Stop him! stop him! Murder! Thief! Fire!—Stop fire! Stop fire!—O Sir Anthony—call! call! bid 'm stop! Murder! Fire!

Sir Anthony. Fire! Murder!—Where?

David. Oons! he's out of sight! and I'm out of breath, for my part! O Sir Anthony, why didn't you stop him? why didn't you stop him?

Sir Anthony. Zounds! the fellow's mad!—Stop whom? stop Jack?

David. Ay, the captain, sir!—there's murder and slaughter——

Sir Anthony. Murder!

David. Ay, please you, Sir Anthony, there's all kinds of murder, all sorts of slaughter to be seen in the fields : there's fighting going on, sir—bloody sword-and-gun fighting !

Sir Anthony. Who are going to fight, dunce ?

David. Everybody that I know of, Sir Anthony : —everybody is going to fight, my poor master, Sir Lucius O'Trigger, your son, the captain——

Sir Anthony. Oh, the dog ! I see his tricks.—Do you know the place ?

David. King's-Mead-Fields.

Sir Anthony. You know the way ?

David. Not an inch ; but I'll call the mayor— aldermen—constables—churchwardens—and beadles —we can't be too many to part them.

Sir Anthony. Come along—give me your shoulder ! we'll get assistance as we go—the lying villain !— Well, I shall be in such a frenzy !—So—this was the history of his trinkets ! I'll bauble him !

(Exeunt.)

SCENE III. *King's-Mead-Fields.*

(Sir Lucius and Acres, with pistols.)

Acres. By my valour ! then, Sir Lucius, forty yards is a good distance. Odds levels and aims !— I say it is a good distance.

Sir Lucius. Is it for muskets or small field-pieces ? Upon my conscience, Mr. Acres, you must leave those things to me.—Stay now—I'll show you.—(*Measures paces along the stage.*) There, now, that is a very pretty distance—a pretty gentleman's distance.

Acres. Zounds ! we might as well fight in a sentry-box ! I tell you, Sir Lucius, the farther he is off, the cooler I shall take my aim.

Sir Lucius. Faith ! then I suppose you would aim at him best of all if he was out of sight !

Acres. No, Sir Lucius ; but I should think forty or eight-and-thirty yards——

Sir Lucius. Pho! pho! nonsense! three or four feet between the mouths of your pistols is as good as a mile.

Acres. Odds bullets, no!—by my valour! there is no merit in killing him so near: do, my dear Sir Lucius, let me bring him down at a long shot:—a long shot, Sir Lucius, if you love me!

Sir Lucius. Well, the gentleman's friend and I must settle that.—But tell me now, Mr. Acres, in case of an accident, is there any little will or commission I could execute for you?

Acres. I am much obliged to you, Sir Lucius—but I don't understand——

Sir Lucius. Why, you may think there's no being shot at without a little risk—and if an unlucky bullet should carry a quietus with it—I say it will be no time then to be bothering you about family matters.

Acres. A quietus!

Sir Lucius. For instance, now—if that should be the case—would you choose to be pickled and sent home?—or would it be the same to you to lie here in the Abbey? I'm told there is very snug lying in the Abbey.

Acres. Pickled!—Snug lying in the Abbey!—Odds tremors! Sir Lucius, don't talk so!

Sir Lucius. I suppose, Mr. Acres, you never were engaged in an affair of this kind before?

Acres. No, Sir Lucius, never before.

Sir Lucius. Ah! that's a pity!—there's nothing like being used to a thing.—Pray now, how would you receive the gentleman's shot?

Acres. Odds files!—I've practised that—there, Sir Lucius—there.—(*Puts himself in an attitude.*) A side-

---

Quietus, Release from life, death. (A *quietus* was originally a receipt: "quietus est," he is quit.)

Abbey, The Abbey Church at Bath; first built by King Offa in 775, and finally rebuilt during the sixteenth century.

front, hey ? Odd ! I'll make myself small enough :
I'll stand edgeways.

Sir Lucius. Now—you're quite out—for if you
stand so when I take my aim—— (*Levelling at him.*)

Acres. Zounds ! Sir Lucius—are you sure it is not
cocked ?

Sir Lucius. Never fear.

Acres. But—but—you don't know—it may go off
of its own head !

Sir Lucius. Pho ! be easy.—Well, now, if I hit you
in the body, my bullet has a double chance—for if it
misses a vital part of your right side—'twill be very
hard if it don't succeed on the left !

Acres. A vital part ?

Sir Lucius. But, there—fix yourself so (*placing
him*)—let him see the broad-side of your full front—
there—now a ball or two may pass clean through your
body, and never do any harm at all.

Acres. Clean through me !—a ball or two clean
through me !

Sir Lucius. Ay, may they—and it is much the
genteelest attitude into the bargain.

Acres. Look'ee ! Sir Lucius—I'd just as lieve be
shot in an awkward posture as a genteel one ; so, by
my valour ! I will stand edgeways.

Sir Lucius (*looking at his watch*). Sure they don't
mean to disappoint us—Hah !—No, faith—I think I
see them coming.

Acres. Hey !—what !—coming !——

Sir Lucius. Ay.—Who are those yonder getting
over the stile ?

Acres. There are two of them indeed !—well—let
them come—hey, Sir Lucius !—we—we—we—we—
won't run.

Sir Lucius. Run !

Acres. No—I say—we *won't* run, by my valour !

Sir Lucius. What the devil's the matter with you ?

Acres. Nothing—nothing—my dear friend—my

107

dear Sir Lucius—but I—I—don't feel quite so bold, somehow, as I did.

Sir Lucius. O fy !—consider your honour.

Acres. Ay—true—my honour. Do, Sir Lucius, edge in a word or two every now and then about my honour.

Sir Lucius. Well, here they're coming. (*Looking.*)

Acres. Sir Lucius—if I wa'n't with you, I should almost think I was afraid.—If my valour should leave me !—Valour will come and go.

Sir Lucius. Then pray keep it fast, while you have it.

Acres. Sir Lucius—I doubt it is going—yes—my valour is certainly going !—it is sneaking off !—I feel it oozing out as it were at the palms of my hands !

Sir Lucius. Your honour—your honour !—Here they are.

Acres. O mercy !—now—that I was safe at *Clod Hall* ! or could be shot before I was aware !

(*Enter Faulkland and Absolute.*)

Sir Lucius. Gentlemen, your most obedient.—Hah !—what, Captain Absolute !—So, I suppose, sir, you are come here, just like myself—to do a kind office, first for your friend—then to proceed to business on your own account.

Acres. What, Jack !—my dear Jack !—my dear friend !

Absolute. Hark'ee, Bob, *Beverley's* at hand.

Sir Lucius. Well, Mr. Acres—I don't blame your saluting the gentleman civilly. So, Mr. Beverley (*to Faulkland*), if you'll choose your weapons, the captain and I will measure the ground.

Faulkland. *My* weapons, sir !

Acres. Odds life ! Sir Lucius, I'm not going to fight Mr. Faulkland ; these are my particular friends.

Sir Lucius. What, sir, did you not come here to fight Mr. Acres ?

Faulkland. Not I, upon my word, sir.

Sir Lucius. Well, now, that's mighty provoking! But I hope, Mr. Faulkland, as there are three of us come on purpose for the game, you won't be so cantankerous as to spoil the party by sitting out.

Absolute. Oh, pray, Faulkland, fight to oblige Sir Lucius.

Faulkland. Nay, if Mr. Acres is so bent on the matter——

Acres. No, no, Mr. Faulkland;—I'll bear my disappointment like a Christian.—Look'ee, Sir Lucius, there's no occasion at all for me to fight; and if it is the same to you, I'd as lieve let it alone.

Sir Lucius. Observe me, Mr. Acres—I must not be trifled with. You have certainly challenged somebody —and you came here to fight him. Now, if that gentleman is willing to represent him, I can't see, for my soul, why it isn't just the same thing.

Acres. Why no—Sir Lucius—I tell you, 'tis one Beverley I've challenged—a fellow, you see, that dare not show his face!—If he were here, I'd make him give up his pretensions directly!

Absolute. Hold, Bob—let me set you right—there is no such man as *Beverley* in the case.—The person who assumed that name is before you; and as his pretensions are the same in both characters, he is ready to support them in whatever way you please.

Sir Lucius. Well, this is lucky.—Now you have an opportunity——

Acres. What, quarrel with my dear friend Jack Absolute!—not if he were fifty Beverleys! Zounds! Sir Lucius, you would not have me so unnatural.

Sir Lucius. Upon my conscience, Mr. Acres, your valour has *oozed* away with a vengeance!

Acres. Not in the least! Odds backs and abettors! I'll be your second with all my heart—and if you should get a *quietus*, you may command me entirely.

Backs and abettors, One's helpers in a given cause.

I'll get you *snug lying* in the *Abbey here* ; or *pickle* you, and send you over to Blunderbuss Hall, or anything of the kind, with the greatest pleasure.

Sir Lucius. Pho ! pho ! you are little better than a coward.

Acres. Mind, gentlemen, he calls me a *coward* ; coward was the word, by my valour !

Sir Lucius. Well, sir ?

Acres. Look'ee, Sir Lucius, 'tisn't that I mind the word coward—*coward* may be said in joke—but if you had called me a *poltroon*, odds daggers and balls——

Sir Lucius. Well, sir ?

Acres. I should have thought you a very ill-bred man.

Sir Lucius. Pho ! you are beneath my notice.

Absolute. Nay, Sir Lucius, you can't have a better second than my friend Acres.—He is a most *determined* dog—called in the country, *Fighting Bob*.—He generally *kills a man a week*—don't you, Bob ?

Acres. Ay—at home !

Sir Lucius, Well, then, captain, 'tis we must begin —so come out, my little counsellor—(*Draws his sword*)—and ask the gentleman, whether he will resign the lady, without forcing you to proceed against him.

Absolute. Come on then, sir—(*Draws*) ; since you won't let it be an amicable suit, here's my reply.

(*Enter Sir Anthony, David, and the Women.*)

David. Knock 'em all down, sweet Sir Anthony ; knock down my master in particular ; and bind his hands over to their good behaviour !

Sir Anthony. Put up, Jack, put up, or I shall be in a frenzy—how came you in a duel, sir ?

Absolute. Faith, sir, that gentleman can tell you better than I ; 'twas he called on me, and you know, sir, I serve his majesty.

Sir Anthony. Here's a pretty fellow ; I catch him going to cut a man's throat, and he tells me, he serves his majesty !—Zounds ! sirrah, then how durst you draw the king's sword against one of his subjects ?

Absolute. Sir, I tell you ! that gentleman called me out, without explaining his reasons.

Sir Anthony. Gad ! sir, how came you to call my son out, without explaining your reasons ?

Sir Lucius. Your son, sir, insulted me in a manner which my honour could not brook.

Sir Anthony. Zounds ! Jack, how durst you insult the gentleman in a manner which his honour could not brook ?

Mrs. Malaprop. Come, come, let's have no honour before ladies.—Captain Absolute, come here—How could you intimidate us so ?—Here's Lydia has been terrified to death for you.

Absolute. For fear I should be killed, or escape, ma'am ?

Mrs. Malaprop. Nay, no delusions to the past— Lydia is convinced ; speak, child.

Sir Lucius. With your leave, ma'am, I must put in a word here : I believe I could interpret the young lady's silence. Now mark——

Lydia. What is it you mean, sir ?

Sir Lucius. Come, come, Delia, we must be serious now—this is no time for trifling.

Lydia. 'Tis true, sir ; and your reproof bids me offer this gentleman my hand, and solicit the return of his affections.

Absolute. Oh ! my little angel, say you so !—Sir Lucius—I perceive there must be some mistake here, with regard to the affront which you affirm I have given you. I can only say, that it could not have been intentional. And as you must be convinced that I should not fear to support a real injury, you shall now see that I am not ashamed to atone for an inadvertency—I ask your pardon.—But for this lady, while honoured with her approbation, I will support my claim against any man whatever.

Sir Anthony. Well said, Jack, and I'll stand by you, my boy.

Acres. Mind, I give up all my claim—I make no pretensions to anything in the world ; and if I can't get a wife without fighting for her, by my valour ! I'll live a bachelor.

Sir Lucius. Captain, give me your hand : an affront handsomely acknowledged becomes an obligation ; and as for the lady, if she chooses to deny her own handwriting, here——   (*Takes out letters.*)

Mrs. Malaprop. Oh, he will dissolve my mystery ! —Sir Lucius, perhaps there's some mistake—perhaps I can illuminate——

Sir Lucius. Pray, old gentlewoman, don't interfere where you have no business.—Miss Languish, are you my Delia, or not ?

Lydia. Indeed, Sir Lucius, I am not.

(*Lydia and Absolute walk aside.*)

Mrs. Malaprop. Sir Lucius O'Trigger—ungrateful as you are—I own the soft impeachment—pardon my blushes, I am Delia.

Sir Lucius. You Delia—pho ! pho ! be easy.

Mrs. Malaprop. Why, thou barbarous Vandyke— those letters are mine—When you are more sensible of my benignity—perhaps I may be brought to encourage your addresses.

Sir Lucius. Mrs. Malaprop, I am extremely sensible of your condescension ; and whether you or Lucy have put this trick on me, I am equally beholden to you.—And, to show you I am not ungrateful, Captain Absolute, since you have taken that lady from me, I'll give you my Delia into the bargain.

Absolute. I am much obliged to you, Sir Lucius ; but here's my friend, Fighting Bob, unprovided for.

Sir Lucius. Hah ! little Valour—here, will you make your fortune ?

Acres. Odds wrinkles ! No.—But give me your hand, Sir Lucius, forget and forgive ; but if ever I give you a chance of *pickling* me again, say Bob Acres is a dunce, that's all.

Sir Anthony. Come, Mrs. Malaprop, don't be cast down—you are in your bloom yet.

Mrs. Malaprop. O Sir Anthony—men are all barbarians.   (*All retire but Julia and Faulkland.*)

Julia (*aside*). He seems dejected and unhappy—not sullen ; there was some foundation, however, for the tale he told me—O woman ! how true should be your judgment, when your resolution is so weak !

Faulkland. Julia !—how can I sue for what I so little deserve ? I dare not presume—yet Hope is the child of Penitence.

Julia. O ! Faulkland, you have not been more faulty in your unkind treatment of me, than I am now in wanting inclination to resent it. As my heart honestly bids me place my weakness to the account of love, I should be ungenerous not to admit the same plea for yours.

Faulkland. Now I shall be blest indeed !
                                (*Sir Anthony comes forward.*)

Sir Anthony. What's going on here ?—So you have been quarrelling too, I warrant ! Come, Julia, I never interfered before ; but let me have a hand in the matter at last.—All the faults I have ever seen in my friend Faulkland seemed to proceed from what he calls the *delicacy* and *warmth* of his affection for you —There, marry him directly, Julia ; you'll find he'll mend surprisingly !   (*The rest come forward.*)

Sir Lucius. Come, now, I hope there is no dissatisfied person, but what is content ; for as I have been disappointed myself, it will be very hard if I have not the satisfaction of seeing other people succeed better.

Acres. You are right, Sir Lucius.—So, Jack, I wish you joy—Mr. Faulkland the same.—Ladies,—come now, to show you I'm neither vexed nor angry, odds tabors and pipes ! I'll order the fiddles in half an hour to the New Rooms—and I insist on your all meeting me there.

Sir Anthony. 'Gad, sir, I like your spirit ; and at night we single lads will drink a health to the young couples, and a husband to Mrs. Malaprop.

Faulkland. Our partners are stolen from us, Jack— I hope to be congratulated by each other—*yours* for having checked in time the errors of an ill-directed imagination, which might have betrayed an innocent heart ; and *mine*, for having, by her gentleness and candour, reformed the unhappy temper of one, who by it made wretched whom he loved most, and tortured the heart he ought to have adored.

Absolute. Well, Jack, we have both tasted the bitters as well as the sweets of love ; with this difference only, that *you* always prepared the bitter cup for yourself, while I——

Lydia. Was always obliged to *me* for it, hey ! Mr. Modesty ?——But, come, no more of that—our happiness is now as unalloyed as general.

Julia. Then let us study to preserve it so : and while Hope pictures to us a flattering scene of future bliss, let us deny its pencil those colours which are too bright to be lasting.—When hearts deserving happiness would unite their fortunes, Virtue would crown them with an unfading garland of modest hurtless flowers ; but ill-judging Passion will force the gaudier rose into the wreath, whose thorn offends them when its leaves are dropped !

The New Rooms, The most exclusive in Bath.
Then let us . . . dropped, Julia points a moral of sensible moderation against sentimental high hopes that are sure to be disappointed.

FINIS.

QUESTIONS ON "THE RIVALS"

PERSONS OF THE PLAY

1. "Captain Absolute is a complete specimen of the type *cad*." Do you agree?

2. Show how Lydia can be (a) romantically sentimental, (b) cynically cunning and pert, (c) truculently independent.

3. "Captain Absolute and Lydia Languish pass well enough as figures in a comedy, but how would they appear if transferred to real life?" Discuss the two characters in the light of this statement.

4. Who are the rivals in *The Rivals*?

5. When is Sir Anthony likeable, and when not?

6. Consider Sir Anthony's opinion on circulating libraries, and Mrs. Malaprop's on the education of girls. What do they show of the *manners* of the period?

7. Show that Mrs. Malaprop is (a) Sentimental, (b) artful, and tyrannical, (c) smug, (d) pretentious in the use of words.

8. Compare and contrast Mrs. Malaprop and Bob Acres as humorous types. How do they affect the working out of the plot?

9. How much of a coward and how much of a "sport" is Bob Acres?

10. Compare and contrast Julia and Faulkland. Is either a true comedy figure?

11. "Sir Lucius is something more than the professional fire-eater." Give your view on the character. Is it clear how he learns that his rival is Captain Absolute?

12. Show shortly how Fag and Lucy have something in common, and how both contrast with David.

13. What sort of fellow is Fag? Why does he exaggerate so much?

14. Show how Thomas makes consistent references to his experience as a "whip."

QUESTIONS ON "THE RIVALS"

15. Do the country or the town characters seem to you the more worthy ?

16. Illustrate Sheridan's use of " label " names ; and show in *three* instances how aptly they apply to the given characters.

17. Contrast is essential to interesting characterization. Point out some outstanding examples of it.

CONSTRUCTION

1. By what means do we learn in the opening scene the facts we need to know for understanding the later action ? What do we gather ? And how is the scene kept interesting ?

2. How is it contrived so that when Sir Anthony wants his son to marry the very girl of his choice (IV. ii.) there is still a big difficulty to overcome, and the play is not abruptly ended ?

3. How does the end of the play (*a*) resolve the complicated situations, (*b*) present a moral ?

4. Do you think the play would be better without the Julia-Faulkland scenes ?

5. Give examples of *surprise* in the working out of the plot.

6. Show what an important part is played by deception, coincidence, and misunderstanding in *The Rivals*.

WIT, SATIRE

1. *The Rivals* satirizes certain features in the life of eighteenth-century society. Indicate some of these, and show *how* they are made a mock of.

2. Would " over-civilized " be an accurate description of the social group presented in *The Rivals* ? Or " spoilt " ?

3. Comedy of Humours exhibits personages with a strongly marked quality belonging to them as individuals, Comedy of Manners with a quality derived from social intercourse. Single out some Humours and some Manners types in *The Rivals*.

QUESTIONS ON "THE RIVALS"

4. "Servants in Sheridan talk as wittily as their masters." Is this true in *The Rivals* ?

5. In what different ways do townsfolk and country folk receive the lash ?

6. Humour arises from character, outlook, or situation; Wit from words and ideas. Give examples of both in *The Rivals*.

7. Give a dozen examples of Malapropisms. Divide them into three or four groups according to their types.

THE SCHOOL FOR SCANDAL

INTRODUCTION TO
"THE SCHOOL FOR SCANDAL"

How it came to be written.—In the same year as
The Rivals (1775) came *St. Patrick's Day*, or *The
Scheming Lieutenant*, a light-hearted piece, of entertainment value only, first produced as a benefit
performance for Lawrence Clinch, the popular Sir
Lucius of *The Rivals*. In November of the same year
followed a comic opera, *The Duenna*. This was an
adaptation of Wycherley's *The Country Wife* (1675),
set to music by Sheridan's father-in-law, Linley. Not
unlike *The Rivals* in character types, wit, and situations, it scored a great success, and ran at Covent
Garden for seventy-five nights. But as literature
the interspersed lyrics have the only permanent
interest. The following year (1776) Sheridan, Linley,
and a friend bought out Garrick's share in Drury
Lane Theatre (later Sheridan's own), where in February 1777 another adaptation of Sheridan's was
produced. This was *A Trip to Scarborough*, a neater
and less rakish version of Vanbrugh's farce, *The
Relapse* (1696). It had sparkling qualities, and a
moonlit garden scene not unlike the screen scene in
The School for Scandal. But it failed.

All this was prentice work for Sheridan, who was
busy at a second big play of his own, more mature
than *The Rivals*. This was *The School for Scandal*,
which was presented at Drury Lane on May 8, 1777.
It was an instant success.

Kind of play.—Like the earlier plays, this was a
handling of the faults of leisured society by neat

exaggeration of well-known types in conflict with their own better selves. It showed, as it were, how society gradually "conditioned the reflexes" of its members so that they became animated dolls behaving falsely to their basic decent natures. The crisis of the play enables the chief personages to strip off their acquired false selves. Thus the good-hearted Lady Teazle (Sheridan's most human character creation) realizes the vice beneath the false polish of her associates. Charles casts off his extravagance. Sir Peter casts his prejudices, and the grumpiness which had been a reaction against the others' vices. Besides these, there are two sorts of contrast types, the vicious by ingrained habit like Lady Sneerwell (though originally her scandalmongering had been only defensive), and the "untainted souls" (who are mere background lay figures) Maria, Rowley, and Oliver. There is no profound originality in the characterization, but a consummate skill in hitting off caricatures of normal society types.

The plot, too, makes first-rate "theatre." Instead of the incidental situation of *The Rivals*, brought about by unnecessary additional characters like Acres and Sir Lucius, there are consecutive and natural situations vitally involving the main figures. The crown of all these is Sheridan's greatest single triumph, the Screen Scene. Here the various motives and interests culminate in a breathless situation that reveals the chief figures in their true light to each other and to the audience : the intersection of the various plots is perfect, and their resolution is completely convincing.

Not less excellent is the dialogue. It is the epigrammatic perfection of speech in a wit-conscious coterie like Oscar Wilde's in *The Importance of Being Earnest* (1895),* and akin to Shaw's wit of competi-

* There is similar wit to-day in the comedies of Noel Coward, Frederick Lonsdale, and Somerset Maugham.

tive viewpoints in his comedies of social purpose. Indeed, the consummate perfection of the repartee lifts the play out of the world of reality, enabling us to enjoy the satire without a feeling of cynicism.

The play is true high comedy except for the sentimental central (but actually negligible) Maria-Charles love plot, and the unreal " angels in disguise " Rowley and Oliver. It is the English masterpiece of comedy of manners, its only rival Congreve's *The Way of the World* (1700).

THE SCHOOL FOR SCANDAL

DRAMATIS PERSONÆ

(With the cast of the first production at Drury
Lane Theatre, May 8, 1777)

SIR PETER TEAZLE	Mr. King
SIR OLIVER SURFACE	Mr. Yates
SIR BENJAMIN BACKBITE . . .	Mr. Dodd
JOSEPH SURFACE	Mr. Palmer
CHARLES SURFACE	Mr. Smith
CARELESS	Mr. Farren
SNAKE	Mr. Packer
CRABTREE	Mr. Parsons
ROWLEY	Mr. Aickin
MOSES	Mr. Baddeley
TRIP	Mr. Lamash
SIR HARRY BUMPER	Mr. Gawdry
LADY TEAZLE	Mrs. Abington
LADY SNEERWELL	Miss Sherry
MRS. CANDOUR	Miss Pope
MARIA	Miss P. Hopkins

Gentlemen, Maid, and Servants.

SCENE.—London.

THE SCHOOL

THE SCHOOL FOR SCANDAL

ACT I

SCENE I. *Lady Sneerwell's Dressing-room.*

(*Lady Sneerwell discovered at her toilet; Snake drinking chocolate.*)

Lady Sneerwell. The paragraphs, you say, Mr. Snake, were all inserted?

Snake. They were, madam; and, as I copied them myself in a feigned hand, there can be no suspicion whence they came.

Lady Sneerwell. Did you circulate the report of Lady Brittle's intrigue with Captain Boastall?

Snake. That's in as fine a train as your ladyship could wish. In the common course of things, I think it must reach Mrs. Clackitt's ears within four-and-twenty hours; and then, you know, the business is as good as done.

Lady Sneerwell. Why, truly, Mrs. Clackitt has a very pretty talent, and a great deal of industry.

Snake. True, madam, and has been tolerably successful in her day. To my knowledge, she has been the cause of six matches being broken off, and three sons being disinherited; of four forced elopements, and as many close confinements; nine separate

Stage Direction.—Lady Sneerwell, Snake, etc. A custom of the period, ladies receiving gentlemen in their rooms while they completed their toilet. (A feminine parallel with the king's levee— Fr. " lever," to rise—which was originally the receiving of nobles by the king while getting up.)

maintenances, and two divorces. Nay, I have more than once traced her causing a *tête-à-tête* in the *Town and Country Magazine*, when the parties, perhaps, had never seen each other's face before in the course of their lives.

Lady Sneerwell. She certainly has talents, but her manner is gross.

Snake. 'Tis very true. She generally designs well, has a free tongue and a bold invention ; but her colouring is too dark, and her outlines often extravagant. She wants that delicacy of tint, and mellowness of sneer, which distinguish your ladyship's scandal.

Lady Sneerwell. You are partial, Snake.

Snake. Not in the least ; everybody allows that Lady Sneerwell can do more with a word or look than many can with the most laboured detail, even when they happen to have a little truth on their side to support it.

Lady Sneerwell. Yes, my dear Snake ; and I am no hypocrite to deny the satisfaction I reap from the success of my efforts. Wounded myself, in the early part of my life, by the envenomed tongue of slander, I confess I have since known no pleasure equal to the reducing others to the level of my own injured reputation.

Snake. Nothing can be more natural. But, Lady Sneerwell, there is one affair in which you have lately employed me, wherein, I confess, I am at a loss to guess your motives.

Lady Sneerwell. I conceive you mean with respect to my neighbour, Sir Peter Teazle, and his family ?

Snake. I do. Here are two young men, to whom Sir Peter has acted as a kind of guardian since their father's death ; the eldest possessing the most amiable

---

Tête-à-tête, Serial name given to portraits of fashionable people suspected of an intrigue, and published monthly in the *Town and Country Magazine* (established 1769).

character, and universally well spoken of—the youngest, the most dissipated and extravagant young fellow in the kingdom, without friends or character : the former an avowed admirer of your ladyship, and apparently your favourite ; the latter attached to Maria, Sir Peter's ward, and confessedly beloved by her. Now, on the face of these circumstances, it is utterly unaccountable to me, why you, the widow of a city knight, with a good jointure, should not close with the passion of a man of such character and expectations as Mr. Surface ; and more so why you should be so uncommonly earnest to destroy the mutual attachment subsisting between his brother Charles and Maria.

Lady Sneerwell. Then, at once to unravel this mystery, I must inform you that love has no share whatever in the intercourse between Mr. Surface and me.

Snake. No !

Lady Sneerwell. His real attachment is to Maria or her fortune ; but, finding in his brother a favoured rival, he has been obliged to mask his pretensions, and profit by my assistance.

Snake. Yet still I am more puzzled why you should interest yourself in his success.

Lady Sneerwell. Heavens ! how dull you are ! Cannot you surmise the weakness which I hitherto, through shame, have concealed even from you ? Must I confess that Charles—that libertine, that extravagant, that bankrupt in fortune and reputation—that he it is for whom I am thus anxious and malicious, and to gain whom I would sacrifice everything ?

Snake. Now, indeed, your conduct appears consistent ; but how came you and Mr. Surface so confidential ?

Lady Sneerwell. For our mutual interest. I have found him out a long time since. I know him to be artful, selfish, and malicious—in short, a sentimental knave ; while with Sir Peter, and indeed with all his acquaintance, he passes for a youthful miracle of prudence, good sense, and benevolence.

Snake. Yes ; yet Sir Peter vows he has not his equal in England ; and, above all, he praises him as a man of sentiment.

Lady Sneerwell. True ; and with the assistance of his sentiment and hypocrisy he has brought Sir Peter entirely into his interest with regard to Maria ; while poor Charles has no friend in the house—though, I fear, he has a powerful one in Maria's heart, against whom we must direct our schemes.

(*Enter Servant.*)

Servant. Mr. Surface.

Lady Sneerwell. Show him up.—(*Exit Servant.*) He generally calls about this time. I don't wonder at people giving him to me for a lover.

(*Enter Joseph Surface.*)

Joseph Surface. My dear Lady Sneerwell, how do you do to-day ? Mr. Snake, your most obedient.

Lady Sneerwell. Snake has just been rallying me on our mutual attachment ; but I have informed him of our real views. You know how useful he has been to us ; and, believe me, the confidence is not ill-placed.

Joseph Surface. Madam, it is impossible for me to suspect a man of Mr. Snake's sensibility and discernment.

Lady Sneerwell. Well, well, no compliments now ; but tell me when you saw your mistress, Maria—or, what is more material to me, your brother.

Joseph Surface. I have not seen either since I left you ; but I can inform you that they never meet. Some of your stories have taken a good effect on Maria.

Lady Sneerwell. Ah, my dear Snake ! the merit of this belongs to you. But do your brother's distresses increase ?

Joseph Surface. Every hour. I am told that he has

had another execution in the house yesterday. In short, his dissipation and extravagance exceed anything I have ever heard of.

Lady Sneerwell. Poor Charles !

Joseph Surface. True, madam ; notwithstanding his vices, one can't help feeling for him. Poor Charles ! I'm sure I wish it were in my power to be of any essential service to him ; for the man who does not share in the distresses of a brother, even though merited by his own misconduct, deserves——

Lady Sneerwell. O Lud ! you are going to be moral, and forget that you are among friends.

Joseph Surface. Egad, that's true ! I'll keep that sentiment till I see Sir Peter. However, it is certainly a charity to rescue Maria from such a libertine, who, if he is to be reclaimed, can be so only by a person of your ladyship's superior accomplishments and understanding.

Snake. I believe, Lady Sneerwell, here's company coming : I'll go and copy the letter I mentioned to you. Mr. Surface, your most obedient.

Joseph Surface. Sir, your very devoted.—(*Exit Snake.*) Lady Sneerwell, I am very sorry you have put any further confidence in that fellow.

Lady Sneerwell. Why so ?

Joseph Surface. I have lately detected him in frequent conference with old Rowley, who was formerly my father's steward, and has never, you know, been a friend of mine.

Lady Sneerwell. And do you think he would betray us ?

Joseph Surface. Nothing more likely : take my word for't, Lady Sneerwell, that fellow hasn't virtue enough to be faithful even to his own villainy. Ah, Maria !

(Enter Maria.)

Lady Sneerwell. Maria, my dear, how do you do ? What's the matter ?

Maria. Oh! there's that disagreeable lover of mine, Sir Benjamin Backbite, has just called at my guardian's, with his odious uncle, Crabtree; so I slipped out, and ran hither to avoid them.

Lady Sneerwell. Is that all?

Joseph Surface. If my brother Charles had been of the party, madam, perhaps you would not have been so much alarmed.

Lady Sneerwell. Nay, now you are severe; for I dare swear the truth of the matter is, Maria heard you were here. But, my dear, what has Sir Benjamin done, that you should avoid him so?

Maria. Oh, he has done nothing—but 'tis for what he has said: his conversation is a perpetual libel on all his acquaintance.

Joseph Surface. Ay, and the worst of it is, there is no advantage in not knowing him; for he'll abuse a stranger just as soon as his best friend: and his uncle's as bad.

Lady Sneerwell. Nay, but we should make allowance; Sir Benjamin is a wit and a poet.

Maria. For my part, I own, madam, wit loses its respect with me, when I see it in company with malice. What do you think, Mr. Surface?

Joseph Surface. Certainly, madam; to smile at the jest which plants a thorn in another's breast is to become a principal in the mischief.

Lady Sneerwell. Pshaw! there's no possibility of being witty without a little ill-nature; the malice of a good thing is the barb that makes it stick. What's your opinion, Mr. Surface?

Joseph Surface. To be sure, madam; that conversation, where the spirit of raillery is suppressed, will ever appear tedious and insipid.

Maria. Well, I'll not debate how far scandal may be allowable; but in a man, I am sure, it is always contemptible. We have pride, envy, rivalship, and a thousand motives to depreciate each other; but the male slanderer must have the cowardice of a woman before he can traduce one.

(Re-enter Servant.)

Servant. Madam, Mrs. Candour is below, and, if your ladyship's at leisure, will leave her carriage.

Lady Sneerwell. Beg her to walk in.—*(Exit Servant.)* Now, Maria, here is a character to your taste ; for, though Mrs. Candour is a little talkative, everybody knows her to be the best-natured and best sort of woman.

Maria. Yes, with a very gross affectation of good nature and benevolence, she does more mischief than the direct malice of old Crabtree.

Joseph Surface. I'faith that's true, Lady Sneerwell : whenever I hear the current running against the characters of my friends, I never think them in such danger as when Candour undertakes their defence.

Lady Sneerwell. Hush !—here she is !

(Enter Mrs. Candour.)

Mrs. Candour. My dear Lady Sneerwell, how have you been this century ?—Mr. Surface, what news do you hear ?—though indeed it is no matter, for I think one hears nothing else but scandal.

Joseph Surface. Just so, indeed, ma'am.

Mrs. Candour. Oh, Maria ! child,—what, is the whole affair off between you and Charles ? His extravagance, I presume—the town talks of nothing else.

Maria. I am very sorry, ma'am, the town has so little to do.

Mrs. Candour. True, true, child : but there's no stopping people's tongues. I own I was hurt to hear it, as I indeed was to learn, from the same quarter, that your guardian, Sir Peter, and Lady Teazle have not agreed lately as well as could be wished.

Maria. 'Tis strangely impertinent for people to busy themselves so.

Mrs. Candour. Very true, child ; but what's to be

done ? People will talk—there's no preventing it. Why, it was but yesterday I was told that Miss Gad-about had eloped with Sir Filigree Flirt. But, Lord ! there's no minding what one hears ; though, to be sure, I had this from very good authority.

Maria. Such reports are highly scandalous.

Mrs. Candour. So they are, child—shameful, shameful ! But the world is so censorious, no charac-ter escapes. Lord, now who would have suspected your friend, Miss Prim, of an indiscretion ! Yet such is the ill-nature of people, that they say her uncle stopped her last week, just as she was stepping into the York Mail with her dancing-master.

Maria. I'll answer for't there are no grounds for that report.

Mrs. Candour. Ah, no foundation in the world, I dare swear : no more, probably, than for the story circulated last month, of Mrs. Festino's affair with Colonel Cassino ;—though, to be sure, that matter was never rightly cleared up.

Joseph Surface. The licence of invention some people take is monstrous indeed.

Maria. 'Tis so , but, in my opinion, those who report such things are equally culpable.

Mrs. Candour. To be sure they are ; tale-bearers are as bad as the tale-makers—'tis an old observation, and a very true one : but what's to be done, as I said before ? how will you prevent people from talking ? To-day, Mrs. Clackitt assured me, Mr. and Mrs. Honeymoon were at last become mere man and wife, like the rest of their acquaintance. And at the same time Miss Tattle, who was by, affirmed, that Lord Buffalo had discovered his lady at a house of no extraordinary fame ; and that Sir Harry Bouquet and Tom Saunter were to measure swords on a similar provocation. But, Lord, do you think I would report these things ! No, no ! tale-bearers, as I said before, are just as bad as the tale-makers.

Joseph Surface. Ah! Mrs. Candour, if everybody had your forbearance and good nature!

Mrs. Candour. I confess, Mr. Surface, I cannot bear to hear people attacked behind their backs; and when ugly circumstances come out against our acquaintance I own I always love to think the best. By-the-bye, I hope 'tis not true that your brother is absolutely ruined?

Joseph Surface. I am afraid his circumstances are very bad indeed, ma'am.

Mrs. Candour. Ah!—I heard so—but you must tell him to keep up his spirits; everybody almost is in the same way: Lord Spindle, Sir Thomas Splint, Captain Quinze, and Mr. Nickit—all up, I hear, within this week; so, if Charles is undone, he'll find half his acquaintance ruined too; and that, you know, is a consolation.

Joseph Surface. Doubtless, ma'am—a very great one.

(Re-enter Servant.)

Servant. Mr. Crabtree and Sir Benjamin Backbite.
(Exit.)

Lady Sneerwell. So, Maria, you see your lover pursues you; positively you shan't escape.

(Enter Crabtree and Sir Benjamin Backbite.)

Crabtree. Lady Sneerwell, I kiss your hand. Mrs. Candour, I don't believe you are acquainted with my nephew, Sir Benjamin Backbite? Egad, ma'am, he has a pretty wit, and is a pretty poet too. Isn't he, Lady Sneerwell?

Sir Benjamin. Oh, fie, uncle!

Crabtree. Nay, egad it's true: I back him at a rebus or a charade against the best rhymer in the kingdom. Has your ladyship heard the epigram he wrote last week on Lady Frizzle's feather catching fire?—Do, Benjamin, repeat it, or the charade

Rebus, A riddle in which words are guessed from puzzle pictures.

you made last night extempore at Mrs. Drowzie's conversazione. Come now; your first is the name of a fish, your second a great naval commander, and——

Sir Benjamin. Uncle, now—pr'ythee——

Crabtree. I'faith, ma'am, 'twould surprise you to hear how ready he is at all these sort of things.

Lady Sneerwell. I wonder, Sir Benjamin, you never publish anything.

Sir Benjamin. To say truth, ma'am, 'tis very vulgar to print; and, as my little productions are mostly satires and lampoons on particular people, I find they circulate more by giving copies in confidence to the friends of the parties. However, I have some love elegies, which, when favoured with this lady's smiles, I mean to give the public.

(Pointing to Maria.)

Crabtree (*to Maria*). 'Fore heaven, ma'am, they'll immortalize you!—you will be handed down to posterity like Petrarch's Laura, or Waller's Sacharissa.

Sir Benjamin (*to Maria*). Yes, madam, I think you will like them, when you shall see them on a beautiful quarto page, where a neat rivulet of text shall meander through a meadow of margin. 'Fore Gad, they will be the most elegant things of their kind!

Crabtree. But, ladies, that's true—have you heard the news?

Mrs. Candour. What, sir, do you mean the report of——

Crabtree. No, ma'am, that's not it.—Miss Nicely is going to be married to her own footman.

Mrs. Candour. Impossible!

Crabtree. Ask Sir Benjamin.

Laura, A Frenchwoman of Avignon to whom the Italian poet Petrarch (1304–74) wrote nearly three hundred sonnets, the classical examples of that form. *Sacharissa*, Lady Dorothea Sidney, daughter of the Earl of Leicester. Edmund Waller (1606–87) wrote love poems to her.

Sir Benjamin. 'Tis very true, ma'am : everything is fixed, and the wedding liveries bespoke.

Lady Sneerwell. Why, I have heard something of this before.

Mrs. Candour. It can't be—and I wonder any one should believe such a story of so prudent a lady as Miss Nicely.

Sir Benjamin. O Lud ! ma'am, that's the very reason 'twas believed at once. She has always been so cautious and so reserved, that everybody was sure there was some reason for it at bottom.

Mrs. Candour. Why, to be sure, a tale of scandal is as fatal to the credit of a prudent lady of her stamp as a fever is generally to those of the strongest constitutions. But there is a sort of puny sickly reputation, that is always ailing, yet will outlive the robuster characters of a hundred prudes.

Sir Benjamin. True, madam, there are valetudinarians in reputation as well as constitution, who, being conscious of their weak part, avoid the least breath of air, and supply their want of stamina by care and circumspection.

Mrs. Candour. Well, but this may be all a mistake. You know, Sir Benjamin, very trifling circumstances often give rise to the most injurious tales.

Crabtree. That they do, I'll be sworn, ma'am. Did you ever hear how Miss Piper came to lose her lover and her character last summer at Tunbridge ?—Sir Benjamin, you remember it ?

Sir Benjamin. Oh, to be sure !—the most whimsical circumstance.

Lady Sneerwell. How was it, pray ?

Crabtree. Why, one evening, at Mrs. Ponto's assembly, the conversation happened to turn on the breeding Nova Scotia sheep in this country. Says a young lady in company, I have known instances of it ; for Miss Letitia Piper, a first cousin of mine, had a Nova Scotia sheep that produced her twins.

" What ! " cries the Lady Dowager Dundizzy (who you know is as deaf as a post), " has Miss Piper had twins ? " This mistake, as you may imagine, threw the whole company into a fit of laughter. However, 'twas the next morning everywhere reported, and in a few days believed by the whole town, that Miss Letitia Piper had actually been brought to bed of a fine boy and girl ; and in less than a week there were some people who could name the father, and the farmhouse where the babies were put to nurse.

Lady Sneerwell. Strange, indeed !

Crabtree. Matter of fact, I assure you. O Lud ! Mr. Surface, pray is it true that your uncle, Sir Oliver, is coming home ?

Joseph Surface. Not that I know of, indeed, sir.

Crabtree. He has been in the East Indies a long time. You can scarcely remember him, I believe ? Sad comfort, whenever he returns, to hear how your brother has gone on !

Joseph Surface. Charles has been imprudent, sir, to be sure ; but I hope no busy people have already prejudiced Sir Oliver against him. He may reform.

Sir Benjamin. To be sure he may ; for my part I never believed him to be so utterly void of principle as people say ; and though he has lost all his friends, I am told nobody is better spoken of by the Jews.

Crabtree. That's true, egad, nephew. If the old Jewry was a ward, I believe Charles would be an alderman : no man more popular there, 'fore Gad ! I hear he pays as many annuities as the Irish tontine ; and that, whenever he is sick, they have prayers for the recovery of his health in all the synagogues.

Sir Benjamin. Yet no man lives in greater splendour. They tell me, when he entertains his friends he

Old Jewry, The former Jewish quarter, near the Bank of England.
Annuities, Annual sums paid out.
Irish tontine, System of life insurance, called after Lorenzo Tonti, a
  Naples banker, who started the scheme in 1773. As each member
  of the scheme died, the annuity of those left became bigger.

will sit down to dinner with a dozen of his own securities; have a score of tradesmen in the ante-chamber, and an officer behind every guest's chair.

Joseph Surface. This may be entertainment to you, gentlemen, but you pay very little regard to the feelings of a brother.

Maria (*aside*). Their malice is intolerable!—(*Aloud*.) Lady Sneerwell, I must wish you a good morning: I'm not very well. (*Exit*.)

Mrs. Candour. O dear! she changes colour very much.

Lady Sneerwell. Do, Mrs. Candour, follow her; she may want your assistance.

Mrs. Candour. That I will, with all my soul, ma'am.—Poor dear girl, who knows what her situation may be! (*Exit*.)

Lady Sneerwell. 'Twas nothing but that she could not bear to hear Charles reflected on, notwithstanding their difference.

Sir Benjamin. The young lady's *penchant* is obvious.

Crabtree. But, Benjamin, you must not give up the pursuit for that: follow her, and put her into good humour. Repeat her some of your own verses. Come, I'll assist you.

Sir Benjamin. Mr. Surface, I did not mean to hurt you; but depend on't your brother is utterly undone.

Crabtree. O Lud, ay! undone as ever man was—can't raise a guinea.

Sir Benjamin. And everything sold, I'm told, that was movable.

Crabtree. I have seen one that was at his house. Not a thing left but some empty bottles that were overlooked, and the family pictures, which I believe are framed in the wainscots.

Sir Benjamin. And I'm very sorry also to hear some bad stories against him. (*Going*.)

Crabtree. Oh, he has done many mean things, that's certain.

Sir Benjamin. But, however, as he's your brother——
                                       (*Going.*)

Crabtree. We'll tell you all another opportunity.
                 (*Exeunt Crabtree and Sir Benjamin.*)

Lady Sneerwell. Ha, ha ! 'tis very hard for them to leave a subject they have not quite run down.

Joseph Surface. And I believe the abuse was no more acceptable to your ladyship than to Maria.

Lady Sneerwell. I doubt her affections are further engaged than we imagine. But the family are to be here this evening, so you may as well dine where you are, and we shall have an opportunity of observing further ; in the meantime, I'll go and plot mischief, and you shall study sentiment.   (*Exeunt.*)

SCENE II. *A Room in Sir Peter Teazle's House.*

(*Enter Sir Peter Teazle.*)

Sir Peter. When an old bachelor marries a young wife, what is he to expect ? 'Tis now six months since Lady Teazle made me the happiest of men—and I have been the most miserable dog ever since ! We tiffed a little going to church, and fairly quarrelled before the bells had done ringing. I was more than once nearly choked with gall during the honeymoon, and had lost all comfort in life before my friends had done wishing me joy. Yet I chose with caution—a girl bred wholly in the country, who never knew luxury beyond one silk gown, nor dissipation above the annual gala of a race ball. Yet she now plays her part in all the extravagant fopperies of fashion and the town, with as ready a grace as if she never had seen a bush or a grass-plot out of Grosvenor Square ! I am sneered at by all my acquaintance, and paragraphed in the newspapers. She dissipates my fortune, and contradicts all my humours ; yet the worst of it is, I doubt I love her, or I should never bear all this. However, I'll never be weak enough to own it.

(Enter Rowley.)

Rowley. Oh! Sir Peter, your servant: how is it with you, sir?

Sir Peter. Very bad, Master Rowley, very bad. I meet with nothing but crosses and vexations.

Rowley. What can have happened since yesterday?

Sir Peter. A good question to a married man!

Rowley. Nay, I'm sure, Sir Peter, your lady can't be the cause of your uneasiness.

Sir Peter. Why, has anybody told you she was dead?

Rowley. Come, come, Sir Peter, you love her, notwithstanding your tempers don't exactly agree.

Sir Peter. But the fault is entirely hers, Master Rowley. I am, myself, the sweetest-tempered man alive, and hate a teasing temper; and so I tell her a hundred times a day.

Rowley. Indeed!

Sir Peter. Ay; and what is very extraordinary, in all our disputes she is always in the wrong! But Lady Sneerwell, and the set she meets at her house, encourage the perverseness of her disposition. Then, to complete my vexation, Maria, my ward, whom I ought to have the power of a father over, is determined to turn rebel too, and absolutely refuses the man whom I have long resolved on for her husband; meaning, I suppose, to bestow herself on his profligate brother.

Rowley. You know, Sir Peter, I have always taken the liberty to differ with you on the subject of these two young gentlemen. I only wish you may not be deceived in your opinion of the elder. For Charles, my life on't! he will retrieve his errors yet. Their worthy father, once my honoured master, was, at his years, nearly as wild a spark; yet, when he died, he did not leave a more benevolent heart to lament his loss.

Sir Peter. You are wrong, Master Rowley. On their father's death, you know, I acted as a kind of guardian to them both, till their uncle Sir Oliver's liberality gave them an early independence : of course no person could have more opportunities of judging of their hearts, and I was never mistaken in my life. Joseph is indeed a model for the young men of the age. He is a man of sentiment, and acts up to the sentiments he professes ; but, for the other, take my word for't, if he had any grain of virtue by descent, he has dissipated it with the rest of his inheritance. Ah ! my old friend, Sir Oliver, will be deeply mortified when he finds how part of his bounty has been misapplied.

Rowley. I am sorry to find you so violent against the young man, because this may be the most critical period of his fortune. I came hither with news that will surprise you.

Sir Peter. What ! let me hear.

Rowley. Sir Oliver is arrived, and at this moment in town.

Sir Peter. How ! you astonish me! I thought you did not expect him this month.

Rowley. I did not : but his passage has been remarkably quick.

Sir Peter. Egad, I shall rejoice to see my old friend. 'Tis sixteen years since we met. We have had many a day together : but does he still enjoin us not to inform his nephews of his arrival ?

Rowley. Most strictly. He means, before it is known, to make some trial of their dispositions.

Sir Peter. Ah ! There needs no art to discover their merits—however, he shall have his way ; but, pray, does he know I am married ?

Rowley. Yes, and will soon wish you joy.

Sir Peter. What, as we drink health to a friend in

consumption ! Ah, Oliver will laugh at me. We used to rail at matrimony together, but he has been steady to his text. Well, he must be soon at my house, though—I'll instantly give orders for his reception. But, Master Rowley, don't drop a word that Lady Teazle and I ever disagree.

Rowley. By no means.

Sir Peter. For I should never be able to stand Noll's jokes ; so I'll have him think, Lord forgive me ! that we are a very happy couple.

Rowley. I understand you ;—but then you must be very careful not to differ while he is in the house with you.

Sir Peter. Egad, and so we must—and that's impossible. Ah ! Master Rowley, when an old bachelor marries a young wife, he deserves—no—the crime carries its punishment along with it.   (*Exeunt.*)

ACT II

SCENE I. *A Room in Sir Peter Teazle's House.*

(*Enter Sir Peter and Lady Teazle.*)

Sir Peter. Lady Teazle, Lady Teazle, I'll not bear it !

Lady Teazle. Sir Peter, Sir Peter, you may bear it or not, as you please ; but I ought to have my own way in everything, and what's more, I will too. What though I was educated in the country, I know very well that women of fashion in London are accountable to nobody after they are married.

Sir Peter. Very well, ma'am, very well ; so a husband is to have no influence, no authority ?

Lady Teazle. Authority ! No, to be sure :—if you wanted authority over me, you should have adopted me, and not married me : I am sure you were old enough.

Sir Peter. Old enough !—ay, there it is ! Well, well, Lady Teazle, though my life may be made unhappy by your temper, I'll not be ruined by your extravagance !

Lady Teazle. My extravagance ! I'm sure I'm not more extravagant than a woman of fashion ought to be.

Sir Peter. No, no, madam, you shall throw away no more sums on such unmeaning luxury. 'Slife ! to spend as much to furnish your dressing-room with flowers in winter as would suffice to turn the Pantheon

'*Slife*, Oath (" God's life ").
Pantheon, A large London concert hall, in Oxford Street. (Burnt down, 1789, and not afterwards rebuilt.)

into a greenhouse, and give a *fête champêtre* at Christmas.

Lady Teazle. And am I to blame, Sir Peter, because flowers are dear in cold weather ? You should find fault with the climate, and not with me. For my part, I'm sure I wish it was spring all the year round, and that roses grew under our feet !

Sir Peter. Oons ! madam—if you had been born to this, I shouldn't wonder at your talking thus ; but you forget what your situation was when I married you.

Lady Teazle. No, no, I don't ; 'twas a very disagreeable one, or I should never have married you.

Sir Peter. Yes, yes, madam, you were then in somewhat a humbler style—the daughter of a plain country squire. Recollect, Lady Teazle, when I saw you first sitting at your tambour, in a pretty figured linen gown, with a bunch of keys at your side, your hair combed smooth over a roll, and your apartment hung round with fruits in worsted, of your own working.

Lady Teazle. Oh, yes ! I remember it very well, and a curious life I led. My daily occupation to inspect the dairy, superintend the poultry, make extracts from the family receipt-book, and comb my aunt Deborah's lap-dog.

Sir Peter. Yes, yes, ma'am, 'twas so indeed.

Lady Teazle. And then, you know, my evening amusements ! To draw patterns for ruffles, which I had not the materials to make up ; to play Pope Joan with the curate ; to read a sermon to my aunt ; or to be stuck down to an old spinet to strum my father to sleep after a fox-chase.

Sir Peter. I am glad you have so good a memory. Yes, madam, these were the recreations I took you from ; but now you must have your coach—*vis-à-vis*

Oons, Zounds (*i.e.* God's wounds). *Pope Joan*, A card game.
Vis-à-vis, Facing each other (viz. the occupants). So a large coach.

—and three powdered footmen before your chair; and, in the summer, a pair of white cats to draw you to Kensington Gardens. No recollection, I suppose, when you were content to ride double, behind the butler, on a docked coach-horse?

Lady Teazle. No—I swear I never did that: I deny the butler and the coach-horse.

Sir Peter. This, madam, was your situation; and what have I done for you? I have made you a woman of fashion, of fortune, of rank—in short, I have made you my wife.

Lady Teazle. Well, then, and there is but one thing more you can make me to add to the obligation, that is——

Sir Peter. My widow, I suppose?

Lady Teazle. Hem! hem!

Sir Peter. I thank you, madam—but don't flatter yourself; for, though your ill-conduct may disturb my peace of mind, it shall never break my heart, I promise you: however, I am equally obliged to you for the hint.

Lady Teazle. Then why will you endeavour to make yourself so disagreeable to me, and thwart me in every little elegant expense?

Sir Peter. 'Slife, madam, I say, had you any of these little elegant expenses when you married me?

Lady Teazle. Lud, Sir Peter! would you have me be out of the fashion?

Sir Peter. The fashion, indeed! what had you to do with the fashion before you married me?

Lady Teazle. For my part, I should think you would like to have your wife thought a woman of taste.

Sir Peter. Ay — there again — taste! Zounds! madam, you had no taste when you married me!

Lady Teazle. That's very true, indeed, Sir Peter!

Chair, Sedan chair.   *Cats*, Smart ponies.

and, after having married you, I should never pretend to taste again, I allow. But now, Sir Peter, since we have finished our daily jangle, I presume I may go to my engagement at Lady Sneerwell's?

Sir Peter. Ay, there's another precious circumstance—a charming set of acquaintance you have made there!

Lady Teazle. Nay, Sir Peter, they are all people of rank and fortune, and remarkably tenacious of reputation.

Sir Peter. Yes, egad, they are tenacious of reputation with a vengeance; for they don't choose anybody should have a character but themselves! Such a crew! Ah! many a wretch has rid on a hurdle who has done less mischief than these utterers of forged tales, coiners of scandal, and clippers of reputation.

Lady Teazle. What, would you restrain the freedom of speech?

Sir Peter. Ah! they have made you just as bad as any one of the society.

Lady Teazle. Why, I believe I do bear a part with a tolerable grace. But I vow I bear no malice against the people I abuse: when I say an ill-natured thing, 'tis out of pure good-humour; and I take it for granted they deal exactly in the same manner with me. But, Sir Peter, you know you promised to come to Lady Sneerwell's too.

Sir Peter. Well, well, I'll call in just to look after my own character.

Lady Teazle. Then, indeed, you must make haste after me or you'll be too late. So good-bye to ye.

(*Exit.*)

Sir Peter. So—I have gained much by my intended expostulation! Yet with what a charming air she

Hurdle, On which criminals were dragged to the place of execution —from Newgate Prison to Tyburn.
Clippers, Clipping the edges of coins, and diminishing their value. (Checked in Charles II.'s reign by having the coins milled.)

contradicts everything I say, and how pleasantly she shows her contempt for my authority! Well, though I can't make her love me, there is great satisfaction in quarrelling with her; and I think she never appears to such advantage as when she is doing everything in her power to plague me.　　　　　(*Exit.*)

SCENE II.　*A Room in Lady Sneerwell's House.*

(*Lady Sneerwell, Mrs. Candour, Crabtree, Sir Benjamin Backbite, and Joseph Surface, discovered.*)
Lady Sneerwell. Nay, positively, we will hear it.
Joseph Surface. Yes, yes, the epigram, by all means.
Sir Benjamin. O plague on't, uncle! 'tis mere nonsense.
Crabtree. No, no; 'fore Gad, very clever for an extempore!
Sir Benjamin. But, ladies, you should be acquainted with the circumstance. You must know, that one day last week, as Lady Betty Curricle was taking the dust in Hyde Park, in a sort of duodecimo phaeton, she desired me to write some verses on her ponies; upon which I took out my pocket-book, and in one moment produced the following:

Sure never were seen two such beautiful ponies;
Other horses are clowns, but these macaronies:
To give them this title I am sure can't be wrong,
Their legs are so slim, and their tails are so long.

Crabtree. There, ladies, done in the smack of a whip, and on horseback too.

Macaronies, Dandies, "swells." The Macaroni Club introduced continental elegances of dress into England. One of the fashions was hair hanging down the back in a grotesque pigtail—"their tails are so long."

Joseph Surface. A very Phœbus, mounted—indeed, Sir Benjamin !

Sir Benjamin. Oh dear, sir !—trifles—trifles.

(*Enter Lady Teazle and Maria.*)

Mrs. Candour. I must have a copy.

Lady Sneerwell. Lady Teazle, I hope we shall see Sir Peter ?

Lady Teazle. I believe he'll wait on your ladyship presently.

Lady Sneerwell. Maria, my love, you look grave. Come, you shall sit down to piquet with Mr. Surface.

Maria. I take very little pleasure in cards—however, I'll do as your ladyship pleases.

Lady Teazle (*aside*). I am surprised Mr. Surface should sit down with her ; I thought he would have embraced this opportunity of speaking to me before Sir Peter came.

Mrs. Candour. Now, I'll die ; but you are so scandalous, I'll forswear your society.

Lady Teazle. What's the matter, Mrs. Candour ?

Mrs. Candour. They'll not allow our friend Miss Vermilion to be handsome.

Lady Sneerwell. Oh, surely she is a pretty woman.

Crabtree. I am very glad you think so, ma'am.

Mrs. Candour. She has a charming fresh colour.

Lady Teazle. Yes, when it is fresh put on.

Mrs. Candour. Oh, fie ! I'll swear her colour is natural : I have seen it come and go !

Lady Teazle. I dare swear you have, ma'am : it goes off at night, and comes again in the morning.

Sir Benjamin. True, ma'am, it not only comes and goes ; but, what's more, egad, her maid can fetch and carry it !

Mrs. Candour. Ha ! ha ! ha ! how I hate to hear you talk so ! But surely, now, her sister is, or was, very handsome.

Crabtree. Who ? Mrs. Evergreen ? O Lord ! she's six-and-fifty if she's an hour !

Mrs. Candour. Now positively you wrong her; fifty-two or fifty-three is the utmost—and I don't think she looks more.

Sir Benjamin. Ah! there's no judging by her looks, unless one could see her face.

Lady Sneerwell. Well, well, if Mrs. Evergreen does take some pains to repair the ravages of time, you must allow she effects it with great ingenuity; and surely that's better than the careless manner in which the widow Ochre caulks her wrinkles.

Sir Benjamin. Nay, now, Lady Sneerwell, you are severe upon the widow. Come, come, 'tis not that she paints so ill—but, when she has finished her face, she joins it on so badly to her neck, that she looks like a mended statue, in which the connoisseur may see at once that the head's modern, though the trunk's antique!

Crabtree. Ha! ha! ha! Well said, nephew!

Mrs. Candour. Ha! ha! ha! Well, you make me laugh; but I vow I hate you for it. What do you think of Miss Simper?

Sir Benjamin. Why, she has very pretty teeth.

Lady Teazle. Yes; and on that account, when she is neither speaking nor laughing (which very seldom happens), she never absolutely shuts her mouth, but leaves it always ajar, as it were—thus.

(*Shows her teeth.*)

Mrs. Candour. How can you be so ill-natured?

Lady Teazle. Nay, I allow even that's better than the pains Mrs. Prim takes to conceal her losses in front. She draws her mouth till it positively resembles the aperture of a poor's-box, and all her words appear to slide out edgewise, as it were—thus: *How do you do, madam? Yes, madam.*

Ochre, Yellow-brown colour; referring to the treatment she gives herself.

Poor's-box, Poor box (to take contributions for the poor), with a slot in the lid.

Lady Sneerwell. Very well, Lady Teazle ; I see you can be a little severe.

Lady Teazle. In defence of a friend it is but justice. But here comes Sir Peter to spoil our pleasantry.

(*Enter Sir Peter Teazle.*)

Sir Peter. Ladies, your most obedient—(*Aside.*) Mercy on me, here is the whole set ! a character dead at every word, I suppose.

Mrs. Candour. I am rejoiced you are come, Sir Peter. They have been so censorious—and Lady Teazle as bad as any one.

Sir Peter. That must be very distressing to you, Mrs. Candour, I dare swear.

Mrs. Candour. Oh, they will allow good qualities to nobody ; not even good nature to our friend Mrs. Pursy.

Lady Teazle. What, the fat dowager who was at Mrs. Quadrille's last night ?

Mrs. Candour. Nay, her bulk is her misfortune ; and, when she takes so much pains to get rid of it, you ought not to reflect on her.

Lady Sneerwell. That's very true, indeed.

Lady Teazle. Yes, I know she almost lives on acids and small whey ; laces herself by pulleys ; and often, in the hottest noon in summer, you may see her on a little squat pony, with her hair plaited up behind like a drummer's, and puffing round the Ring on a full trot.

Mrs. Candour. I thank you, Lady Teazle, for defending her.

Sir Peter. Yes, a good defence, truly.

Mrs. Candour. Truly, Lady Teazle is as censorious as Miss Sallow.

Crabtree. Yes, and she is a curious being to pretend to be censorious—an awkward gawky, without any one good point under heaven.

The Ring, The circular drive in Hyde Park, called Rotten Row (*i.e. route du roi*, King's Road, because laid out by Charles II.).

Mrs. Candour. Positively you shall not be so very severe.   Miss Sallow is a near relation of mine by marriage, and as for her person, great allowance is to be made ; for, let me tell you, a woman labours under many disadvantages who tries to pass for a girl of six-and-thirty.

Lady Sneerwell. Though, surely, she is handsome still—and for the weakness in her eyes, considering how much she reads by candle-light, it is not to be wondered at.

Mrs. Candour. True ; and then as to her manner, upon my word I think it is particularly graceful, considering she never had the least education ; for you know her mother was a Welsh milliner, and her father a sugar-baker at Bristol.

Sir Benjamin. Ah ! you are both of you too good-natured !

Sir Peter (*aside*). Yes, damned good-natured ! This their own relation ! mercy on me !

Mrs. Candour. For my part, I own I cannot bear to hear a friend ill-spoken of.

Sir Peter. No, to be sure !

Sir Benjamin. Oh ! you are of a moral turn. Mrs. Candour and I can sit for an hour and hear Lady Stucco talk sentiment.

Lady Teazle. Nay, I vow Lady Stucco is very well with the dessert after dinner ; for she's just like the French fruit one cracks for mottoes—made up of paint and proverb.

Mrs. Candour. Well, I will never join in ridiculing a friend ; and so l constantly tell my cousin Ogle, and you all know what pretensions she has to be critical on beauty.

Crabtree. Oh, to be sure ! she has herself the oddest countenance that ever was seen ; 'tis a collection of features from all the different countries of the globe.

Sugar-baker, Sugar-refiner.

Sir Benjamin. So she has, indeed—an Irish front—
Crabtree. Caledonian locks——
Sir Benjamin. Dutch nose——
Crabtree. Austrian lips——
Sir Benjamin. Complexion of a Spaniard——
Crabtree. And teeth *à la Chinoise*——
Sir Benjamin. In short, her face resembles a *table d'hôte* at Spa—where no two guests are of a nation——
Crabtree. Or a congress at the close of a general war—wherein all the members, even to her eyes, appear to have a different interest, and her nose and chin are the only parties likely to join issue.
Mrs. Candour. Ha! ha! ha!
Sir Peter (*aside*). Mercy on my life!—a person they dine with twice a week!
Lady Sneerwell. Go—go—you are a couple of provoking toads.
Mrs. Candour. Nay, but I vow you shall not carry the laugh off so—for give me leave to say, that Mrs. Ogle——
Sir Peter. Madam, madam, I beg your pardon—there's no stopping these good gentlemen's tongues. But when I tell you, Mrs. Candour, that the lady they are abusing is a particular friend of mine, I hope you'll not take her part.
Lady Sneerwell. Ha! ha! ha! well said, Sir Peter! But you are a cruel creature—too phlegmatic yourself for a jest, and too peevish to allow wit in others.
Sir Peter. Ah, madam, true wit is more nearly allied to good nature than your ladyship is aware of.
Lady Teazle. True, Sir Peter: I believe they are so near akin that they can never be united.
Sir Benjamin. Or rather, madam, suppose them man and wife, because one seldom sees them together.
Lady Teazle. But Sir Peter is such an enemy to

"*Table d'hôte*" *at Spa*, Dinner comprising items to suit all the mixed guests present, at Spa, the Belgian watering-place.

scandal, I believe he would have it put down by parliament.

Sir Peter. 'Fore heaven, madam, if they were to consider the sporting with reputation of as much importance as poaching on manors, and pass an act for the preservation of fame, I believe many would thank them for the bill.

Lady Sneerwell. O Lud! Sir Peter; would you deprive us of our privileges?

Sir Peter. Ay, madam; and then no person should be permitted to kill characters and run down reputations, but qualified old maids and disappointed widows.

Lady Sneerwell. Go, you monster!

Mrs. Candour. But, surely, you would not be quite so severe on those who only report what they hear?

Sir Peter. Yes, madam, I would have law merchant for them too; and in all cases of slander currency, whenever the drawer of the lie was not to be found, the injured parties should have a right to come on any of the indorsers.

Crabtree. Well, for my part, I believe there never was a scandalous tale without some foundation.

Lady Sneerwell. Come, ladies, shall we sit down to cards in the next room?

(*Enter Servant, who whispers Sir Peter.*)

Sir Peter. I'll be with them directly.—(*Exit Servant.*) (*Aside.*) I'll get away unperceived.

Lady Sneerwell. Sir Peter, you are not going to leave us?

Law merchant, Mercantile law, here relating to bills and banking.

Slander currency, Slander passed round from person to person.

Drawer, Person signing a promise to repay money borrowed. So, the inventor of a piece of scandal; one who " borrows " the good reputation of the victim, to make it bad.

Indorsers, Those who have signed their name on the back of the bill, and must pay the account if the drawer does not. Repeaters of scandal.

Sir Peter. Your ladyship must excuse me ; I'm called away by particular business. But I leave my character behind me. (*Exit.*)

Sir Benjamin. Well—certainly, Lady Teazle, that lord of yours is a strange being : I could tell you some stories of him would make you laugh heartily if he were not your husband.

Lady Teazle. Oh, pray don't mind that ; come, do let's hear them.

(*Exeunt all but Joseph Surface and Maria.*)

Joseph Surface. Maria, I see you have no satisfaction in this society.

Maria. How is it possible I should ! If to raise malicious smiles at the infirmities or misfortunes of those who have never injured us be the province of wit or humour, Heaven grant me a double portion of dullness !

Joseph Surface. Yet they appear more ill-natured than they are ; they have no malice at heart.

Maria. Then is their conduct still more contemptible ; for, in my opinion, nothing could excuse the intemperance of their tongues but a natural and uncontrollable bitterness of mind.

Joseph Surface. Undoubtedly, madam ; and it has always been a sentiment of mine, that to propagate a malicious truth wantonly is more despicable than to falsify from revenge. But can you, Maria, feel thus for others, and be unkind to me alone ? Is hope to be denied the tenderest passion ?

Maria. Why will you distress me by renewing this subject ?

Joseph Surface. Ah, Maria ! you would not treat me thus, and oppose your guardian, Sir Peter's will, but that I see that profligate Charles is still a favoured rival.

Maria. Ungenerously urged ! But, whatever my sentiments are for that unfortunate young man, be assured I shall not feel more bound to give him up, because his distresses have lost him the regard even of a brother.

Joseph Surface. Nay, but, Maria, do not leave me with a frown : by all that's honest, I swear——

(Kneels.)

(Re-enter Lady Teazle behind.)

(Aside.) Gad's life, here's Lady Teazle.—*(Aloud to Maria.)* You must not—no, you shall not—for, though I have the greatest regard for Lady Teazle——

Maria. Lady Teazle ?

Joseph Surface. Yet were Sir Peter to suspect——

Lady Teazle (coming forward). What is this, pray ? Do you take her for me ?—Child, you are wanted in the next room.—*(Exit Maria.)* What is all this, pray ?

Joseph Surface. Oh, the most unlucky circumstance in nature ! Maria has somehow suspected the tender concern I have for your happiness, and threatened to acquaint Sir Peter with her suspicions, and I was just endeavouring to reason with her when you came in.

Lady Teazle. Indeed ! but you seemed to adopt a very tender mode of reasoning—do you usually argue on your knees ?

Joseph Surface. Oh, she's a child, and I thought a little bombast—but, Lady Teazle, when are you to give me your judgment on my library, as you promised ?

Lady Teazle. No, no ; I begin to think it would be imprudent, and you know I admit you as a lover no further than fashion requires.

Joseph Surface. True—a mere Platonic cicisbeo, what every wife is entitled to.

Lady Teazle. Certainly, one must not be out of the fashion. However, I have so many of my country prejudices left, that, though Sir Peter's ill-humour

---

Platonic cicisbeo, Equivalent to-day to a "dancing partner," or "boy-friend" of a married woman to take her out to entertainments.

may vex me ever so, it never shall provoke me
to——

Joseph Surface. The only revenge in your power.
Well, I applaud your moderation.

Lady Teazle. Go—you are an insinuating wretch!
But we shall be missed—let us join the company.

Joseph Surface. But we had best not return
together.

Lady Teazle. Well, don't stay; for Maria shan't
come to hear any more of your reasoning, I promise
you. (*Exit.*)

Joseph Surface. A curious dilemma, truly, my
politics have run me into! I wanted, at first, only to
ingratiate myself with Lady Teazle, that she might
not be my enemy with Maria; and I have, I don't
know how, become her serious lover. Sincerely I
begin to wish I had never made such a point of gain-
ing so very good a character, for it has led me into
so many cursed rogueries that I doubt I shall be
exposed at last. (*Exit.*)

SCENE. III. *A Room in Sir Peter Teazle's House.*

(*Enter Sir Oliver Surface and Rowley.*)

Sir Oliver. Ha! ha! ha! so my friend is married,
hey?—a young wife out of the country. Ha! ha!
ha! that he should have stood bluff to old bachelor
so long, and sink into a husband at last!

Rowley. But you must not rally him on the subject,
Sir Oliver; 'tis a tender point, I assure you, though
he has been married only seven months.

Sir Oliver. Then he has been just half a year on
the stool of repentance!—Poor Peter! But you say
he has entirely given up Charles—never sees him,
hey?

Rowley. His prejudice against him is astonishing, and I am sure greatly increased by a jealousy of him with Lady Teazle, which he has industriously been led into by a scandalous society in the neighbourhood, who have contributed not a little to Charles's ill name. Whereas the truth is, I believe, if the lady is partial to either of them, his brother is the favourite.

Sir Oliver. Ay, I know there are a set of malicious, prating, prudent gossips, both male and female, who murder characters to kill time, and will rob a young fellow of his good name before he has years to know the value of it. But I am not to be prejudiced against my nephew by such, I promise you! No, no: if Charles has done nothing false or mean, I shall compound for his extravagance.

Rowley. Then, my life on't, you will reclaim him. Ah, sir, it gives me new life to find that your heart is not turned against him, and that the son of my good old master has one friend, however, left.

Sir Oliver. What! shall I forget, Master Rowley, when I was at his years myself? Egad, my brother and I were neither of us very prudent youths; and yet, I believe, you have not seen many better men than your old master was?

Rowley. Sir, 'tis this reflection gives me assurance that Charles may yet be a credit to his family. But here comes Sir Peter.

Sir Oliver. Egad, so he does! Mercy on me, he's greatly altered, and seems to have a settled married look! One may read husband in his face at this distance!

(*Enter Sir Peter Teazle.*)

Sir Peter. Ha! Sir Oliver—my old friend! Welcome to England a thousand times!

Sir Oliver. Thank you, thank you, Sir Peter! and i'faith I am glad to find you well, believe me!

Compound, Make allowance; *i.e.* pardon.

Sir Peter. Oh! 'tis a long time since we met—fifteen years, I doubt, Sir Oliver, and many a cross accident in the time.

Sir Oliver. Ay, I have had my share. But, what! I find you are married, hey, my old boy? Well, well, it can't be helped; and so—I wish you joy with all my heart!

Sir Peter. Thank you, thank you, Sir Oliver.—Yes, I have entered into—the happy state; but we'll not talk of that now.

Sir Oliver. True, true, Sir Peter; old friends should not begin on grievances at first meeting. No, no, no.

Rowley (*aside to Sir Oliver*). Take care, pray, sir.

Sir Oliver. Well, so one of my nephews is a wild rogue, hey?

Sir Peter. Wild! Ah! my old friend, I grieve for your disappointment there; he's a lost young man, indeed. However, his brother will make you amends; Joseph is, indeed, what a youth should be—everybody in the world speaks well of him.

Sir Oliver. I am sorry to hear it; he has too good a character to be an honest fellow. Everybody speaks well of him! Pshaw! then he has bowed as low to knaves and fools as to the honest dignity of genius and virtue.

Sir Peter. What, Sir Oliver! do you blame him for not making enemies?

Sir Oliver. Yes, if he has merit enough to deserve them.

Sir Peter. Well, well—you'll be convinced when you know him. 'Tis edification to hear him converse; he professes the noblest sentiments.

Sir Oliver. Oh, plague of his sentiments! If he salutes me with a scrap of morality in his mouth, I shall be sick directly. But, however, don't mistake me, Sir Peter; I don't mean to defend Charles's errors; but, before I form my judgment of either of them, I intend to make a trial of their hearts; and my friend Rowley and I have planned something for the purpose.

Rowley. And Sir Peter shall own for once he has been mistaken.

Sir Peter. Oh, my life on Joseph's honour !

Sir Oliver. Well—come, give us a bottle of good wine, and we'll drink the lads' health, and tell you our scheme.

Sir Peter. Allons, then !

Sir Oliver. And don't, Sir Peter, be so severe against your old friend's son. Odds my life ! I am not sorry that he has run out of course a little : for my part, I hate to see prudence clinging to the green suckers of youth ; 'tis like ivy round a sapling, and spoils the growth of the tree.   (*Exeunt.*)

ACT III

SCENE I. *A Room in Sir Peter Teazle's House.*

(*Enter Sir Peter Teazle, Sir Oliver Surface,
and Rowley.*)

Sir Peter. Well, then, we will see this fellow first, and have our wine afterwards. But how is this, Master Rowley ? I don't see the jet of your scheme.

Rowley. Why, sir, this Mr. Stanley, whom I was speaking of, is nearly related to them by their mother, He was once a merchant in Dublin, but has been ruined by a series of undeserved misfortunes. He has applied, by letter, since his confinement, both to Mr. Surface and Charles : from the former he has received nothing but evasive promises of future service, while Charles has done all that his extravagance has left him power to do ; and he is, at this time, endeavouring to raise a sum of money, part of which, in the midst of his own distresses, I know he intends for the service of poor Stanley.

Sir Oliver. Ah ! he is my brother's son.

Sir Peter. Well, but how is Sir Oliver personally to——

Rowley. Why, sir, I will inform Charles and his brother that Stanley has obtained permission to apply personally to his friends ; and, as they have neither of them ever seen him, let Sir Oliver assume his character, and he will have a fair opportunity of judging, at least, of the benevolence of their dispositions : and believe me, sir, you will find in the

Jet, Point.

youngest brother one who, in the midst of folly and dissipation, has still, as our immortal bard expresses it,—

> " a heart to pity, and a hand
> Open as day, for melting charity."

Sir Peter. Pshaw! What signifies his having an open hand or purse either, when he has nothing left to give? Well, well, make the trial, if you please. But where is the fellow whom you brought for Sir Oliver to examine, relative to Charles's affairs?

Rowley. Below, waiting his commands, and no one can give him better intelligence.—This, Sir Oliver, is a friendly Jew, who, to do him justice, has done everything in his power to bring your nephew to a proper sense of his extravagance.

Sir Peter. Pray let us have him in.

Rowley. Desire Mr. Moses to walk upstairs.

(Calls to Servant.)

Sir Peter. But, pray, why should you suppose he will speak the truth?

Rowley. Oh, I have convinced him that he has no chance of recovering certain sums advanced to Charles but through the bounty of Sir Oliver, who he knows is arrived; so that you may depend on his fidelity to his own interests. I have also another evidence in my power, one Snake, whom I have detected in a matter little short of forgery, and shall shortly produce to remove some of your prejudices, Sir Peter, relative to Charles and Lady Teazle.

Sir Peter. I have heard too much on that subject.

Rowley. Here comes the honest Israelite.

(Enter Moses.)

—This is Sir Oliver.

Sir Oliver. Sir, I understand you have lately had great dealings with my nephew Charles.

Immortal bard, Shakespeare. See 2 *Henry IV.*, IV. iv. 31–32. " A heart to pity " should be " He hath a tear for pity."

Moses. Yes, Sir Oliver, I have done all I could for him; but he was ruined before he came to me for assistance.

Sir Oliver. That was unlucky, truly; for you have had no opportunity of showing your talents.

Moses. None at all; I hadn't the pleasure of knowing his distresses till he was some thousands worse than nothing.

Sir Oliver. Unfortunate, indeed! But I suppose you have done all in your power for him, honest Moses?

Moses. Yes, he knows that. This very evening I was to have brought him a gentleman from the city, who does not know him, and will, I believe, advance him some money.

Sir Peter. What, one Charles had never had money from before?

Moses. Yes, Mr. Premium, of Crutched Friars, formerly a broker.

Sir Peter. Egad, Sir Oliver, a thought strikes me! —Charles, you say, does not know Mr. Premium?

Moses. Not at all.

Sir Peter. Now then, Sir Oliver, you may have a better opportunity of satisfying yourself by than an old romancing tale of a poor relation: go with my friend Moses, and represent Premium, and then, I'll answer for it, you'll see your nephew in all his glory.

Sir Oliver. Egad, I like this idea better than the other, and I may visit Joseph afterwards as old Stanley.

Sir Peter. True—so you may.

Rowley. Well, this is taking Charles rather at a disadvantage, to be sure. However, Moses, you understand Sir Peter, and will be faithful?

Crutched Friars, London street, near the Tower. (After a monastery of Friars with a cross—" crutch "—on their sleeve: a minor order.)

Moses. You may depend upon me.—(*Looks at his watch.*) This is near the time I was to have gone.

Sir Oliver. I'll accompany you as soon as you please, Moses—— But hold! I have forgot one thing—how the plague shall I be able to pass for a Jew?

Moses. There's no need—the principal is Christian.

Sir Oliver. Is he? I'm very sorry to hear it. But, then again, an't I rather too smartly dressed to look like a money-lender?

Sir Peter. Not at all; 'twould not be out of character, if you went in your carriage—would it, Moses?

Moses. Not in the least.

Sir Oliver. Well, but how must I talk? there's certainly some cant of usury and mode of treating that I ought to know.

Sir Peter. Oh, there's not much to learn. The great point, as I take it, is to be exorbitant enough in your demands. Hey, Moses?

Moses. Yes, that's a very great point.

Sir Oliver. I'll answer for't I'll not be wanting in that. I'll ask him eight or ten per cent. on the loan, at least.

Moses. If you ask him no more than that, you'll be discovered immediately.

Sir Oliver. Hey! what, the plague! how much then?

Moses. That depends upon the circumstances. If he appears not very anxious for the supply, you should require only forty or fifty per cent.; but if you find him in great distress, and want the moneys very bad, you may ask double.

Sir Peter. A good honest trade you're learning, Sir Oliver!

Sir Oliver. Truly, I think so—and not unprofitable.

Moses. Then, you know, you haven't the moneys

Cant of usury, Catchwords used by moneylenders.

yourself, but are forced to borrow them for him of a friend.

Sir Oliver. Oh! I borrow it of a friend, do I?

Moses. And your friend is an unconscionable dog: but you can't help that.

Sir Oliver. My friend an unconscionable dog, is he?

Moses. Yes, and he himself has not the moneys by him, but is forced to sell stock at a great loss.

Sir Oliver. He is forced to sell stock at a great loss, is he? Well, that's very kind of him.

Sir Peter. I'faith, Sir Oliver—Mr. Premium, I mean—you'll soon be master of the trade. But, Moses! would not you have him run out a little against the Annuity Bill? That would be in character, I should think.

Moses. Very much.

Rowley. And lament that a young man now must be at years of discretion before he is suffered to ruin himself?

Moses. Ay, great pity!

Sir Peter. And abuse the public for allowing merit to an act whose only object is to snatch misfortune and imprudence from the rapacious grip of usury, and give the minor a chance of inheriting his estate without being undone by coming into possession.

Sir Oliver. So, so—Moses shall give me further instructions as we go together.

Sir Peter. You will not have much time, for your nephew lives hard by.

Sir Oliver. Oh, never fear! my tutor appears so able, that though Charles lived in the next street, it must be my own fault if I am not a complete rogue before I turn the corner. (*Exit with Moses.*)

Annuity Bill, Passed in 1777, to put an end to annuity contracts with minors. This was a loss to moneylenders, who could no longer take advantage of young simpletons and spendthrifts who would barter away their future estates for a present income.

Sir Peter. So, now, I think Sir Oliver will be convinced : you are partial, Rowley, and would have prepared Charles for the other plot.

Rowley. No, upon my word, Sir Peter.

Sir Peter. Well, go bring me this Snake, and I'll hear what he has to say presently. I see Maria, and want to speak with her.—(*Exit Rowley.*) I should be glad to be convinced my suspicions of Lady Teazle and Charles were unjust. I have never yet opened my mind on this subject to my friend Joseph—I am determined I will do it—he will give me his opinion sincerely.

(*Enter Maria.*)

So, child, has Mr. Surface returned with you ?

Maria. No, sir ; he was engaged.

Sir Peter. Well, Maria, do you not reflect, the more you converse with that amiable young man, what return his partiality for you deserves ?

Maria. Indeed, Sir Peter, your frequent importunity on this subject distresses me extremely—you compel me to declare, that I know no man who has ever paid me a particular attention whom I would not prefer to Mr. Surface.

Sir Peter. So—here's perverseness ! No, no, Maria, 'tis Charles only whom you would prefer. 'Tis evident his vices and follies have won your heart.

Maria. This is unkind, sir. You know I have obeyed you in neither seeing nor corresponding with him : I have heard enough to convince me that he is unworthy my regard. Yet I cannot think it culpable, if, while my understanding severely condemns his vices, my heart suggests pity for his distresses.

Sir Peter. Well, well, pity him as much as you please ; but give your heart and hand to a worthier object.

Maria. Never to his brother !

Sir Peter. Go, perverse and obstinate ! But take care, madam ; you have never yet known what the authority of a guardian is : don't compel me to inform you of it.

Maria. I can only say, you shall not have just reason. 'Tis true, by my father's will, I am for a short period bound to regard you as his substitute ; but must cease to think you so, when you would compel me to be miserable. (*Exit.*)

Sir Peter. Was ever man so crossed as I am, everything conspiring to fret me ! I had not been involved in matrimony a fortnight, before her father, a hale and hearty man, died, on purpose, I believe, for the pleasure of plaguing me with the care of his daughter. —(*Lady Teazle sings without.*) But here comes my helpmate ! She appears in great good humour. How happy I should be if I could tease her into loving me, though but a little !

(*Enter Lady Teazle.*)

Lady Teazle. Lud ! Sir Peter, I hope you haven't been quarrelling with Maria ? It is not using me well to be ill-humoured when I am not by.

Sir Peter. Ah, Lady Teazle, you might have the power to make me good-humoured at all times.

Lady Teazle. I am sure I wish I had ; for I want you to be in a charming sweet temper at this moment. Do be good-humoured now, and let me have two hundred pounds, will you ?

Sir Peter. Two hundred pounds ; what, an't I to be in a good humour without paying for it ! But speak to me thus, and i'faith there's nothing I could refuse you. You shall have it ; but seal me a bond for the repayment.

Lady Teazle. Oh, no—there—my note of hand will do as well. (*Offering her hand.*)

Sir Peter. And you shall no longer reproach me with not giving you an independent settlement. I mean shortly to surprise you ; but shall we always live thus, hey ?

Lady Teazle. If you please. I'm sure I don't care

how soon we leave off quarrelling, provided you'll own you were tired first.

Sir Peter. Well—then let our future contest be, who shall be most obliging.

Lady Teazle. I assure you, Sir Peter, good nature becomes you. You look now as you did before we were married, when you used to walk with me under the elms, and tell me stories of what a gallant you were in your youth, and chuck me under the chin, you would; and ask me if I thought I could love an old fellow, who would deny me nothing—didn't you ?

Sir Peter. Yes, yes, and you were as kind and attentive——

Lady Teazle. Ay, so I was, and would always take your part, when my acquaintance used to abuse you, and turn you into ridicule.

Sir Peter. Indeed !

Lady Teazle. Ay, and when my cousin Sophy has called you a stiff, peevish old bachelor, and laughed at me for thinking of marrying one who might be my father, I have always defended you, and said, I didn't think you so ugly by any means, and that you'd make a very good sort of a husband.

Sir Peter. And you prophesied right; and we shall now be the happiest couple——

Lady Teazle. And never differ again ?

Sir Peter. No, never—though at the same time, indeed, my dear Lady Teazle, you must watch your temper very seriously; for in all our little quarrels, my dear, if you recollect, my love, you always began first.

Lady Teazle. I beg your pardon, my dear Sir Peter; indeed, you always gave the provocation.

Sir Peter. Now, see, my angel ! take care—contradicting isn't the way to keep friends.

Lady Teazle. Then, don't you begin it, my love !

Sir Peter. There, now ! you—you are going on. You don't perceive, my life, that you are just doing

166

the very thing which you know always makes me angry.

Lady Teazle. Nay, you know if you will be angry without any reason, my dear——

Sir Peter. There ! now you want to quarrel again.

Lady Teazle. No, I'm sure I don't : but, if you will be so peevish——

Sir Peter. There now ! who begins first ?

Lady Teazle. Why, you, to be sure. I said nothing —but there's no bearing your temper.

Sir Peter. No, no, madam : the fault's in your own temper.

Lady Teazle. Ay, you are just what my cousin Sophy said you would be.

Sir Peter. Your cousin Sophy is a forward, impertinent gipsy.

Lady Teazle. You are a great bear, I am sure, to abuse my relations.

Sir Peter. Now may all the plagues of marriage be doubled on me, if ever I try to be friends with you any more !

Lady Teazle. So much the better.

Sir Peter. No, no, madam : 'tis evident you never cared a pin for me, and I was a madman to marry you —a pert, rural coquette, that had refused half the honest squires in the neighbourhood !

Lady Teazle. And I am sure I was a fool to marry you—an old dangling bachelor, who was single at fifty, only because he never could meet with any one who would have him.

Sir Peter. Ay, ay, madam ; but you were pleased enough to listen to me : you never had such an offer before.

Lady Teazle. No ! didn't I refuse Sir Tivy Terrier, who everybody said would have been a better match ? for his estate is just as good as yours, and he has broke his neck since we have been married.

Sir Peter. I have done with you, madam ! You

are an unfeeling, ungrateful—but there's an end of everything. I believe you capable of everything that is bad. Yes, madam, I now believe the reports relative to you and Charles, madam. Yes, madam, you and Charles are, not without grounds——

Lady Teazle. Take care, Sir Peter ! you had better not insinuate any such thing ! I'll not be suspected without cause, I promise you.

Sir Peter. Very well, madam ! very well ! a separate maintenance as soon as you please. Yes, madam, or a divorce ! I'll make an example of myself for the benefit of all old bachelors. Let us separate, madam.

Lady Teazle. Agreed ! agreed ! And now, my dear Sir Peter, we are of a mind once more, we may be the happiest couple, and never differ again, you know : ha ! ha ! ha ! Well, you are going to be in a passion, I see, and I shall only interrupt you—so, bye ! bye !
(*Exit.*)

Sir Peter. Plagues and tortures ! can't I make her angry either ! Oh, I am the most miserable fellow ! But I'll not bear her presuming to keep her temper : no ! she may break my heart, but she shan't keep her temper.   (*Exit.*)

SCENE II. *A Room in Charles Surface's House.*

(*Enter Trip, Moses, and Sir Oliver Surface.*)

Trip. Here, Master Moses ! if you'll stay a moment, I'll try whether—what's the gentleman's name ?

Sir Oliver (*aside to Moses*). Mr. Moses, what is my name ?

Moses. Mr. Premium.

Trip. Premium—very well.   (*Exit, taking snuff.*)

Sir Oliver. To judge by the servants, one wouldn't believe the master was ruined. But what ! sure, this was my brother's house ?

Moses. Yes, sir; Mr. Charles bought it of Mr. Joseph, with the furniture, pictures, etc., just as the old gentleman left it. Sir Peter thought it a piece of extravagance in him.

Sir Oliver. In my mind, the other's economy in selling it to him was more reprehensible by half.

(*Re-enter Trip.*)

Trip. My master says you must wait, gentlemen: he has company, and can't speak with you yet.

Sir Oliver. If he knew who it was wanted to see him, perhaps he would not send such a message.

Trip. Yes, yes, sir; he knows you are here—I did not forget little Premium: no, no, no.

Sir Oliver. Very well; and I pray, sir, what may be your name?

Trip. Trip, sir; my name is Trip, at your service.

Sir Oliver. Well, then, Mr. Trip, you have a pleasant sort of place here, I guess?

Trip. Why, yes—here are three or four of us pass our time agreeably enough; but then our wages are sometimes a little in arrear—and not very great either—but fifty pounds a year, and find our own bags and bouquets.

Sir Oliver (*aside.*) Bags and bouquets! halters and bastinadoes!

Trip. And *à propos*, Moses, have you been able to get me that little bill discounted?

Sir Oliver (*aside*). Wants to raise money, too!— mercy on me! Has his distresses too, I warrant, like a lord, and affects creditors and duns.

Moses. 'Twas not to be done, indeed, Mr. Trip.

Trip. Good lack, you surprise me! My friend

Bags, Pouches, made of silk, to hold the back hair; " bag-wig."
Bouquets, Adornments like a bunch of flowers; finery.
Bill, Bill of exchange, or promissory note; binding the one who signs it to pay the stated sum by a given date. If it is presented before that date the amount of the interest on the sum for the difference of time is taken off, or *discounted.* Here, turned into cash at present price.

Brush has endorsed it, and I thought when he put his name at the back of a bill 'twas the same as cash.

Moses. No, 'twouldn't do.

Trip. A small sum—but twenty pounds. Hark'ee, Moses, do you think you couldn't get it me by way of annuity ?

Sir Oliver (*aside*). An annuity ! ha ! ha ! a footman raise money by way of annuity ! Well done, luxury, egad !

Moses. Well, but you must insure your place.

Trip. Oh, with all my heart ! I'll insure my place, and my life, too, if you please.

Sir Oliver (*aside*). It's more than I would your neck.

Moses. But is there nothing you could deposit ?

Trip. Why, nothing capital of my master's wardrobe has dropped lately ; but I could give you a mortgage on some of his winter clothes, with equity of redemption before November—or you shall have the reversion of the French velvet, or a post-obit on the blue and silver ;—these, I should think, Moses, with a few pair of point ruffles, as a collateral security —hey, my little fellow ?

Moses. Well, well.   (*Bell rings.*)

Trip. Egad, I heard the bell ! I believe, gentlemen, I can now introduce you. Don't forget the annuity, little Moses ! This way, gentlemen, I'll insure my place, you know.

Sir Oliver (*aside*). If the man be a shadow of the master, this is the temple of dissipation indeed !

                                        (*Exeunt.*)

Capital, Valuable.   *Dropped*, Come to me (when discarded).
Mortgage . . . November, Promise of the clothes, given for a loan of money, the clothes to be handed over by November or else the loan returned.
Reversion, Right to a thing after the owner's death (here, disuse).
Post-obit, Bond for a loan payable on a given person's death (*i.e.* Charles's ceasing to wear the clothes).
Collateral, Extra.

SCENE III.   *Another Room in the same.*

(*Charles Surface, Sir Harry Bumper, Careless, and Gentlemen, discovered drinking.*)

Charles Surface. 'Fore heaven, 'tis true!—there's the great degeneracy of the age. Many of our acquaintance have taste, spirit, and politeness; but plague on't they won't drink.

Careless. It is so, indeed, Charles! they give in to all the substantial luxuries of the table, and abstain from nothing but wine and wit. Oh, certainly society suffers by it intolerably! for now, instead of the social spirit of raillery that used to mantle over a glass of bright Burgundy, their conversation is become just like the Spa-water they drink, which has all the pertness and flatulency of champagne, without its spirit or flavour.

First Gentleman. But what are they to do who love play better than wine?

Careless. True! there's Sir Harry diets himself for gaming, and is now under a hazard regimen.

Charles Surface. Then he'll have the worst of it. What! you wouldn't train a horse for the course by keeping him from corn? For my part, egad, I'm never so successful as when I am a little merry: let me throw on a bottle of champagne, and I never lose—at least I never feel my losses, which is exactly the same thing.

Second Gentleman. Ay, that I believe.

Charles Surface. And, then, what man can pretend to be a believer in love, who is an abjurer of wine? 'Tis the test by which the lover knows his own heart. Fill a dozen bumpers to a dozen beauties, and she that floats at the top is the maid that has bewitched you.

Mantle, Rise.   *Flatulency*, Gassiness.
Hazard, Game of dice.   *Regimen*, diet; *viz.* keeping off wine, in training for hazard.

171

Careless. Now then, Charles, be honest, and give us your real favourite.

Charles Surface. Why, I have withheld her only in compassion to you. If I toast her, you must give a round of her peers, which is impossible—on earth.

Careless. Oh, then we'll find some canonized vestals or heathen goddesses that will do, I warrant !

Charles Surface. Here then, bumpers, you rogues ! bumpers ! Maria ! Maria——

Sir Harry. Maria who ?

Charles Surface. Oh, damn the surname !—'tis too formal to be registered in Love's calendar—but now, Sir Harry, beware, we must have beauty superlative.

Careless. Nay, never study, Sir Harry : we'll stand to the toast, though your mistress should want an eye, and you know you have a song will excuse you.

Sir Harry. Egad, so I have ! and I'll give him the song instead of the lady.   (*Sings.*)

Here's to the maiden of bashful fifteen ;
    Here's to the widow of fifty ;
Here's to the flaunting extravagant quean,
    And here's to the housewife that's thrifty.

Chorus.
    Let the toast pass,—
    Drink to the lass,
I'll warrant she'll prove an excuse for the glass.

Here's to the charmer whose dimples we prize ;
    Now to the maid who has none, sir ;
Here's to the girl with a pair of blue eyes,
    And here's to the nymph with but one, sir.

Chorus.
    Let the toast pass,—
    Drink to the lass,
I'll warrant she'll prove an excuse for the glass.

Here's to the maid with a bosom of snow ;
 Now to her that's as brown as a berry ;
Here's to the wife with a face full of woe,
 And now to the damsel that's merry.

    Chorus.
 Let the toast pass,—
 Drink to the lass,
I'll warrant she'll prove an excuse for the glass.

For let 'em be clumsy, or let 'em be slim,
 Young or ancient, I care not a feather ;
So fill a pint bumper quite up to the brim,
So fill up your glasses, nay, fill to the brim,
 And let us e'en toast them together.

    Chorus.
 Let the toast pass,—
 Drink to the lass,
I'll warrant she'll prove an excuse for the glass.

All. Bravo ! Bravo !
 (*Enter Trip, and whispers Charles Surface.*)
Charles Surface. Gentlemen, you must excuse me a little.—Careless, take the chair, will you ?

Careless. Nay, pr'ythee, Charles, what now ? This is one of your peerless beauties, I suppose, dropped in by chance ?

Charles Surface. No, faith ! To tell you the truth, 'tis a Jew and a broker, who are come by appointment.

Careless. Oh, damn it ! let's have the Jew in.

First Gentleman. Ay, and the broker too, by all means.

Second Gentleman. Yes, yes, the Jew and the broker.

Charles Surface. Egad, with all my heart !—Trip, bid the gentlemen walk in.—(*Exit Trip.*) Though there's one of them a stranger, I can tell you.

Careless. Charles, let us give them some generous Burgundy, and perhaps they'll grow conscientious.

Charles Surface. Oh, hang 'em, no! wine does but draw forth a man's natural qualities; and to make them drink would only be to whet their knavery.

(*Re-enter Trip, with Sir Oliver Surface and Moses.*)

Charles Surface. So, honest Moses; walk in, pray, Mr. Premium—that's the gentleman's name, isn't it, Moses?

Moses. Yes, sir.

Charles Surface. Set chairs, Trip.—Sit down, Mr. Premium.—Glasses, Trip. (*Trip gives chairs and glasses, and exit.*) Sit down, Moses.—Come, Mr. Premium, I'll give you a sentiment; here's *Success to usury !*—Moses, fill the gentleman a bumper.

Moses. Success to usury!   (*Drinks.*)

Careless. Right, Moses—usury is prudence and industry, and deserves to succeed.

Sir Oliver. Then here's—All the success it deserves!
                                               (*Drinks.*)

Careless. No, no, that won't do! Mr. Premium, you have demurred at the toast, and must drink it in a pint bumper.

First Gentleman. A pint bumper, at least.

Moses. Oh, pray, sir, consider—Mr. Premium's a gentleman.

Careless. And therefore loves good wine.

Second Gentleman. Give Moses a quart glass—this is mutiny, and a high contempt for the chair.

Careless. Here, now for't! I'll see justice done to the last drop of my bottle.

Sir Oliver. Nay, pray, gentlemen—I did not expect this usage.

Charles Surface. No, hang it, you shan't; Mr. Premium's a stranger.

Sir Oliver (*aside*). Odd! I wish I was well out of their company.

Odd, " God."

Careless. Plague on 'em, then! if they won't drink, we'll not sit down with them. Come, Harry, the dice are in the next room.—Charles, you'll join us when you have finished your business with the gentlemen?

Charles Surface. I will! I will!—(*Exeunt Sir Harry Bumper and Gentlemen; Careless following.*) Careless.

Careless (*returning*). Well!

Charles Surface. Perhaps I may want you.

Careless. Oh, you know I am always ready: word, note, or bond, 'tis all the same to me. (*Exit.*)

Moses. Sir, this is Mr. Premium, a gentleman of the strictest honour and secrecy; and always performs what he undertakes. Mr. Premium, this is——

Charles Surface. Pshaw! have done. Sir, my friend Moses is a very honest fellow, but a little slow at expression: he'll be an hour giving us our titles. Mr. Premium, the plain state of the matter is this: I am an extravagant young fellow who wants to borrow money; you I take to be a prudent old fellow, who has got money to lend. I am blockhead enough to give fifty per cent. sooner than not have it! and you, I presume, are rogue enough to take a hundred if you can get it. Now, sir, you see we are acquainted at once, and may proceed to business without further ceremony.

Sir Oliver. Exceeding frank, upon my word. I see, sir, you are not a man of many compliments.

Charles Surface. Oh no, sir! plain dealing in business I always think best.

Sir Oliver. Sir, I like you the better for it. However, you are mistaken in one thing; I have no money to lend, but I believe I could procure some of a friend; but then he's an unconscionable dog. Isn't he, Moses? And must sell stock to accommodate you. Mustn't he, Moses?

Moses. Yes, indeed! You know I always speak the truth, and scorn to tell a lie!

Charles Surface. Right. People that speak truth

generally do. But these are trifles, Mr. Premium. What! I know money isn't to be bought without paying for't!

Sir Oliver. Well, but what security could you give? You have no land, I suppose?

Charles Surface. Not a mole-hill, nor a twig, but what's in the bough-pots out of the window!

Sir Oliver. Nor any stock, I presume?

Charles Surface. Nothing but live stock—and that's only a few pointers and ponies. But pray, Mr. Premium, are you acquainted at all with any of my connections?

Sir Oliver. Why, to say the truth, I am.

Charles Surface. Then you must know that I have a devilish rich uncle in the East Indies, Sir Oliver Surface, from whom I have the greatest expectations?

Sir Oliver. That you have a wealthy uncle, I have heard; but how your expectations will turn out is more, I believe, than you can tell.

Charles Surface. Oh, no!—there can be no doubt. They tell me I'm a prodigious favourite, and that he talks of leaving me everything.

Sir Oliver. Indeed! this is the first I've heard of it.

Charles Surface. Yes, yes, 'tis just so. Moses knows 'tis true; don't you, Moses?

Moses. Oh, yes! I'll swear to't.

Sir Oliver (*aside*). Egad, they'll persuade me presently I'm at Bengal.

Charles Surface. Now I propose, Mr. Premium, if it's agreeable to you, a post-obit on Sir Oliver's life: though at the same time the old fellow has been so liberal to me, that I give you my word, I should be very sorry to hear that anything had happened to him.

Sir Oliver. Not more than I should, I assure you. But the bond you mention happens to be just the

---

Bough-pots, Flower-pots, window-boxes.

worst security you could offer me—for I might live to a hundred and never see the principal.

Charles Surface. Oh, yes, you would! the moment Sir Oliver dies, you know, you would come on me for the money.

Sir Oliver. Then I believe I should be the most unwelcome dun you ever had in your life.

Charles Surface. What! I suppose you're afraid that Sir Oliver is too good a life?

Sir Oliver. No, indeed I am not; though I have heard he is as hale and healthy as any man of his years in Christendom.

Charles Surface. There again, now, you are misinformed. No, no, the climate has hurt him considerably, poor uncle Oliver. Yes, yes, he breaks apace, I'm told—and is so much altered lately that his nearest relations would not know him.

Sir Oliver. No! Ha! ha! ha! so much altered lately that his nearest relations would not know him! Ha! ha! ha! egad—ha! ha! ha!

Charles Surface. Ha! ha!—you're glad to hear that, little Premium?

Sir Oliver. No, no, I'm not.

Charles Surface. Yes, yes, you are—ha! ha! ha! —you know that mends your chance.

Sir Oliver. But I'm told Sir Oliver is coming over; nay, some say he has actually arrived.

Charles Surface. Pshaw! sure I must know better than you whether he's come or not. No, no, rely on't he's at this moment at Calcutta. Isn't he, Moses?

Moses. Oh, yes, certainly.

Sir Oliver. Very true, as you say, you must know better than I, though I have it from pretty good authority. Haven't I, Moses?

Moses. Yes, most undoubted!

Sir Oliver. But, sir, as I understand you want a few hundreds immediately, is there nothing you could dispose of?

Charles Surface. How do you mean ?

Sir Oliver. For instance, now, I have heard that your father left behind him a great quantity of massy old plate.

Charles Surface. O Lud ! that's gone long ago. Moses can tell you how better than I can.

Sir Oliver (*aside*). Good lack ! all the family race-cups and corporation-bowls !—(*Aloud.*) Then it was also supposed that his library was one of the most valuable and compact.

Charles Surface. Yes, yes, so it was—vastly too much so for a private gentleman. For my part, I was always of a communicative disposition, so I thought it a shame to keep so much knowledge to myself.

Sir Oliver (*aside*). Mercy upon me ! learning that had run in the family like an heirloom !—(*Aloud.*) Pray, what are become of the books ?

Charles Surface. You must inquire of the auctioneer, Master Premium, for I don't believe even Moses can direct you.

Moses. I know nothing of books.

Sir Oliver. So, so, nothing of the family property left, I suppose ?

Charles Surface. Not much, indeed ; unless you have a mind to the family pictures. I have got a room full of ancestors above : and if you have a taste for old paintings, egad, you shall have 'em a bargain !

Sir Oliver. Hey ! what the devil ! sure, you wouldn't sell your forefathers, would you ?

Charles Surface. Every man of them, to the best bidder.

Sir Oliver. What ! your great-uncles and aunts ?

Charles Surface. Ay, and my great-grandfathers and grandmothers too.

Sir Oliver (*aside*). Now I give him up !—(*Aloud.*) What the plague, have you no bowels for your own

Corporation-bowls, Gold and silver bowls presented to the family by city corporations.

kindred? Odd's life! do you take me for Shylock in the play, that you would raise money of me on your own flesh and blood?

Charles Surface. Nay, my little broker, don't be angry : what need you care, if you have your money's worth?

Sir Oliver. Well, I'll be the purchaser : I think I can dispose of the family canvas.—(*Aside.*) Oh, I'll never forgive him this! never!

(Re-enter Careless.)

Careless. Come, Charles, what keeps you?

Charles Surface. I can't come yet. I'faith, we are going to have a sale above stairs; here's little Premium will buy all my ancestors!

Careless. Oh, burn your ancestors!

Charles Surface. No, he may do that afterwards, if he pleases. Stay, Careless, we want you : egad, you shall be auctioneer—so come along with us.

Careless. Oh, have with you, if that's the case. I can handle a hammer as well as a dice-box! Going! going!

Sir Oliver (*aside*). Oh, the profligates!

Charles Surface. Come, Moses, you shall be appraiser, if we want one. Gad's life, little Premium, you don't seem to like the business?

Sir Oliver. Oh, yes, I do, vastly! Ha! ha! ha! yes, yes, I think it a rare joke to sell one's family by auction—ha! ha!—(*Aside.*) Oh, the prodigal!

Charles Surface. To be sure! when a man wants money, where the plague should he get assistance, if he can't make free with his own relations! (*Exeunt.*)

Sir Oliver. I'll never forgive him ; never! never!

ACT IV

SCENE I. *A Picture Room in Charles Surface's House.*

(*Enter Charles Surface, Sir Oliver Surface, Moses, and Careless.*)

Charles Surface. Walk in, gentlemen, pray walk in ;—here they are, the family of the Surfaces, up to the Conquest.

Sir Oliver. And, in my opinion, a goodly collection.

Charles Surface. Ay, ay, these are done in the true spirit of portrait-painting ; no *volontier grace* or expression. Not like the works of your modern Raphaels who give you the strongest resemblance, yet contrive to make your portrait independent of you ; so that you may sink the original and not hurt the picture. No, no ; the merit of these is the inveterate likeness —all stiff and awkward as the originals, and like nothing in human nature besides.

Sir Oliver. Ah ! we shall never see such figures of men again.

Charles Surface. I hope not. Well, you see, Master Premium, what a domestic character I am ; here I sit of an evening surrounded by my family. But come, get to your pulpit, Mr. Auctioneer ; here's an old gouty chair of my grandfather's will answer the purpose.

Careless. Ay, ay, this will do. But, Charles, I haven't a hammer ; and what's an auctioneer without his hammer ?

Volontier grace, Charm added by the painter.
Raphaels, Painters who, like Raphael (1483–1520), idealized their sitters, in contrast with the realistic Dutch school.

Charles Surface. Egad, that's true. What parchment have we here? Oh, our genealogy in full. (*Taking pedigree down.*) Here, Careless, you shall have no common bit of mahogany, here's the family tree for you, you rogue! This shall be your hammer, and now you may knock down my ancestors with their own pedigree.

Sir Oliver (aside). What an unnatural rogue!—an *ex post facto* parricide!

Careless. Yes, yes, here's a list of your generation indeed ;—faith, Charles, this is the most convenient thing you could have found for the business, for it will not only serve as a hammer, but a catalogue into the bargain. Come, begin—A-going, a-going, a-going!

Charles Surface. Bravo, Careless! Well, here's my great-uncle, Sir Richard Ravelin, a marvellous good general in his day, I assure you. He served in all the Duke of Marlborough's wars, and got that cut over his eye at the battle of Malplaquet. What say you, Mr. Premium? look at him—there's a hero! not cut out of his feathers, as your modern clipped captains are, but enveloped in wig and regimentals, as a general should be. What do you bid?

Sir Oliver (aside to Moses). Bid him speak.

Moses. Mr. Premium would have you speak.

Charles Surface. Why, then, he shall have him for ten pounds, and I'm sure that's not dear for a staff-officer.

Sir Oliver (aside). Heaven deliver me! His famous uncle Richard for ten pounds!—(*Aloud.*) Very well, sir, I take him at that.

Charles Surface. Careless, knock down my uncle Richard.—Here, now, is a maiden sister of his, my

Ex post facto parricide, One who, as looked at after his father's death, has been the virtual cause of it (*i.e.* Charles was going to " knock down " his father, who was already dead).

Ravelin, A fortified outwork.

Malplaquet, 1709, A village in N. France.

Not cut out of his feathers, Not deprived of his ornamental dress.

great-aunt Deborah, done by Kneller, in his best manner, and esteemed a very formidable likeness. There she is, you see, a shepherdess feeding her flock. You shall have her for five pounds ten—the sheep are worth the money.

Sir Oliver (*aside*). Ah! poor Deborah! a woman who set such a value on herself!—(*Aloud.*) Five pounds ten—she's mine.

Charles Surface. Knock down my aunt Deborah! Here, now, are two that were a sort of cousins of theirs.—You see, Moses, these pictures were done some time ago, when beaux wore wigs, and the ladies their own hair.

Sir Oliver. Yes, truly, head-dresses appear to have been a little lower in those days.

Charles Surface. Well, take that couple for the same.

Moses. 'Tis a good bargain.

Charles Surface. Careless!—This, now, is a grandfather of my mother's, a learned judge, well known on the western circuit.—What do you rate him at, Moses?

Moses. Four guineas.

Charles Surface. Four guineas! Gad's life, you don't bid me the price of his wig.—Mr. Premium, you have more respect for the woolsack; do let us knock his lordship down at fifteen.

Sir Oliver. By all means.

Careless. Gone!

Charles Surface. And there are two brothers of his, William and Walter Blunt, Esquires, both Members of Parliament, and noted speakers; and, what's

---

Kneller, 1646–1723, German-English portrait-painter. Court-painter to Charles II. and three following sovereigns.

Beaux, Men of fashion. Wigs were at their most elaborate (for men) under Queen Anne (1702–14). At this time (1777) they were almost out of fashion for men; but women were wearing them, because of the high style of hair-dress, whereas in Anne's reign a low style had allowed women to wear their own hair.

very extraordinary, I believe, this is the first time they were ever bought or sold.

Sir Oliver. That is very extraordinary, indeed! I'll take them at your own price, for the honour of Parliament.

Careless. Well said, little Premium! I'll knock them down at forty.

Charles Surface. Here's a jolly fellow—I don't know what relation, but he was mayor of Norwich: take him at eight pounds.

Sir Oliver. No, no; six will do for the mayor.

Charles Surface. Come, make it guineas, and I'll throw you the two aldermen there into the bargain.

Sir Oliver. They're mine.

Charles Surface. Careless, knock down the mayor and aldermen. But, plague on't! we shall be all day retailing in this manner; do let us deal whole-sale: what say you, little Premium? Give me three hundred pounds for the rest of the family in the lump.

Careless. Ay, ay, that will be the best way.

Sir Oliver. Well, well, anything to accommodate you; they are mine. But there is one portrait which you have always passed over.

Careless. What, that ill-looking little fellow over the settee?

Sir Oliver. Yes, sir, I mean that: though I don't think him so ill-looking a little fellow, by any means.

Charles Surface. What, that? Oh, that's my uncle Oliver! 'Twas done before he went to India.

Careless. Your uncle Oliver! Gad, then you'll never be friends, Charles. That, now, to me, is as stern a looking rogue as ever I saw; an unforgiving eye, and a damned disinheriting countenance! an in-veterate knave, depend on't. Don't you think so, little Premium?

Sir Oliver. Upon my soul, sir, I do not; I think it is as honest a looking face as any in the room, dead or alive. But I suppose uncle Oliver goes with the rest of the lumber ?

Charles Surface. No, hang it ! I'll not part with poor Noll. The old fellow has been very good to me, and, egad, I'll keep his picture while I've a room to put it in.

Sir Oliver (*aside*). The rogue's my nephew after all !—(*Aloud.*) But, sir, I have somehow taken a fancy to that picture.

Charles Surface. I'm sorry for't, for you certainly will not have it. Oons, haven't you got enough of them ?

Sir Oliver (*aside*). I forgive him everything !—(*Aloud.*) But, sir, when I take a whim in my head, I don't value money. I'll give you as much for that as for all the rest.

Charles Surface. Don't tease me, master broker ; I tell you I'll not part with it, and there's an end of it.

Sir Oliver (*aside*). How like his father the dog is. —(*Aloud.*) Well, well, I have done.—(*Aside.*) I did not perceive it before, but I think I never saw such a striking resemblance.—(*Aloud.*) Here is a draft for your sum.

Charles Surface. Why, 'tis for eight hundred pounds !

Sir Oliver. You will not let Sir Oliver go ?

Charles Surface. Zounds ! no ! I tell you, once more.

Sir Oliver. Then never mind the difference, we'll balance that another time. But give me your hand on the bargain ; you are an honest fellow, Charles— I beg pardon, sir, for being so free.—Come, Moses.

Charles Surface. Egad, this is a whimsical old fellow !—But, hark'ee, Premium, you'll prepare lodgings for these gentlemen.

Sir Oliver. Yes, yes, I'll send for them in a day or two.

Charles Surface. But hold ; do now send a genteel

conveyance for them, for, I assure you, they were most of them used to ride in their own carriages.

Sir Oliver. I will, I will—for all but Oliver.

Charles Surface. Ay, all but the little nabob.

Sir Oliver. You're fixed on that?

Charles Surface. Peremptorily.

Sir Oliver (aside). A dear extravagant rogue!—(*Aloud.*) Good day! Come, Moses.—(*Aside.*) Let me hear now who dares call him profligate!

(*Exit with Moses.*)

Careless. Why, this is the oddest genius of the sort I ever met with!

Charles Surface. Egad, he's the prince of brokers, I think. I wonder how the devil Moses got acquainted with so honest a fellow?—Ha! here's Rowley.—Do, Careless, say I'll join the company in a few moments.

Careless. I will—but don't let that old blockhead persuade you to squander any of that money on old musty debts, or any such nonsense; for tradesmen, Charles, are the most exorbitant fellows.

Charles Surface. Very true, and paying them is only encouraging them.

Careless. Nothing else.

Charles Surface. Ay, ay, never fear.—(*Exit Careless.*) So! this was an odd old fellow, indeed. Let me see, two-thirds of these five hundred and thirty odd pounds are mine by right. 'Fore Heaven! I find one's ancestors are more valuable relations than I took them for!—Ladies and gentlemen, your most obedient and very grateful servant.

(*Bows ceremoniously to the pictures.*)
(*Enter Rowley.*)

Ha! old Rowley! egad, you are just come in time to take leave of your old acquaintance.

Rowley. Yes, I heard they were a-going. But I wonder you can have such spirits under so many distresses.

Genius, Character, " customer."

Charles Surface. Why, there's the point! my distresses are so many, that I can't afford to part with my spirits; but I shall be rich and splenetic, all in good time. However, I suppose you are surprised that I am not more sorrowful at parting with so many near relations; to be sure, 'tis very affecting; but you see they never move a muscle, so why should I?

Rowley. There's no making you serious a moment.

Charles Surface. Yes, faith, I am so now. Here, my honest Rowley, here, get me this changed directly, and take a hundred pounds of it immediately to old Stanley.

Rowley. A hundred pounds! Consider only——

Charles Surface. God's life, don't talk about it! poor Stanley's wants are pressing, and, if you don't make haste, we shall have some one call that has a better right to the money.

Rowley. Ah! there's the point! I never will cease dunning you with the old proverb——

Charles Surface. *Be just before you're generous.*— Why, so I would if I could; but Justice is an old hobbling beldame, and I can't get her to keep pace with Generosity, for the soul of me.

Rowley. Yet, Charles, believe me, one hour's reflection——

Charles Surface. Ay, ay, it's very true; but, hark'ee, Rowley, while I have, by Heaven, I'll give; so, damn your economy! and now for hazard.   (*Exeunt.*)

SCENE II.   *Another room in the same.*

(*Enter Sir Oliver Surface and Moses.*)

Moses. Well, sir, I think, as Sir Peter said, you have seen Mr. Charles in high glory; 'tis great pity he's so extravagant.

Sir Oliver. True, but he would not sell my picture.

Moses. And loves wine and women so much.

Sir Oliver. But he would not sell my picture.

Moses. And games so deep.

Sir Oliver. But he would not sell my picture. Oh, here's Rowley.

(Enter Rowley.)

Rowley. So, Sir Oliver, I find you have made a purchase——

Sir Oliver. Yes, yes, our young rake has parted with his ancestors like old tapestry.

Rowley. And here has he commissioned me to redeliver you part of the purchase-money—I mean, though, in your necessitous character of old Stanley.

Moses. Ah! there is the pity of all: he is so damned charitable.

Rowley. And I left a hosier and two tailors in the hall, who, I'm sure, won't be paid, and this hundred would satisfy them.

Sir Oliver. Well, well, I'll pay his debts, and his benevolence too. But now I am no more a broker, and you shall introduce me to the elder brother as old Stanley.

Rowley. Not yet awhile ; Sir Peter, I know, means to call there about this time.

(Enter Trip.)

Trip. Oh, gentlemen, I beg pardon for not showing you out ; this way—Moses, a word.

(Exit with Moses.)

Sir Oliver. There's a fellow for you ! Would you believe it, that puppy intercepted the Jew on our coming, and wanted to raise money before he got to his master !

Rowley. Indeed.

Sir Oliver. Yes, they are now planning an annuity business. Ah, Master Rowley, in my days servants were content with the follies of their masters, when they were worn a little threadbare ; but now they have their vices, like their birthday clothes, with the gloss on. *(Exeunt.)*

SCENE III.　*A Library in Joseph Surface's House.*

(*Enter Joseph Surface and Servant.*)
Joseph Surface. No letter from Lady Teazle?
Servant. No, sir.
Joseph Surface (*aside*). I am surprised she has not sent, if she is prevented from coming. Sir Peter certainly does not suspect me. Yet I wish I may not lose the heiress, through the scrape I have drawn myself into with the wife; however, Charles's imprudence and bad character are great points in my favour.　　　　　　　　　(*Knocking without.*)
Servant. Sir, I believe that must be Lady Teazle.
Joseph Surface. Hold! See whether it is or not, before you go to the door: I have a particular message for you if it should be my brother.
Servant. 'Tis her ladyship, sir; she always leaves the chair at the milliner's in the next street.
Joseph Surface. Stay: draw that screen before the window—that will do;—my opposite neighbour is a maiden lady of so curious a temper. —(*Servant draws the screen, and exit.*) I have a difficult hand to play in this affair. Lady Teazle has lately suspected my views on Maria; but she must by no means be let into that secret,—at least, till I have her more in my power.
(*Enter Lady Teazle.*)
Lady Teazle. What, sentiment in soliloquy now? Have you been very impatient? O Lud! don't pretend to look grave. I vow I couldn't come before.
Joseph Surface. O madam, punctuality is a species of constancy very unfashionable in a lady of quality.
(*Places chairs, and sits after Lady Teazle is seated.*)
Lady Teazle. Upon my word, you ought to pity

Milliner's, Shop selling ribbons and dresses. (Fr. Milan, where ribbons and trimmings came from.)

me. Do you know Sir Peter is grown so ill-natured to me of late, and so jealous of Charles too—that's the best of the story, isn't it ?

Joseph Surface (*aside*). I am glad my scandalous friends keep that up.

Lady Teazle. I am sure I wish he would let Maria marry him, and then perhaps he would be convinced ; don't you, Mr. Surface ?

Joseph Surface (*aside*). Indeed I do not.—(*Aloud.*) Oh, certainly I do ! for then my dear Lady Teazle would also be convinced how wrong her suspicions were of my having any design on the silly girl.

Lady Teazle. Well, well, I'm inclined to believe you. But isn't it provoking, to have the most ill-natured things said of one ? And there's my friend Lady Sneerwell has circulated I don't know how many scandalous tales of me, and all without any foundation too ; that's what vexes me.

Joseph Surface. Ay, madam, to be sure, that is the provoking circumstance—without foundation ; yes, yes, there's the mortification, indeed ; for, when a scandalous story is believed against one, there certainly is no comfort like the consciousness of having deserved it.

Lady Teazle. No, to be sure, then I'd forgive their malice ; but to attack me, who am really so innocent and who never say an ill-natured thing of anybody —that is, of any friend ; and then Sir Peter, too, to have him so peevish, and so suspicious, when I know the integrity of my own heart—indeed 'tis monstrous !

Joseph Surface. But, my dear Lady Teazle, 'tis your own fault if you suffer it. When a husband entertains a groundless suspicion of his wife, and withdraws his confidence from her, the original compact is broken, and she owes it to the honour of her sex to endeavour to outwit him.

Lady Teazle. Indeed ! So that, if he suspects me

without cause, it follows, that the best way of curing his jealousy is to give him reason for't?

Joseph Surface. Undoubtedly—for your husband should never be deceived in you : and in that case it becomes you to be frail in compliment to his discernment.

Lady Teazle. To be sure, what you say is very reasonable, and when the consciousness of my innocence——

Joseph Surface. Ah, my dear madam, there is the great mistake ; 'tis this very conscious innocence that is of the greatest prejudice to you. What is it makes you negligent of forms, and careless of the world's opinion ? why, the consciousness of your own innocence. What makes you thoughtless in your conduct, and apt to run into a thousand little imprudences ? why, the consciousness of your own innocence. What makes you impatient of Sir Peter's temper, and outrageous at his suspicions ? why, the consciousness of your innocence.

Lady Teazle. 'Tis very true !

Joseph Surface. Now, my dear Lady Teazle, if you would but once make a trifling *faux pas*, you can't conceive how cautious you would grow, and how ready to humour and agree with your husband.

Lady Teazle. Do you think so ?

Joseph Surface. Oh, I'm sure on't ; and then you would find all scandal would cease at once, for—in short, your character at present is like a person in a plethora, absolutely dying from too much health.

Lady Teazle. So, so ; then I perceive your prescription is, that I must sin in my own defence, and part with my virtue to preserve my reputation ?

Joseph Surface. Exactly so, upon my credit, ma'am.

Lady Teazle. Well, certainly this is the oddest doctrine, and the newest receipt for avoiding calumny?

Plethora, Diseased condition supposed to be due to having too much blood (actually to excess of red corpuscles).

Joseph Surface. An infallible one, believe me. Prudence, like experience, must be paid for.

Lady Teazle. Why, if my understanding were once convinced——

Joseph Surface. Oh, certainly, madam, your understanding should be convinced. Yes, yes—Heaven forbid I should persuade you to do anything you thought wrong. No, no, I have too much honour to desire it.

Lady Teazle. Don't you think we may as well leave honour out of the argument ? (*Rises.*)

Joseph Surface. Ah, the ill effects of your country education, I see, still remain with you.

Lady Teazle. I doubt they do, indeed ; and I will fairly own to you, that if I could be persuaded to do wrong, it would be by Sir Peter's ill-usage sooner than your honourable logic, after all.

Joseph Surface (*taking her hand*). Then, by this hand, which he is unworthy of——

(*Re-enter Servant.*)

'Sdeath, you blockhead—what do you want ?

Servant. I beg your pardon, sir, but I thought you would not choose Sir Peter to come up without announcing him.

Joseph Surface. Sir Peter !—Oons—the devil !

Lady Teazle. Sir Peter ! O Lud ! I'm ruined ! I'm ruined !

Servant. Sir, 'twasn't I let him in.

Lady Teazle. Oh ! I'm quite undone ! What will become of me ? Now, Mr. Logic—Oh ! mercy, sir, he's on the stairs—I'll get behind here—and if ever I'm so imprudent again—— (*Goes behind the screen.*)

Joseph Surface. Give me that book.

(*Sits down. Servant pretends to adjust his chair.*)
(*Enter Sir Peter Teazle.*)

Sir Peter. Ay, ever improving himself. Mr. Surface. Mr. Surface—— (*Pats Joseph on the shoulder.*)

Joseph Surface. Oh, my dear Sir Peter, I beg your

pardon. (*Gaping, throws away the book.*) I have been dozing over a stupid book. Well, I am much obliged to you for this call. You haven't been here, I believe, since I fitted up this room. Books, you know, are the only things I am a coxcomb in.

Sir Peter. 'Tis very neat indeed. Well, well, that's proper : and you can make even your screen a source of knowledge—hung, I perceive, with maps.

Joseph Surface. Oh, yes, I find great use in that screen.

Sir Peter. I dare say you must, certainly, when you want to find anything in a hurry.

Joseph Surface (*aside*). Ay, or to hide anything in a hurry either.

Sir Peter. Well, I have a little private business——

Joseph Surface (*to Servant*). You need not stay.

Servant. No, sir.　　　　　　　　　　　　(*Exit.*)

Joseph Surface. Here's a chair, Sir Peter—I beg——

Sir Peter. Well, now we are alone, there is a subject, my dear friend, on which I wish to unburden my mind to you—a point of the greatest moment to my peace ; in short, my good friend, Lady Teazle's conduct of late has made me very unhappy.

Joseph Surface. Indeed ! I am very sorry to hear it.

Sir Peter. Yes, 'tis but too plain she has not the least regard for me ; but, what's worse, I have pretty good authority to suppose she has formed an attachment to another.

Joseph Surface. Indeed ! you astonish me !

Sir Peter. Yes ! and, between ourselves, I think I've discovered the person.

Joseph Surface. How ! you alarm me exceedingly.

Sir Peter. Ay, my dear friend, I knew you would sympathize with me !

Joseph Surface. Yes, believe me, Sir Peter, such a

A coxcomb in, Vain, fussy about.

discovery would hurt me just as much as it would you.

Sir Peter. I am convinced of it. Ah! it is a happiness to have a friend whom we can trust even with one's family secrets. But have you no guess who I mean?

Joseph Surface. I haven't the most distant idea. It can't be Sir Benjamin Backbite?

Sir Peter. Oh, no! What say you to Charles?

Joseph Surface. My brother! impossible!

Sir Peter. Oh, my dear friend, the goodness of your own heart misleads you. You judge of others by yourself.

Joseph Surface. Certainly, Sir Peter, the heart that is conscious of its own integrity is ever slow to credit another's treachery.

Sir Peter. True; but your brother has no sentiment—you never hear him talk so.

Joseph Surface. Yet I can't but think Lady Teazle herself has too much principle.

Sir Peter. Ay; but what is principle against the flattery of a handsome, lively young fellow?

Joseph Surface. That's very true.

Sir Peter. And then, you know, the difference of our ages makes it very improbable that she should have any great affection for me; and if she were to be frail, and I were to make it public, why the town would only laugh at me, the foolish old bachelor, who had married a girl.

Joseph Surface. That's true, to be sure—they would laugh.

Sir Peter. Laugh! ay, and make ballads, and paragraphs, and the devil knows what of me.

Joseph Surface. No, you must never make it public.

Sir Peter. But then again—that the nephew of my old friend, Sir Oliver, should be the person to attempt such a wrong, hurts me more nearly.

Joseph Surface. Ay, there's the point. When

ingratitude barbs the dart of injury, the wound has double danger in it.

Sir Peter. Ay—I, that was, in a manner, left his guardian : in whose house he had been so often entertained ; who never in my life denied him—my advice !

Joseph Surface. Oh, 'tis not to be credited ! There may be a man capable of such baseness, to be sure ; but, for my part, till you can give me positive proofs, I cannot but doubt it. However, if it should be proved on him, he is no longer a brother of mine—I disclaim kindred with him : for the man who can break the laws of hospitality, and tempt the wife of his friend, deserves to be branded as the pest of society.

Sir Peter. What a difference there is between you ! What noble sentiments !

Joseph Surface. Yet I cannot suspect Lady Teazle's honour.

Sir Peter. I am sure I wish to think well of her, and to remove all ground of quarrel between us. She has lately reproached me more than once with having made no settlement on her ; and, in our last quarrel, she almost hinted that she should not break her heart if I was dead. Now, as we seem to differ in our ideas of expense, I have resolved she shall have her own way, and be her own mistress in that respect for the future ; and, if I were to die, she will find I have not been inattentive to her interest while living. Here, my friend, are the drafts of two deeds, which I wish to have your opinion on. By one, she will enjoy eight hundred a year independent while I live ; and, by the other, the bulk of my fortune at my death.

Joseph Surface. This conduct, Sir Peter, is indeed truly generous.—(*Aside.*) I wish it may not corrupt my pupil.

Sir Peter. Yes, I am determined she shall have no cause to complain, though I would not have her acquainted with the latter instance of my affection yet awhile.

Joseph Surface (*aside*). Nor I, if I could help it.

Sir Peter. And now, my dear friend, if you please, we will talk over the situation of your hopes with Maria.

Joseph Surface (*softly*). Oh, no, Sir Peter, another time, if you please.

Sir Peter. I am sensibly chagrined at the little progress you seem to make in her affections.

Joseph Surface (*softly*). I beg you will not mention it. What are my disappointments when your happiness is in debate !—(*Aside.*) 'Sdeath, I shall be ruined every way !

Sir Peter. And though you are averse to my acquainting Lady Teazle with your passion, I'm sure she's not your enemy in the affair.

Joseph Surface. Pray, Sir Peter, now oblige me. I am really too much affected by the subject we have been speaking of to bestow a thought on my own concerns. The man who is entrusted with his friend's distresses can never——

(*Re-enter Servant.*)

Well, sir ?

Servant. Your brother, sir, is speaking to a gentleman in the street, and says he knows you are within.

Joseph Surface. 'Sdeath, blockhead, I'm not within —I'm out for the day.

Sir Peter. Stay—hold—a thought has struck me : —you shall be at home.

Joseph Surface. Well, well, let him up.—(*Exit Servant.*) (*Aside.*) He'll interrupt Sir Peter, however.

Sir Peter. Now, my good friend, oblige me, I entreat you. Before Charles comes, let me conceal myself somewhere ; then do you tax him on the point we have been talking, and his answer may satisfy me at once.

Joseph Surface. Oh, fie, Sir Peter ! would you have

me join in so mean a trick ?—to trepan my brother too ?

Sir Peter. Nay, you tell me you are sure he is innocent ; if so, you do him the greatest service by giving him an opportunity to clear himself, and you will set my heart at rest. Come, you shall not refuse me : (*Going up*) here, behind the screen will be— Hey ! what the devil ! there seems to be one listener here already—I'll swear I saw a petticoat !

Joseph Surface. Ha ! ha ! ha ! Well, this is ridiculous enough. I'll tell you, Sir Peter, though I hold a man of intrigue to be a most despicable character, yet you know, it does not follow that one is to be an absolute Joseph either ! Hark'ee, 'tis a little French milliner, a silly rogue that plagues me ; and having some character to lose, on your coming, sir, she ran behind the screen.

Sir Peter. Ah, a rogue—— But, egad, she has overheard all I have been saying of my wife.

Joseph Surface. Oh, 'twill never go any farther, you may depend upon it !

Sir Peter. No ! then, faith, let her hear it out.— Here's a closet will do as well.

Joseph Surface. Well, go in there.

Sir Peter. Sly rogue ! sly rogue !

　　　　　　　　　　　　　(*Goes into the closet.*)

Joseph Surface. A narrow escape, indeed ! and a curious situation I'm in, to part man and wife in this manner.

Lady Teazle (*peeping*). Couldn't I steal off ?

Joseph Surface. Keep close, my angel !

Sir Peter (*peeping*). Joseph, tax him home.

Joseph Surface. Back, my dear friend !

Lady Teazle (*peeping*). Couldn't you lock Sir Peter in ?

Joseph Surface. Be still, my life !

Trepan, Trap.

Sir Peter (*peeping*). You're sure the little milliner won't blab ?

Joseph Surface. In, in, my dear Sir Peter !—'Fore Gad, I wish I had a key to the door.

(*Enter Charles Surface.*)

Charles Surface. Holla ! brother, what has been the matter ? Your fellow would not let me up at first. What ! have you had a Jew or a wench with you ?

Joseph Surface. Neither, brother, I assure you.

Charles Surface. But what has made Sir Peter steal off ? I thought he had been with you.

Joseph Surface. He was, brother; but, hearing you were coming, he did not choose to stay.

Charles Surface. What ! was the old gentleman afraid I wanted to borrow money of him !

Joseph Surface. No, sir : but I am sorry to find, Charles, you have lately given that worthy man grounds for great uneasiness.

Charles Surface. Yes, they tell me I do that to a great many worthy men. But how so, pray ?

Joseph Surface. To be plain with you, brother, he thinks you are endeavouring to gain Lady Teazle's affections from him.

Charles Surface. Who, I ? O Lud ! not I, upon my word.—Ha ! ha ! ha ! ha ! so the old fellow has found out that he has got a young wife, has he ?—or, what is worse, Lady Teazle has found out she has an old husband ?

Joseph Surface. This is no subject to jest on, brother. He who can laugh——

Charles Surface. True, true, as you were going to say—then, seriously, I never had the least idea of what you charge me with, upon my honour.

Joseph Surface (*raising his voice*). Well, it will give Sir Peter great satisfaction to hear this.

Charles Surface. To be sure, I once thought the lady seemed to have taken a fancy to me ; but, upon

my soul, I never gave her the least encouragement.
Besides, you know my attachment to Maria.

Joseph Surface. But sure, brother, even if Lady
Teazle had betrayed the fondest partiality for you——

Charles Surface. Why, look'ee, Joseph, I hope I
shall never deliberately do a dishonourable action;
but if a pretty woman was purposely to throw herself
in my way—and that pretty woman married to a
man old enough to be her father——

Joseph Surface. Well!

Charles Surface. Why, I believe I should be obliged
to borrow a little of your morality, that's all. But,
brother, do you know now that you surprise me
exceedingly, by naming me with Lady Teazle; for
i'faith, I always understood you were her favourite.

Joseph Surface. Oh, for shame, Charles! This
retort is foolish!

Charles Surface. Nay, I swear I have seen you
exchange such significant glances——

Joseph Surface. Nay, nay, sir, this is no jest.

Charles Surface. Egad, I'm serious! Don't you
remember one day, when I called here——

Joseph Surface. Nay, prithee, Charles——

Charles Surface. And found you together——

Joseph Surface. Zounds, sir, I insist——

Charles Surface. And another time, when your
servant——

Joseph Surface. Brother, brother, a word with you!
—(*Aside.*) Gad, I must stop him.

Charles Surface. Informed, I say, that——

Joseph Surface. Hush! I beg your pardon, but Sir
Peter has overheard all we have been saying. I knew
you would clear yourself, or I should not have con-
sented.

Charles Surface. How, Sir Peter! Where is he?

Joseph Surface. Softly, there! (*Points to the closet.*)

Charles Surface. Oh, 'fore Heaven, I'll have him
out. Sir Peter, come forth!

Joseph Surface. No, no——

Charles Surface. I say, Sir Peter, come into court. —(*Pulls in Sir Peter.*) What! my old guardian! —What!—turn inquisitor, and take evidence incog.? Oh, fie! Oh, fie!

Sir Peter. Give me your hand, Charles—I believe I have suspected you wrongfully; but you mustn't be angry with Joseph—'twas my plan!

Charles Surface. Indeed!

Sir Peter. But I acquit you. I promise you I don't think near so ill of you as I did. What I have heard has given me great satisfaction.

Charles Surface. Egad, then, 'twas lucky you didn't hear any more. Wasn't it, Joseph?

Sir Peter. Ah! you would have retorted on him.

Charles Surface. Ah, ay, that was a joke.

Sir Peter. Yes, yes, I know his honour too well.

Charles Surface. But you might as well have suspected him as me in this matter, for all that. Mightn't he, Joseph?

Sir Peter. Well, well, I believe you.

Joseph Surface (*aside*). Would they were both out of the room!

Sir Peter. And in future, perhaps, we may not be such strangers.

(*Re-enter Servant, and whispers Joseph Surface.*)

Servant. Lady Sneerwell is below, and says she will come up.

Joseph Surface. Gentlemen, I beg pardon—I must wait on you downstairs; here's a person come on particular business.

Charles Surface. Well, you can see him in another room. Sir Peter and I have not met a long time, and I have something to say to him.

Joseph Surface (*aside*). They must not be left together.—(*Aloud.*) I'll send Lady Sneerwell away,

Inquisitor, Detective.

and return directly.—(*Aside to Sir Peter.*) Sir Peter, not a word of the French milliner.

Sir Peter (*aside to Joseph Surface*). I! not for the world!—(*Exit Joseph Surface.*) Ah, Charles, if you associated more with your brother, one might indeed hope for your reformation. He is a man of sentiment. Well, there is nothing in the world as noble as a man of sentiment.

Charles Surface. Pshaw! he is too moral by half; and so apprehensive of his good name, as he calls it, that I suppose he would as soon let a priest into his house as a wench.

Sir Peter. No, no,—come, come,—you wrong him. No, no, Joseph is no rake, but he is no such saint either, in that respect.—(*Aside.*) I have a great mind to tell him—we should have such a laugh at Joseph.

Charles Surface. Oh, hang him! he's a very anchorite, a young hermit!

Sir Peter. Hark'ee—you must not abuse him: he may chance to hear of it again, I promise you.

Charles Surface. Why, you won't tell him?

Sir Peter. No—but—this way.—(*Aside.*) Egad, I'll tell him.—(*Aloud.*) Hark'ee, have you a mind to have a good laugh at Joseph?

Charles Surface. I should like it of all things.

Sir Peter. Then, i'faith, we will! I'll be quit with him for discovering me.—(*Whispers.*) He had a girl with him when I called.

Charles Surface. What! Joseph? You jest.

Sir Peter. Hush!—a little French milliner—and the best of the jest is—she's in the room now.

Charles Surface. The devil she is!

Sir Peter. Hush! I tell you. (*Points to the screen.*)

Charles Surface. Behind the screen? Odds life, let's unveil her!

Sir Peter. No, no, he's coming:—you shan't, indeed!

Discovering me, Revealing my hiding-place.

Charles Surface. Oh, egad, we'll have a peep at the little milliner !

Sir Peter. Not for the world !—Joseph will never forgive me.

Charles Surface. I'll stand by you——

Sir Peter. Odds, here he is !

(*Charles Surface throws down the screen.*)

(*Re-enter Joseph Surface.*)

Charles Surface. Lady Teazle, by all that's wonderful !

Sir Peter. Lady Teazle, by all that's damnable !

Charles Surface. Sir Peter, this is one of the smartest French milliners I ever saw. Egad, you seem all to have been diverting yourselves here at hide and seek, and I don't see who is out of the secret. Shall I beg your ladyship to inform me ? Not a word !—Brother, will you be pleased to explain this matter ? What ! is Morality dumb too ?—Sir Peter, though I found you in the dark, perhaps you are not so now ! All mute ! Well—though I can make nothing of the affair, I suppose you perfectly understand one another; so I'll leave you to yourselves.—(*Going.*) Brother, I'm sorry to find you have given that worthy man grounds for so much uneasiness.—Sir Peter ! there's nothing in the world so noble as a man of sentiment !

(*Exit.*)

Joseph Surface. Sir Peter—notwithstanding—I confess—that appearances are against me—if you will afford me your patience—I make no doubt—but I shall explain everything to your satisfaction.

Sir Peter. If you please, sir.

Joseph Surface. The fact is, sir, that Lady Teazle, knowing my pretensions to your ward Maria—I say, sir, Lady Teazle, being apprehensive of the jealousy of your temper—and knowing my friendship to the family—she, sir, I say—called here—in order that—I might explain these pretensions—but on your coming—being apprehensive—as I said—of **your** jealousy—she withdrew—and this, you may depend on it, is the whole truth of the matter.

Sir Peter. A very clear account, upon my word; and I dare swear the lady will vouch for every article of it.

Lady Teazle. For not one word of it, Sir Peter!

Sir Peter. How! don't you think it worth while to agree in the lie?

Lady Teazle. There is not one syllable of truth in what that gentleman has told you.

Sir Peter. I believe you, upon my soul, ma'am!

Joseph Surface (aside to Lady Teazle). 'Sdeath, madam, you will betray me?

Lady Teazle. Good Mr. Hypocrite, by your leave, I'll speak for myself.

Sir Peter. Ay, let her alone, sir; you'll find she'll make out a better story than you, without prompting.

Lady Teazle. Hear me, Sir Peter!—I came here on no matter relating to your ward, and even ignorant of this gentleman's pretensions to her. But I came, seduced by his insidious arguments, at least to listen to his pretended passion, if not to sacrifice your honour to his baseness.

Sir Peter. Now, I believe, the truth is coming, indeed!

Joseph Surface. The woman's mad!

Lady Teazle. No, sir, she has recovered her senses, and your own arts have furnished her with the means. —Sir Peter, I do not expect you to credit me—but the tenderness you expressed for me, when I am sure you could not think I was a witness to it, has penetrated so to my heart, that had I left the place without the shame of this discovery, my future life should have spoken the sincerity of my gratitude. As for that smooth-tongued hypocrite, who would have seduced the wife of his too credulous friend, while he affected honourable addresses to his ward—I behold him now in a light so truly despicable, that I shall never again respect myself for having listened to him.   (*Exit.*)

Joseph Surface. Notwithstanding all this, Sir Peter, Heaven knows——

Sir Peter. That you are a villain! and so I leave you to your conscience.

Joseph Surface. You are too rash, Sir Peter; you shall hear me. The man who shuts out conviction by refusing to——

Sir Peter. Oh, damn your sentiments!

(*Exeunt Sir Peter and Joseph Surface, talking.*)

ACT V

SCENE I. *The Library in Joseph Surface's House.*

(*Enter Joseph Surface and Servant.*)

Joseph Surface. Mr. Stanley! and why should you think I would see him? you must know he comes to ask something.

Servant. Sir, I should not have let him in, but that Mr. Rowley came to the door with him.

Joseph Surface. Pshaw! blockhead! to suppose that I should now be in a temper to receive visits from poor relations!—Well, why don't you show the fellow up?

Servant. I will, sir.—Why, sir, it was not my fault that Sir Peter discovered my lady——

Joseph Surface. Go, fool!—(*Exit Servant.*) Sure Fortune never played a man of my policy such a trick before! My character with Sir Peter, my hopes with Maria, destroyed in a moment! I'm in a rare humour to listen to other people's distresses! I shan't be able to bestow even a benevolent sentiment on Stanley. —So! here he comes, and Rowley with him. I must try to recover myself, and put a little charity into my face, however.   (*Exit.*)

(*Enter Sir Oliver Surface and Rowley.*)

Sir Oliver. What! does he avoid us? That was he, was it not?

Rowley. It was, sir. But I doubt you are come a little too abruptly. His nerves are so weak, that the sight of a poor relation may be too much for him. I should have gone first to break it to him.

Sir Oliver. Oh, plague of his nerves! Yet this is

he whom Sir Peter extols as a man of the most
benevolent way of thinking !

Rowley. As to his way of thinking, I cannot pretend to decide ; for, to do him justice, he appears to
have as much speculative benevolence as any private
gentleman in the kingdom, though he is seldom so
sensual as to indulge himself in the exercise of it.

Sir Oliver. Yet he has a string of charitable sentiments at his fingers' ends.

Rowley. Or, rather, at his tongue's end, Sir Oliver ;
for I believe there is no sentiment he has such faith
in as that *Charity begins at home.*

Sir Oliver. And his, I presume, is of that domestic
sort which never stirs abroad at all.

Rowley. I doubt you'll find it so ;—but he's coming.
I mustn't seem to interrupt you ; and you know,
immediately as you leave him, I come in to announce
your arrival in your real character.

Sir Oliver. True ; and afterwards you'll meet me
at Sir Peter's.

Rowley. Without losing a moment.   (*Exit.*)

Sir Oliver. I don't like the complaisance of his
features.

(*Re-enter Joseph Surface.*)

Joseph Surface. Sir, I beg you ten thousand pardons
for keeping you a moment waiting.—Mr. Stanley, I
presume.

Sir Oliver. At your service.

Joseph Surface. Sir, I beg you will do me the
honour to sit down—I entreat you, sir.

Sir Oliver. Dear sir—there's no occasion.—(*Aside.*)
Too civil by half !

Joseph Surface. I have not the pleasure of knowing
you, Mr. Stanley ; but I am extremely happy to see
you look so well. You were nearly related to my
mother, I think, Mr. Stanley ?

Sir Oliver. I was, sir ; so nearly that my present

Sensual, Practical, matter-of-fact.

poverty, I fear, may do discredit to her wealthy children, else I should not have presumed to trouble you.

Joseph Surface. Dear sir, there needs no apology : he that is in distress, though a stranger, has a right to claim kindred with the wealthy. I am sure I wish I was one of that class, and had it in my power to offer you even a small relief.

Sir Oliver. If your uncle, Sir Oliver, were here, I should have a friend.

Joseph Surface. I wish he was, sir, with all my heart : you should not want an advocate with him, believe me, sir.

Sir Oliver. I should not need one—my distresses would recommend me. But I imagined his bounty would enable you to become the agent of his charity.

Joseph Surface. My dear sir, you were strangely misinformed. Sir Oliver is a worthy man, a very worthy man ; but avarice, Mr. Stanley, is the vice of age. I will tell you, my good sir, in confidence, what he has done for me has been a mere nothing ; though people, I know, have thought otherwise, and, for my part, I never chose to contradict the report.

Sir Oliver. What ! has he never transmitted you bullion—rupees—pagodas ?

Joseph Surface. Oh, dear sir, nothing of the kind ! No, no ; a few presents now and then—china, shawls, congou tea, avadavats, and Indian crackers—little more, believe me.

Sir Oliver (*aside*). Here's gratitude for twelve thousand pounds !—Avadavats and Indian crackers !

Joseph Surface. Then, my dear sir, you have heard, I doubt not, of the extravagance of my brother; there are very few would credit what I have done for that unfortunate young man.

Bullion, Gold or silver in the mass.
Rupees, Indian silver coins (worth about 2s.).
Pagodas, Indian gold or silver coins (of higher value than the rupee).
Congou tea, Black China tea.
Avadavats, Small Indian song-birds ; strawberry finches.

Sir Oliver (*aside*). Not I, for one !

Joseph Surface. The sums I have lent him ! Indeed I have been exceedingly to blame ; it was an amiable weakness ; however, I don't pretend to defend it—and now I feel it doubly culpable, since it has deprived me of the pleasure of serving you, Mr. Stanley, as my heart dictates.

Sir Oliver (*aside*). Dissembler !—(*Aloud.*) Then, sir, you can't assist me ?

Joseph Surface. At present, it grieves me to say, I cannot ; but, whenever I have the ability, you may depend upon hearing from me.

Sir Oliver. I am extremely sorry——

Joseph Surface. Not more than I, believe me ; to pity, without the power to relieve, is still more painful than to ask and be denied.

Sir Oliver. Kind sir, your most obedient humble servant.

Joseph Surface. You leave me deeply affected, Mr. Stanley.—William, be ready to open the door.

(Calls to Servant.)

Sir Oliver. Oh, dear sir, no ceremony.

Joseph Surface. Your very obedient.

Sir Oliver. Your most obsequious.

Joseph Surface. You may depend upon hearing from me, whenever I can be of service.

Sir Oliver. Sweet sir, you are too good.

Joseph Surface. In the meantime I wish you health and spirits.

Sir Oliver. Your ever grateful and perpetual humble servant.

Joseph Surface. Sir, yours as sincerely.

Sir Oliver. Charles !—you are my heir. (*Exit.*)

Joseph Surface. This is one bad effect of a good character ; it invites application from the unfortunate, and there needs no small degree of address to gain the reputation of benevolence without incurring the expense. The silver ore of pure charity is an expensive article in the catalogue of a man's good qualities ; whereas the sentimental French plate I use instead of it makes just as good a show, and pays no tax.

(*Re-enter Rowley.*)

Rowley. Mr. Surface, your servant : I was apprehensive of interrupting you, though my business demands immediate attention, as this note will inform you.

Joseph Surface. Always happy to see Mr. Rowley. —(*Aside. Reads the letter.*) Sir Oliver Surface !— My uncle arrived !

Rowley. He is, indeed : we have just parted— quite well, after a speedy voyage, and impatient to embrace his worthy nephew.

Joseph Surface. I am astonished !—William ! stop Mr. Stanley, if he's not gone. (*Calls to Servant.*)

Rowley. Oh ! he's out of reach, I believe.

Joseph Surface. Why did you not let me know this when you came in together ?

Rowley. I thought you had particular business. But I must be gone to inform your brother, and appoint him here to meet your uncle. He will be with you in a quarter of an hour.

Joseph Surface. So he says. Well, I am strangely overjoyed at his coming.—(*Aside.*) Never, to be sure, was anything so damned unlucky !

Rowley. You will be delighted to see how well he looks.

Joseph Surface. Oh ! I'm overjoyed to hear it.— (*Aside.*)—Just at this time !

Rowley. I'll tell him how impatiently you expect him.

Joseph Surface. Do, do ; pray give my best duty and affection. Indeed, I cannot express the sensations I feel at the thought of seeing him.—(*Exit Rowley.*) Certainly his coming just at this time is the cruellest piece of ill fortune. (*Exit.*)

SCENE II. *A Room in Sir Peter Teazle's House.*

(Enter Mrs. Candour and Maid.)

Maid. Indeed, ma'am, my lady will see nobody at present.

Mrs. Candour. Did you tell her it was her friend Mrs. Candour ?

Maid. Yes, ma'am ; but she begs you will excuse her.

Mrs. Candour. Do go again ; I shall be glad to see her, if it be only for a moment, for I am sure she must be in great distress. *(Exit Maid.)* Dear heart, how provoking ! I'm not mistress of half the circumstances ! We shall have the whole affair in the newspapers, with the names of the parties at length, before I have dropped the story at a dozen houses.

(Enter Sir Benjamin Backbite.)

Oh, dear Sir Benjamin ! you have heard, I suppose——

Sir Benjamin. Of Lady Teazle and Mr. Surface——

Mrs. Candour. And Sir Peter's discovery——

Sir Benjamin. Oh, the strangest piece of business, to be sure !

Mrs. Candour. Well, I never was so surprised in my life. I am so sorry for all parties, indeed.

Sir Benjamin. Now, I don't pity Sir Peter at all : he was so extravagantly partial to Mr. Surface.

Mrs. Candour. Mr. Surface ! Why, 'twas with Charles Lady Teazle was detected.

Sir Benjamin. No, no, I tell you : Mr. Surface is the gallant.

Mrs. Candour. No such thing ! Charles is the man. 'Twas Mr. Surface brought Sir Peter on purpose to discover them.

Sir Benjamin. I tell you I had it from one——

Mrs. Candour. And I have it from one——

Sir Benjamin. Who had it from one, who had it——

Mrs. Candour. From one immediately—— But here comes Lady Sneerwell ; perhaps she knows the whole affair.

(*Enter Lady Sneerwell.*)

Lady Sneerwell. So, my dear Mrs. Candour, here's a sad affair of our friend Lady Teazle !

Mrs. Candour. Ay, my dear friend, who would have thought——

Lady Sneerwell. Well, there is no trusting to appearances ; though, indeed, she was always too lively for me.

Mrs. Candour. To be sure, her manners were a little too free ; but then she was so young !

Lady Sneerwell. And had, indeed, some good qualities.

Mrs. Candour. So she had, indeed. But have you heard the particulars ?

Lady Sneerwell. No ; but everybody says that Mr. Surface——

Sir Benjamin. Ah, there ; I told you Mr. Surface was the man.

Mrs. Candour. No, no ; indeed the assignation was with Charles.

Lady Sneerwell. With Charles ! You alarm me, Mrs. Candour.

Mrs. Candour. Yes, yes ; he was the lover. Mr. Surface, to do him justice, was only the informer.

Sir Benjamin. Well, I'll not dispute with you, Mrs. Candour ; but, be it which it may, I hope that Sir Peter's wound will not——

Mrs. Candour. Sir Peter's wound ! Oh, mercy ! I didn't hear a word of their fighting.

Lady Sneerwell. Nor I, a syllable.

Sir Benjamin. No ! what, no mention of the duel ?

Mrs. Candour. Not a word.

Sir Benjamin. Oh, yes : they fought before they left the room.

Lady Sneerwell. Pray let us hear.

Mrs. Candour. Ay, do oblige us with the duel.

Sir Benjamin. "Sir," says Sir Peter, immediately after the discovery, "*you are a most ungrateful fellow.*"

Mrs. Candour. Ay, to Charles——

Sir Benjamin. No, no—to Mr. .Surface—"*a most ungrateful fellow ; and old as I am, sir,*" says he, "*I insist on immediate satisfaction.*"

Mrs. Candour. Ay, that must have been to Charles ; for 'tis very unlikely Mr. Surface should fight in his own house.

Sir Benjamin. 'Gad's life, ma'am, not at all—"*giving me immediate satisfaction.*"—On this, ma'am, Lady Teazle, seeing Sir Peter in such danger, ran out of the room in strong hysterics, and Charles after her, calling out for hartshorn and water ; then, madam, they began to fight with swords——

(*Enter Crabtree.*)

Crabtree. With pistols, nephew—pistols ! I have it from undoubted authority.

Mrs. Candour. Oh, Mr. Crabtree, then it is all true !

Crabtree. Too true, madam, and Sir Peter is dangerously wounded——

Sir Benjamin. By a thrust in segoon quite through his left side——

Crabtree. By a bullet lodged in the thorax.

Mrs. Candour. Mercy on me ! Poor Sir Peter !

Crabtree. Yes, madam ; though Charles would have avoided the matter, if he could.

Mrs. Candour. I knew Charles was the person.

Sir Benjamin. My uncle, I see, knows nothing of the matter.

In segoon, In *seconde,* or second position in fencing. A parry at waist level.

Crabtree. But Sir Peter taxed him with the basest ingratitude——

Sir Benjamin. That I told you, you know——

Crabtree. Do, nephew, let me speak !—and insisted on immediate——

Sir Benjamin. Just as I said——

Crabtree. Odds life, nephew, allow others to know something too ! A pair of pistols lay on the bureau (for Mr. Surface, it seems, had come home the night before late from Salthill, where he had been to see the Montem with a friend, who has a son at Eton), so, unluckily, the pistols were left charged.

Sir Benjamin. I heard nothing of this.

Crabtree. Sir Peter forced Charles to take one, and they fired, it seems, pretty nearly together. Charles's shot took effect, as I tell you, and Sir Peter's missed ; but, what is very extraordinary, the ball struck against a little bronze Shakespeare that stood over the fireplace, grazed out of the window at a right angle, and wounded the postman, who was just coming to the door with a double letter from North-amptonshire.

Sir Benjamin. My uncle's account is more circumstantial, I confess ; but I believe mine is the true one, for all that.

Lady Sneerwell (aside). I am more interested in this affair than they imagine, and must have better information.   (*Exit.*)

Sir Benjamin. Ah ! Lady Sneerwell's alarm is very easily accounted for.

Crabtree. Yes, yes, they certainly do say—but that's neither here nor there.

Salthill . . . Eton, Refers to a former Etonian custom. Every third year, on Whit-Tuesday, the boys used to proceed to the mound (*ad montem*) called Salthill, on the Bath Road, to collect money from passers-by, to pay the university expenses of the senior scholars. The proceeds were called *salt-money*. (*Cf.* the origin of " salary.")   *Grazed*, Glanced off.
Double letter, Letter on two sheets, costing double postage.

Mrs. Candour. But, pray, where is Sir Peter at present?

Crabtree. Oh! they brought him home, and he is now in the house, though the servants are ordered to deny him.

Mrs. Candour. I believe so, and Lady Teazle, I suppose, attending him.

Crabtree. Yes, yes; and I saw one of the faculty enter just before me.

Sir Benjamin. Hey! who comes here?

Crabtree. Oh, this is he: the physician, depend on't.

Mrs. Candour. Oh, certainly! it must be the physician; and now we shall know.

(Enter Sir Oliver Surface.)

Crabtree. Well, doctor, what hopes?

Mrs. Candour. Ay, doctor, how's your patient?

Sir Benjamin. Now, doctor, isn't it a wound with a small-sword?

Crabtree. A bullet lodged in the thorax, for a hundred!

Sir Oliver. Doctor! a wound with a small-sword! and a bullet in the thorax?—Oons! are you mad, good people?

Sir Benjamin. Perhaps, sir, you are not a doctor?

Sir Oliver. Truly, I am to thank you for my degree, if I am.

Crabtree. Only a friend of Sir Peter's, then, I presume. But, sir, you must have heard of his accident?

Sir Oliver. Not a word!

Crabtree. Not of his being dangerously wounded?

Sir Oliver. The devil he is!

Sir Benjamin. Run through the body——

Crabtree. Shot in the breast——

Sir Benjamin. By one Mr. Surface——

Faculty, viz. medical.   *Small-sword*, Fencing sword.

Crabtree. Ay, the younger.

Sir Oliver. Hey! what the plague! you seem to differ strangely in your accounts; however, you agree that Sir Peter is dangerously wounded.

Sir Benjamin. Oh, yes, we agree in that.

Crabtree. Yes, yes, I believe there can be no doubt of that.

Sir Oliver. Then, upon my word, for a person in that situation, he is the most imprudent man alive; for here he comes, walking as if nothing at all was the matter.

(Enter Sir Peter Teazle.)

Odds heart, Sir Peter! you are come in good time, I promise you; for we had just given you over!

Sir Benjamin (aside to Crabtree). Egad, uncle, this is the most sudden recovery!

Sir Oliver. Why, man! what do you do out of bed with a small-sword through your body, and a bullet lodged in your thorax?

Sir Peter. A small-sword and a bullet?

Sir Oliver. Ay; these gentlemen would have killed you without law or physic, and wanted to dub me a doctor, to make me an accomplice.

Sir Peter. Why, what is all this?

Sir Benjamin. We rejoice, Sir Peter, that the story of the duel is not true, and are sincerely sorry for your other misfortune.

Sir Peter (aside). So, so; all over the town already.

Crabtree. Though, Sir Peter, you were certainly vastly to blame to marry at your years.

Sir Peter. Sir, what business is that of yours?

Mrs. Candour. Though, indeed, as Sir Peter made so good a husband, he's very much to be pitied.

Sir Peter. Plague on your pity, ma'am! I desire none of it.

Sir Benjamin. However, Sir Peter, you must not mind the laughing and jests you will meet with on the occasion.

Sir Peter. Sir, sir ! I desire to be master in my own house.

Crabtree. 'Tis no uncommon case, that's one comfort.

Sir Peter. I insist on being left to myself : without ceremony, I insist on your leaving my house directly !

Mrs. Candour. Well, well, we are going ; and depend on't, we'll make the best report of it we can.

(*Exit.*)

Sir Peter. Leave my house !

Crabtree. And tell how hardly you've been treated.

(*Exit.*)

Sir Peter. Leave my house !

Sir Benjamin. And how patiently you bear it.

(*Exit.*)

Sir Peter. Fiends ! vipers ! furies ! Oh ! that their own venom would choke them !

Sir Oliver. They are very provoking indeed, Sir Peter.

(*Enter Rowley.*)

Rowley. I heard high words : what has ruffled you, sir ?

Sir Peter. Pshaw ! what signifies asking ? Do I ever pass a day without my vexations ?

Rowley. Well, I'm not inquisitive.

Sir Oliver. Well, Sir Peter, I have seen both my nephews in the manner we proposed.

Sir Peter. A precious couple they are !

Rowley. Yes, and Sir Oliver is convinced that your judgment was right, Sir Peter.

Sir Oliver. Yes, I find Joseph is indeed the man, after all.

Rowley. Ay, as Sir Peter says, he is a man of sentiment.

Sir Oliver. And acts up to the sentiments he professes.

Rowley. It certainly is edification to hear him talk.

Sir Oliver. Oh, he's a model for the young men of

the age ! But how's this, Sir Peter ? you don't join us in your friend Joseph's praise, as I expected.

Sir Peter. Sir Oliver, we live in a damned wicked world, and the fewer we praise the better.

Rowley. What ! do you say so, Sir Peter, who were never mistaken in your life ?

Sir Peter. Pshaw ! plague on you both ! I see by your sneering you have heard the whole affair. I shall go mad among you !

Rowley. Then, to fret you no longer, Sir Peter, we are indeed acquainted with it all. I met Lady Teazle coming from Mr. Surface's so humbled, that she deigned to request me to be her advocate with you.

Sir Peter. And does Sir Oliver know all this ?

Sir Oliver. Every circumstance.

Sir Peter. What, of the closet and the screen, hey ?

Sir Oliver. Yes, yes, and the little French milliner. Oh, I have been vastly diverted with the story ! ha ! ha ! ha !

Sir Peter. 'Twas very pleasant.

Sir Oliver. I never laughed more in my life, I assure you : ha ! ha ! ha !

Sir Peter. Oh, vastly diverting ! ha ! ha ! ha !

Rowley. To be sure, Joseph with his sentiments ! ha ! ha ! ha !

Sir Peter. Yes, his sentiments ! ha ! ha ! ha ! Hypocritical villain !

Sir Oliver. Ay, and that rogue Charles to pull Sir Peter out of the closet : ha ! ha ! ha !

Sir Peter. Ha ! ha ! 'twas devilish entertaining, to be sure !

Sir Oliver. Ha ! ha ! ha ! Egad, Sir Peter, I should like to have seen your face when the screen was thrown down : ha ! ha !

Sir Peter. Yes, my face when the screen was thrown down : ha ! ha ! ha ! Oh, I must never show my head again !

Sir Oliver. But come, come, it isn't fair to laugh at you neither, my old friend, though, upon my soul, I can't help it.

Sir Peter. Oh, pray don't restrain your mirth on my account : it does not hurt me at all ! I laugh at the whole affair myself. Yes, yes, I think being a standing jest for all one's acquaintance a very happy situation. Oh, yes, and then of a morning to read the paragraphs about Mr. S——, Lady T——, and Sir P——, will be so entertaining !

Rowley. Without affectation, Sir Peter, you may despise the ridicule of fools. But I see Lady Teazle going towards the next room ; I am sure you must desire a reconciliation as earnestly as she does.

Sir Oliver. Perhaps my being here prevents her coming to you. Well, I'll leave honest Rowley to mediate between you ; but he must bring you all presently to Mr. Surface's, where I am now returning, if not to reclaim a libertine, at least to expose hypocrisy.

Sir Peter. Ah, I'll be present at your discovering yourself there with all my heart ; though 'tis a vile unlucky place for discoveries.

Rowley. We'll follow. (*Exit Sir Oliver Surface.*)

Sir Peter. She is not coming here, you see, Rowley.

Rowley. No, but she has left the door of that room open, you perceive. See, she is in tears.

Sir Peter. Certainly a little mortification appears very becoming in a wife. Don't you think it will do her good to let her pine a little ?

Rowley. Oh, this is ungenerous in you !

Sir Peter. Well, I know not what to think. You remember the letter I found of hers evidently intended for Charles !

Rowley. A mere forgery, Sir Peter ! laid in your way on purpose. This is one of the points which I intend Snake shall give you conviction of.

Sir Peter. I wish I were once satisfied of that. She

looks this way. What a remarkably elegant turn of the head she has! Rowley, I'll go to her.

Rowley. Certainly.

Sir Peter. Though, when it is known that we are reconciled, people will laugh at me ten times more.

Rowley. Let them laugh, and retort their malice only by showing them you are happy in spite of it.

Sir Peter. I'faith, so I will! and, if I'm not mistaken, we may yet be the happiest couple in the country.

Rowley. Nay, Sir Peter, he who once lays aside suspicion——

Sir Peter. Hold, Master Rowley! if you have any regard for me, never let me hear you utter anything like a sentiment : I have had enough of them to serve me the rest of my life.   (*Exeunt.*)

SCENE III.   *The Library in Joseph Surface's House.*

(*Enter Joseph Surface and Lady Sneerwell.*)

Lady Sneerwell. Impossible! Will not Sir Peter immediately be reconciled to Charles, and of course no longer oppose his union with Maria? The thought is distraction to me.

Joseph Surface. Can passion furnish a remedy?

Lady Sneerwell. No, nor cunning either. Oh, I was a fool and idiot, to league with such a blunderer!

Joseph Surface. Surely, Lady Sneerwell, I am the greatest sufferer ; yet you see I bear the accident with calmness.

Lady Sneerwell. Because the disappointment doesn't reach your heart ; your interest only attached you to Maria. Had you felt for her what I have for that

Retort, Cast back, return.
Sentiment, Moral reflection; short, pithy sentence defining an obvious rule of conduct. Maxim.   *Distraction*, Madness.

ungrateful libertine, neither your temper nor hypocrisy could prevent your showing the sharpness of your vexation.

Joseph Surface. But why should your reproaches fall on me for this disappointment ?

Lady Sneerwell. Are you not the cause of it ? Had you not a sufficient field for your roguery in imposing upon Sir Peter, and supplanting your brother, but you must endeavour to seduce his wife ? I hate such an avarice of crimes ; 'tis an unfair monopoly, and never prospers.

Joseph Surface. Well, I admit I have been to blame. I confess I deviated from the direct road of wrong, but I don't think we're so totally defeated either.

Lady Sneerwell. No ?

Joseph Surface. You tell me you have made a trial of Snake since we met, and that you still believe him faithful to us ?

Lady Sneerwell. I do believe so.

Joseph Surface. And that he has undertaken, should it be necessary, to swear and prove, that Charles is at this time contracted by vows and honour to your ladyship, which some of his former letters to you will serve to support ?

Lady Sneerwell. This, indeed, might have assisted.

Joseph Surface. Come, come ; it is not too late yet.—(*Knocking at the door.*) But hark ! this is probably my uncle, Sir Oliver : retire to that room ; we'll consult further when he's gone.

Lady Sneerwell. Well, but if he should find you out too.

Joseph Surface. Oh, I have no fear of that. Sir Peter will hold his tongue for his own credit's sake— and you may depend on it I shall soon discover Sir Oliver's weak side !

Lady Sneerwell. I have no diffidence of your abilities ! only be constant to one roguery at a time.

219

Joseph Surface. I will, I will !—(*Exit Lady Sneer-well.*)　So !　'tis confounded hard, after such bad fortune, to be baited by one's confederate in evil. Well, at all events, my character is so much better than Charles's, that I certainly—hey !—what—this is not Sir Oliver, but old Stanley again.　Plague on't that he should return to tease me just now !　I shall have Sir Oliver come and find him here—and——

(*Enter Sir Oliver Surface.*)

Gad's life, Mr. Stanley, why have you come back to plague me at this time ?　You must not stay now, upon my word.

Sir Oliver. Sir, I hear your uncle Oliver is expected here, and though he has been so penurious to you, I'll try what he'll do for me.

Joseph Surface. Sir, 'tis impossible for you to stay now, so I must beg——　Come any other time, and I promise you, you shall be assisted.

Sir Oliver. No ; Sir Oliver and I must be acquainted.

Joseph Surface. Zounds, sir ! then I insist on your quitting the room directly.

Sir Oliver. Nay, sir——

Joseph Surface. Sir, I insist on't !—Here, William ! show this gentleman out.　Since you compel me, sir, not one moment—this is such insolence.

(*Going to push him out.*)
(*Enter Charles Surface.*)

Charles Surface. Heyday !　what's the matter now ? What the devil, have you got hold of my little broker here ?　Zounds, brother, don't hurt little Premium. What's the matter, my little fellow ?

Joseph Surface. So !　he has been with you, too, has he ?

Charles Surface. To be sure he has.　Why, he's as honest a little——　But sure, Joseph, you have not been borrowing money too, have you ?

Joseph Surface. Borrowing ?　no !　But, brother, you know we expect Sir Oliver here every——

Charles Surface. O Gad, that's true. Noll mustn't find the little broker here, to be sure.

Joseph Surface. Yet, Mr. Stanley insists——

Charles Surface. Stanley! why, his name's Premium.

Joseph Surface. No, sir, Stanley.

Charles Surface. No, no, Premium.

Joseph Surface. Well, no matter which—but——

Charles Surface. Ay, ay, Stanley or Premium, 'tis the same thing, as you say; for I suppose he goes by half a hundred names, besides A.B. at the coffee-house.   (*Knocking.*)

Joseph Surface. 'Sdeath! here's Sir Oliver at the door. Now I beg, Mr. Stanley——

Charles Surface. Ay, ay, and I beg, Mr. Premium——

Sir Oliver. Gentlemen——

Joseph Surface. Sir, by heaven you shall go!

Charles Surface. Ay, out with him, certainly.

Sir Oliver. This violence——

Joseph Surface. Sir, 'tis your own fault.

Charles Surface. Out with him, to be sure.

(*Both forcing Sir Oliver out.*)

(*Enter Sir Peter and Lady Teazle, Maria, and Rowley.*)

Sir Peter. My old friend, Sir Oliver—hey! What in the name of wonder!—here are dutiful nephews—assault their uncle at a first visit!

Lady Teazle. Indeed, Sir Oliver, 'twas well we came in to rescue you.

Rowley. Truly it was; for I perceive, Sir Oliver, the character of old Stanley was no protection to you.

Sir Oliver. Nor of Premium either: the necessities of the former could not extort a shilling from that benevolent gentleman; and with the other I stood a chance of faring worse than my ancestors, and being knocked down without being bid for.

A.B. at the coffee-house, Any disguise name used for a secret appointment at a coffee-house.

Joseph Surface. Charles !
Charles Surface. Joseph !
Joseph Surface. 'Tis now complete !
Charles Surface. Very.
Sir Oliver. Sir Peter, my friend, and Rowley, too—look on that elder nephew of mine. You know what he has already received from my bounty ; and you also know how gladly I would have regarded half my fortune as held in trust for him ? judge, then, my disappointment in discovering him to be destitute of truth, charity, and gratitude !
Sir Peter. Sir Oliver, I should be more surprised at this declaration, if I had not myself found him to be mean, treacherous, and hypocritical.
Lady Teazle. And if the gentleman pleads not guilty to these, pray let him call me to his character.
Sir Peter. Then, I believe, we need add no more : if he knows himself, he will consider it as the most perfect punishment that he is known to the world.
Charles Surface (*aside*). If they talk this way to Honesty, what will they say to me, by-and-by ?

　　　(*Sir Peter, Lady Teazle, and Maria retire.*)
Sir Oliver. As for that prodigal, his brother, there——
Charles Surface (*aside*). Ay, now comes my turn : the damned family pictures will ruin me !
Joseph Surface. Sir Oliver—uncle, will you honour me with a hearing ?
Charles Surface (*aside*). Now, if Joseph would make one of his long speeches, I might recollect myself a little.
Sir Oliver (*to Joseph Surface*). I suppose you would undertake to justify yourself ?
Joseph Surface. I trust I could.
Sir Oliver (*to Charles Surface*). Well, sir !—and you could justify yourself too, I suppose ?
Charles Surface. Not that I know of, Sir Oliver.

Sir Oliver. What !—Little Premium has been let too much into the secret, I suppose ?

Charles Surface. True, sir ; but they were family secrets, and should not be mentioned again, you know.

Rowley. Come, Sir Oliver, I know you cannot speak of Charles's follies with anger.

Sir Oliver. Odd's heart, no more I can ; nor with gravity either. Sir Peter, do you know the rogue bargained with me for all his ancestors ; sold me judges and generals by the foot, and maiden aunts as cheap as broken china.

Charles Surface. To be sure, Sir Oliver, I did make a little free with the family canvas, that's the truth on't. My ancestors may rise in judgment against me, there's no denying it ; but believe me sincere when I tell you—and upon my soul I would not say so if I was not—that if I do not appear mortified at the exposure of my follies, it is because I feel at this moment the warmest satisfaction at seeing you, my liberal benefactor.

Sir Oliver. Charles, I believe you. Give me your hand again : the ill-looking little fellow over the settee has made your peace.

Charles Surface. Then, sir, my gratitude to the original is still increased.

Lady Teazle (advancing). Yet, I believe, Sir Oliver, here is one whom Charles is still more anxious to be reconciled to. (*Pointing to Maria.*)

Sir Oliver. Oh, I have heard of his attachment there ; and, with the young lady's pardon, if I construe right—that blush——

Sir Peter. Well, child, speak your sentiments.

Maria. Sir, I have little to say, but that I shall rejoice to hear that he is happy ; for me, whatsoever claim I had to his attention, I willingly resign to one who has a better title.

Charles Surface. How, Maria ?

Sir Peter. Heyday! what's the mystery now? While he appeared an incorrigible rake, you would give your hand to no one else; and now that he is likely to reform I'll warrant you won't have him.

Maria. His own heart and Lady Sneerwell know the cause.

Charles Surface. Lady Sneerwell!

Joseph Surface. Brother, it is with great concern I am obliged to speak on this point, but my regard to justice compels me, and Lady Sneerwell's injuries can no longer be concealed.   (*Opens the door.*)

(*Enter Lady Sneerwell.*)

Sir Peter. So! another French milliner! Egad, he has one in every room in the house, I suppose!

Lady Sneerwell. Ungrateful Charles! Well may you be surprised, and feel for the indelicate situation your perfidy has forced me into.

Charles Surface. Pray, uncle, is this another plot of yours? For, as I have life, I don't understand it.

Joseph Surface. I believe, sir, there is but the evidence of one person more necessary to make it extremely clear.

Sir Peter. And that person, I imagine, is Mr. Snake.—Rowley, you were perfectly right to bring him with us, and pray let him appear.

Rowley. Walk in, Mr. Snake.

(*Enter Snake.*)

I thought his testimony might be wanted; however, it happens unluckily, that he comes to confront Lady Sneerwell, not to support her.

Lady Sneerwell. A villain! Treacherous to me at last! Speak, fellow, have you too conspired against me?

Snake. I beg your ladyship ten thousand pardons; you paid me extremely liberally for the lie in question; but I unfortunately have been offered double to speak the truth.

Lady Sneerwell. The torments of shame and disappointment on you all ! *(Going.)*

Lady Teazle. Hold, Lady Sneerwell—before you go, let me thank you for the trouble you and that gentleman have taken, in writing letters from me to Charles, and answering them yourself ; and let me also request you to make my respects to the scandalous college, of which you are president, and inform them, that Lady Teazle, licentiate, begs leave to return the diploma they granted her, as she leaves off practice, and kills characters no longer.

Lady Sneerwell. You too, madam !—provoking— insolent ! May your husband live these fifty years !
(Exit.)

Sir Peter. Oons ! what a fury !

Lady Teazle. A malicious creature, indeed !

Sir Peter. What ! not for her last wish ?

Lady Teazle. Oh, no !

Sir Oliver. Well, sir, and what have you to say now ?

Joseph Surface. Sir, I am so confounded, to find that Lady Sneerwell could be guilty of suborning Mr. Snake in this manner, to impose on us all, that I know not what to say : however, lest her revengeful spirit should prompt her to injure my brother, I had certainly better follow her directly. For the man who attempts to—— *(Exit.)*

Sir Peter. Moral to the last drop !

Sir Oliver. Ay, and marry her, Joseph, if you can. Oil and vinegar !—egad, you'll do very well together.

Rowley. I believe we have no more occasion for Mr. Snake at present ?

Snake. Before I go, I beg pardon once for all, for whatever uneasiness I have been the humble instrument of causing to the parties present.

Sir Peter. Well, well, you have made atonement by a good deed at last.

Snake. But I must request of the company, that it shall never be known.

Sir Peter. Hey ! what the plague ! are you ashamed of having done a right thing once in your life ?

Snake. Ah, sir, consider—I live by the badness of my character ; and, if it were once known that I had been betrayed into an honest action, I should lose every friend I have in the world.

Sir Oliver. Well, well—we'll not traduce you by saying anything in your praise, never fear.

(Exit Snake.)

Sir Peter. There's a precious rogue !

Lady Teazle. See, Sir Oliver, there needs no persuasion now to reconcile your nephew and Maria.

Sir Oliver. Ay, ay, that's as it should be, and, egad, we'll have the wedding to-morrow morning.

Charles Surface. Thank you, dear uncle.

Sir Peter. What, you rogue ! don't you ask the girl's consent first ?

Charles Surface. Oh, I have done that a long time —a minute ago—and she has looked yes.

Maria. For shame, Charles !—I protest, Sir Peter, there has not been a word——

Sir Oliver. Well, then, the fewer the better : may your love for each other never know abatement.

Sir Peter. And may you live as happily together as Lady Teazle and I intend to do !

Charles Surface. Rowley, my old friend, I am sure you congratulate me ; and I suspect that I owe you much.

Sir Oliver. You do indeed, Charles.

Rowley. If my efforts to serve you had not succeeded you would have been in my debt for the attempt—but deserve to be happy—and you over-repay me.

Sir Peter. Ay, honest Rowley always said you would reform.

Charles Surface. Why, as to reforming, Sir Peter, I'll make no promises, and that I take to be a proof that I intend to set about it. But here shall be my

monitor—my gentle guide.—Ah ! can I leave the
virtuous path these eyes illumine ?
Though thou, dear maid, shouldst waive thy beauty's
    sway,
Thou still must rule, because I will obey :
An humble fugitive from Folly view,
No sanctuary near but Love and you :
                        (To the audience.)
You can, indeed, each anxious fear remove,
For even Scandal dies, if you approve.
                        (Exeunt omnes.)

FINIS

QUESTIONS ON
"THE SCHOOL FOR SCANDAL"

Persons of the Play

1. Sketch the character of Charles Surface. Is he suitable for a hero?

2. Would you trust Charles's promise to reform?

3. "A man of sentiment," "a sentimental knave." Comment on the meaning of these phrases, and show how they apply to Joseph Surface.

4. "Joseph Surface is the most artificial, puppet-like figure in the play." Do you agree?

5. Outline the part played by Sir Oliver Surface, and estimate (a) his character, (b) whether he is convincing.

6. Why is *Surface* a good name for the three persons who bear it in the play?

7. Has Maria any personality? Is it suitable?

8. Describe the characters and relationship of Sir Peter and Lady Teazle. Is one or are both at fault?

9. Distinguish Lady Sneerwell, Mrs. Candour, and Sir Benjamin Backbite as three types of scandalmonger.

10. Ought a comedy of manners like this to aim at natural characters or at telling types?

11. Give three examples of how persons in the play behave in accordance with their names.

Construction

1. Is the opening scene successful (a) in providing requisite information about the chief characters, (b) in holding our interest, (c) in indicating the tone of the whole play?

2. "I wish," said a first-nighter in the pit during the scene at Lady Sneerwell's, "that these people would

have done talking and let the play begin." Are the " scandal scenes " necessary ?

3. Describe the quarrel scenes of the Teazles. Do they come under the head of serious or comic situations ?

4. Why are IV. iii. and V. i. the turning-points of the play ?

5. Show how Sheridan manages in III. iii. steadily to lower Charles in Sir Oliver's eyes, and then in IV. i. to raise him again.

6. Explain the plan by which Sir Oliver Surface learned the true character of his nephews.

7. Describe the screen scene. Show how it provides suspense and surprise.

8. From the point of view of "theatre," would the screen scene be better if the audience were not to know till the fall of the screen who was hidden behind it ?

9. How was it embarrassing that Lady Teazle had hidden behind the screen (a) before any one said anything (notice where the screen was), (b) up to the upsetting, (c) after the upsetting ?

10. The play is a tangle of attitudes to the young Surfaces on the part of (a) Sir Peter, (b) Sir Oliver, (c) all the womenfolk. Sort out the tangle.

11. All the scenes are indoors, and much alike. How many actually different settings are there ?

12. Draw stage plans for (a) the first scandal scene, I. i., and (b) the screen scene.

13. Sketch simple sets for (a) Joseph's library, (b) Charles's picture room.

WIT, SATIRE

1. Even though in many details the play is topical and " period," it is still very popular on the stage. Why ?

2. Is it a better play than *The Rivals* ?

3. Is it surprising that this was George Washington's favourite play ?

4. " Here is Sheridan succeeding in true crystal-clear impersonality." Comment on this ; with special reference finally to the characters of Maria, Rowley, and Sir Oliver.

5. Give examples of humour of (a) character, (b) situation.

6. Illustrate, with quotations, the scandal-making of Lady Sneerwell's club.

7. Give five examples of repartee.

8. "True wit is more nearly allied to good nature than your ladyship is aware of." Is this opinion of Sir Peter's true?

9. Is the play as a whole (a) a moral lesson on the evils of scandal, or (b) a witty and enjoyable pattern on a ground of society life?

THE CRITIC

INTRODUCTION TO "THE CRITIC"

When the play was written.—In 1776 Sheridan had become manager of Drury Lane Theatre, in which position he suffered a great deal from self-appointed critics and dabblers who fancied themselves as playwrights. He was the special target of the supporters of sentimental ("sloppy") drama, of the kind written by Richard Cumberland. At last (after three years of sufferance) he turned his incredible gift for mockery to good use in hitting back at his foes, and wrote *The Critic*, or *A Tragedy Rehearsed*. Presented on October 29, 1779, it was a great success.

The kind of play.—It is a burlesque (with running commentary) of high-flown, show (or "heroic") tragedy : a kind of highbrow farce. There had been many examples by earlier writers of such skittish caricature. The best known of these were Shakespeare's *Pyramus and Thisbe* in *A Midsummer Night's Dream*, and the Players' Speeches before Hamlet in *Hamlet* ; Buckingham's *The Rehearsal* (1672) ; Fielding's *Tom Thumb the Great* (1730) ; and Garrick's *A Peep behind the Curtain*, or *The New Rehearsal* (1767). But they had made fun mostly of the actors. Sheridan widened the scope to embrace theatre "fans," critics, playwrights, and amateur producers as well.

There are three acts, of a consecutive kind (*i.e.* there is no worked-up plot).* Act I. is like the scandal scenes in Sheridan's masterpiece, brilliantly sarcastic high comedy of repartee, with Sir Fretful Plagiary (a caricature of Richard Cumberland) as the butt.

* The plot is of a railway line, not a spider's web type.

INTRODUCTION TO "THE CRITIC"

It is a skit on the petty jealousies of stagy people. Then there enters the overwhelming personality of Mr. Puff,* author and producer of the tragedy to be rehearsed, and past-master in the theory and practice of "stunt" publicity. From him we learn the "wangling" and humbug of commercial advertising, and the false taste of the time for staginess and sentiment ("where history gives you a good, heroic outline for a play, you may fill up with a little love at your own discretion" !).

Act II. brings us, after a short scene of explanatory comment before the curtain, to the rehearsal of Mr. Puff's play, *The Spanish Armada*, presenting incidents at Tilbury Fort while the enemy is approaching. The rehearsal is all burlesque, a farcical show underlined by the ridiculous compèring of Mr. Puff. The usual ingredients in a tragedy of the time—an exciting opening, exposition of the situation, noble language, lofty passions, strong episodes, suspense, coincidence, surprise, climax, crisis, recognition of disguised relatives, sub-plots, duels, a grand *scena* as wind-up—all these are made as laughable as possible by exaggeration, deliberate reversal, and anticlimax. Every sensible rule of play-writing and production is turned to mockery, which is underlined by Mr. Puff's voluble approval. The heroic figures speak ranting exaggerations of Othello, the pathetic ones ridiculous flowery gibberings after Ophelia or wailing repetitions in the manner of *Richard III*. Symbolic figures make a hash of common sense, and the play ends with a cinema-like spectacle of the English fleet destroying the Armada, with a procession of all the English rivers, undulating music, and "See, the conquering hero comes"; while Puff pats himself on the back with "My battle! my noise!—and my procession!"

---

* Subtle, in Jonson's *The Alchemist* (1610), has the same gusto and exuberance of language.

INTRODUCTION TO "THE CRITIC"

The whole play shows Sheridan's undiminished talent as a comic writer ; even an increased vitality of dialogue. The sarcastic comments are inimitable—" Where they do agree on the stage, their unanimity is wonderful ! " But excellent in its kind as it was, *The Critic* marked the end of Sheridan's comic writing, almost the end of his career as a dramatist. His only other play was a tragedy, *Pizarro*, in 1799, adapted from the German playwright Kotzebue (1761–1819).

Sheridan's political career.—As playwright, Sheridan was the practitioner, not the natural, inspired genius. He was opportunist : and wanted money and reputation. He had no great insight into human nature. He was indolent ; it being said that *The Critic* would not have been finished at all if the company had not in desperation enticed him into a room at the theatre, with a warm fire, food, wine, and the unfinished script, and there locked him until the last word was written.

So it was not surprising when, always an accomplished orator, he turned to the wider field of politics. He entered Parliament as M.P. for Stafford, 1780, joining the Whig opposition under Burke and Fox. With these last, his generous spirit prompted him to oppose the American War. Two years later he became an Under-Secretary to the Treasury. But though he sat as M.P. for thirty-two years, no high office gratified his ambition. It was largely a question again of indolence. Yet as orator he delivered some of the greatest speeches in the annals of Parliament—notably as accuser of Warren Hastings, and on the mutiny at the Nore. Even Pitt said of Sheridan's first speech on Hastings' impeachment, that it " surpassed all the eloquence of ancient and modern times, and possessed everything that genius or art could furnish, to agitate and control the human mind." In 1812, as the unsuccessful candidate for

Westminster, he ended his political career. He had been not a fixed star but a meteor.

Later years.—His first wife dying in 1792, he married again. But though he was warm-hearted, his thriftlessness made home-life a strain. Constantly in debt, he was often saved only by his fascination and wit from being sold up ; while his seat in Parliament alone protected him from going to a debtor's prison. Servants would starve in his service rather than leave him ; but it was a racketing life.

Then in February 1809 fate played him a cruel blow; his entire fortune together with his means of living perished in the burning down of Drury Lane Theatre. Watching the fire from a coffee-house near by, he ordered a bottle of port, and answered his expostulating friend with the remark, " It is hard if a man can't drink a glass of wine by his own fireside." A few years later, when he was suffering from a fatal disease, bailiffs took possession of his home ; and he would have been carried off to prison in his blankets had not the doctor warned the sheriff's officer that he was dying. An appeal was made to friends for help ; but it arrived too late. On July 7, 1816, shivering and worn out, he died.

The irony he had constantly played with on the small scale now played with him on the grand ; for when he was dead for want of attention, the noblest figures in the land provided him with a magnificent funeral, and his coffin was followed to Westminster Abbey by a dazzling array of earls, marquesses, and dukes. And posterity has elected to remember him not by what he expected, his serious parliamentary speeches, but by his three light comedies.

THE CRITIC

Or, A Tragedy Rehearsed

DRAMATIS PERSONÆ

(With the cast of the original performances at
Drury Lane Theatre in 1779)

SIR FRETFUL PLAGIARY . . .	Mr. Parsons
PUFF	Mr. King
DANGLE	Mr. Dodd
SNEER	Mr. Palmer
SIGNOR PASTICCIO RITORNELLO .	Mr. Delpini
INTERPRETER	Mr. Baddeley
UNDER PROMPTER . . .	Mr. Phillimore
MR. HOPKINS	Mr. Hopkins
MRS. DANGLE	Mrs. Hopkins
SIGNORE PASTICCIO RITORNELLO }	Miss Field and the Miss Abrams

CHARACTERS OF THE TRAGEDY

LORD BURLEIGH . . .	Mr. Moody
GOVERNOR OF TILBURY FORT .	Mr. Wrighten
EARL OF LEICESTER . .	Mr. Farren
SIR WALTER RALEIGH . .	Mr. Burton
SIR CHRISTOPHER HATTON .	Mr. Waldron
MASTER OF THE HORSE . .	Mr. Kenny
DON FEROLO WHISKERANDOS .	Mr. Bannister, jun.
BEEFEATER	Mr. Wright
JUSTICE	Mr. Packer
SON	Mr. Lamash
CONSTABLE	Mr. Fawcett
THAMES	Mr. Gawdry
TILBURINA	Miss Pope
CONFIDANT	Mrs. Bradshaw
JUSTICE'S LADY . . .	Mrs. Johnston
FIRST NIECE	Miss Collett
SECOND NIECE	Miss Kirby

Guards, Constables, Chorus, Rivers, Attendants,
&c., &c.

SCENE.—London: in Dangle's house during the First
Act, and throughout the rest of the play in Drury
Lane Theatre.

237

THE CRITIC

Or, A Tragedy Rehearsed

ACT I

SCENE I. *A Room in Dangle's House.*

(*Mr. and Mrs. Dangle at breakfast, and reading newspapers.*)

Dangle (*reading*). Brutus to Lord North.—*Letter the second on the State of the Army*—Pshaw! *To the first L dash D of the A dash Y.*—*Genuine extract of a Letter from St. Kitts.*—*Coxheath Intelligence.*—*It is now confidently asserted that Sir Charles Hardy*—Pshaw! nothing but about the fleet and the nation !—and I hate all politics but theatrical politics.—Where's the *Morning Chronicle*?

Mrs. Dangle. Yes, that's your Gazette.

Dangle. So, here we have it.—(*Reads.*) "*Theatrical intelligence extraordinary.*—We hear there is a new tragedy in rehearsal at Drury Lane Theatre called the Spanish Armada, said to be written by Mr. Puff, a gentleman well known in the theatrical world. If

Brutus to Lord North, Lord North was Prime Minister at this time (1770–82). "Brutus" is probably an allusion to the famous Letters of Junius, political articles in *The Public Advertiser* between 1769 and 1772. Brutus' name was L. Junius Brutus.
Coxheath, Where militia was encamped, near Maidstone. A French invasion was feared.
Sir Charles Hardy, Commanding the Channel Fleet.
Morning Chronicle, A newspaper specializing in drama and the arts.
Gazette, Official newspaper. (Reference to *The London Gazette*.)
Puff, Boost. So, Mr. Booster.

we may allow ourselves to give credit to the report of the performers, who, truth to say, are in general but indifferent judges, this piece abounds with the most striking and received beauties of modern composition."—So! I am very glad my friend Puff's tragedy is in such forwardness.—Mrs. Dangle, my dear, you will be very glad to hear that Puff's tragedy——

Mrs. Dangle. Lord, Mr. Dangle, why will you plague me about such nonsense ?—Now the plays are begun I shall have no peace.—Isn't it sufficient to make yourself ridiculous by your passion for the theatre, without continually teasing me to join you ? Why can't you ride your hobby-horse without desiring to place me on a pillion behind you, Mr. Dangle ?

Dangle. Nay, my dear, I was only going to read——

Mrs. Dangle. No, no ; you will never read anything that's worth listening to. You hate to hear about your country ; there are letters every day with Roman signatures, demonstrating the certainty of an invasion, and proving that the nation is utterly undone. But you never will read anything to entertain one.

Dangle. What has a woman to do with politics, Mrs. Dangle ?

Mrs. Dangle. And what have you to do with the theatre, Mr. Dangle ! Why should you affect the character of a critic ? I have no patience with you !—Haven't you made yourself the jest of all your acquaintance by your interference in matters where you have no business ? Are you not called a theatrical quidnunc, and a mock Mæcenas to second-hand authors ?

Received, Approved, fashionable.
Roman signatures, Nom-de-plumes like *Brutus*, *Pro Bono Publico*. The letters dealt with a threatened invasion by the French and Spanish fleets, which were in the Channel.
Quidnunc, Know-all ; Nosy Parker.
Mæcenas, Millionaire friend of the Emperor Augustus ; famous for aiding many great authors, including Vergil and Horace. Died 8 B.C.

Dangle. True; my power with the managers is pretty notorious. But is it no credit to have applications from all quarters for my interest—from lords to recommend fiddlers, from ladies to get boxes, from authors to get answers, and from actors to get engagements?

Mrs. Dangle. Yes, truly; you have contrived to get a share in all the plague and trouble of theatrical property, without the profit, or even the credit of the abuse that attends it.

Dangle. I am sure, Mrs. Dangle, you are no loser by it, however; you have all the advantages of it. Mightn't you, last winter, have had the reading of the new pantomime a fortnight previous to its performance? And doesn't Mr. Fosbrook let you take places for a play before it is advertised, and set you down for a box for every new piece through the season? And didn't my friend, Mr. Smatter, dedicate his last farce to you at my particular request, Mrs. Dangle?

Mrs. Dangle. Yes; but wasn't the farce damned, Mr. Dangle? And to be sure it is extremely pleasant to have one's house made the motley rendezvous of all the lackeys of literature; the very high 'Change of trading authors and jobbing critics?—Yes, my drawing-room is an absolute register office for candidate actors, and poets without character.—Then to be continually alarmed with misses and ma'ams piping hysteric changes on Juliets and Dorindas, Pollys, and Ophelias; and the very furniture trembling at the probationary starts and unprovoked rants of would-be Richards and Hamlets!—And what is worse than all, now that the manager has monopolized the Opera

Property, Affairs.   *High 'Change,* Chief Stock Exchange.
Dorindas, In Farquhar's *The Beaux Stratagem,* 1664.
Pollys, In Gay's *Beggar's Opera,* 1727.
Richards and Hamlets, Referring specially to David Garrick's rôles at the time, Richard III. and Hamlet.
Monopolized, Taken over.

House, haven't we the signors and signoras calling
here, sliding their smooth semibreves, and gargling
glib divisions in their outlandish throats—with foreign
emissaries and French spies, for aught I know, disguised like fiddlers and figure-dancers ?

Dangle. Mercy !   Mrs. Dangle !

Mrs. Dangle. And to employ yourself so idly at such
an alarming crisis as this too—when, if you had the
least spirit, you would have been at the head of one
of the Westminster associations—or trailing a volunteer pike in the Artillery Ground ! But you—o' my
conscience, I believe, if the French were landed to-
morrow, your first inquiry would be, whether they
had brought a theatrical troop with them.

Dangle. Mrs. Dangle, it does not signify—I say
the stage is " the Mirror of Nature," and the actors
are " the abstract and brief chronicles of the time " ;
and pray what can a man of sense study better ?—
Besides, you will not easily persuade me that there
is no credit or importance in being at the head of a
band of critics, who take upon them to decide for the
whole town, whose opinion and patronage all writers
solicit, and whose recommendation no manager dares
refuse.

Mrs. Dangle. Ridiculous !—Both managers and
authors of the least merit laugh at your pretensions.—
The public is their critic—without whose fair approbation they know no play can rest on the stage, and
with whose applause they welcome such attacks as
yours, and laugh at the malice of them, where they
can't at the wit.

Dangle. Very well, madam—very well !

(*Enter Servant.*)

Servant. Mr. Sneer, sir, to wait on you.

Divisions, Arpeggios sung to a single syllable in the opera.
Figure-dancers, Ballet dancers.
Mirror of Nature . . . time, References to Hamlet's advice to the
   players, *Hamlet*, III. ii. 24, and description of them, II. ii. 508.

Dangle. Oh, show Mr. Sneer up.—(*Exit Servant.*) Plague on't, now we must appear loving and affection-ate, or Sneer will hitch us into a story.

Mrs. Dangle. With all my heart ; you can't be more ridiculous than you are.

Dangle. You are enough to provoke——

(*Enter Sneer.*)

Ha ! my dear Sneer, I am vastly glad to see you.— My dear, here's Mr. Sneer.

Mrs. Dangle. Good-morning to you, sir.

Dangle. Mrs. Dangle and I have been diverting ourselves with the papers. Pray, Sneer, won't you go to Drury Lane Theatre the first night of Puff's tragedy ?

Sneer. Yes; but I suppose one shan't be able to get in, for on the first night of a new piece they always fill the house with orders to support it. But here, Dangle, I have brought you two pieces, one of which you must exert yourself to make the managers accept, I can tell you that ; for 'tis written by a person of consequence.

Dangle. So ! now my plagues are beginning.

Sneer. Ay, I am glad of it, for now you'll be happy. Why, my dear Dangle, it is a pleasure to see how you enjoy your volunteer fatigue, and your solicited solicitations.

Dangle. It's a great trouble—yet, egad, it's pleas-ant too.—Why, sometimes of a morning I have a dozen people call on me at breakfast-time, whose faces I never saw before, nor ever desire to see again.

Sneer. That must be very pleasant indeed !

Dangle. And not a week but I receive fifty letters, and not a line in them about any business of my own.

Sneer. An amusing correspondence !

Orders, Free seats.
243

Dangle (*reading*). " Bursts into tears, and exit."—
What, is this a tragedy ?

Sneer. No, that's a genteel comedy, not a trans-
lation—only taken from the French : it is written in
a style which they have lately tried to run down ; the
true sentimental, and nothing ridiculous in it from
the beginning to the end.

Mrs. Dangle. Well, if they had kept to that, I
should not have been such an enemy to the stage ;
there was some edification to be got from those
pieces, Mr. Sneer !

Sneer. I am quite of your opinion, Mrs. Dangle :
the theatre, in proper hands, might certainly be made
the school of morality ; but now, I am sorry to say
it, people seem to go there principally for their entertainment !

Mrs. Dangle. It would have been more to the credit
of the managers to have kept it in the other line.

Sneer. Undoubtedly, madam ; and hereafter perhaps to have had it recorded, that in the midst of a
luxurious and dissipated age, they preserved two
houses in the capital, where the conversation was
always moral at least, if not entertaining !

Dangle. Now, egad, I think the worst alteration
is in the nicety of the audience !—No *double-entendre*,
no smart innuendo admitted ; even Vanbrugh and
Congreve obliged to undergo a bungling reformation !

Sneer. Yes, and our prudery in this respect is just
on a par with the artificial bashfulness of a courtesan,

Two houses, Covent Garden and Drury Lane.
Nicety, Squeamishness.
Double-entendre, Joke with a surface meaning that is innocent, and
    an under one that is not.
Vanbrugh, whose play *The Relapse* Sheridan had recast and pre-
    sented as *A Trip to Scarborough* at Drury Lane in 1777. Disap-
    proval of the " bungling reformation " had come from the critics.
    So Sheridan is hitting here at himself.
Congreve, Greatest of the Restoration dramatists. His best comedy
    was *The Way of the World*, 1700.

who increases the blush upon her cheek in an exact proportion to the diminution of her modesty.

Dangle. Sneer can't even give the public a good word! But what have we here?—This seems a very odd——

Sneer. Oh, that's a comedy, on a very new plan; replete with wit and mirth, yet of a most serious moral! You see it is called *The Reformed House-breaker*; where, by the mere force of humour, house-breaking is put into so ridiculous a light, that if the piece has its proper run, I have no doubt but that bolts and bars will be entirely useless by the end of the season.

Dangle. Egad, this is new indeed!

Sneer. Yes; it is written by a particular friend of mine, who has discovered that the follies and foibles of society are subjects unworthy the notice of the comic muse, who should be taught to stoop only at the greater vices and blacker crimes of humanity—gibbeting capital offences in five acts, and pillorying petty larcenies in two.—In short, his idea is to dramatize the penal laws, and make the stage a court of ease to the Old Bailey.

Dangle. It is truly moral.

(*Re-enter Servant.*)

Servant. Sir Fretful Plagiary, sir.

Dangle. Beg him to walk up.—(*Exit Servant.*) Now, Mrs. Dangle, Sir Fretful Plagiary is an author to your own taste.

Mrs. Dangle. I confess he is a favourite of mine, because everybody else abuses him.

Sneer. Very much to the credit of your charity, madam, if not of your judgment.

Dangle. But, egad, he allows no merit to any author but himself, that's the truth on't—though he's my friend.

Court of ease to the Old Bailey, Relief court to the London Central Criminal Court. *Plagiary*, "Copy-cat."

Sneer. Never.—He is as envious as an old maid verging on the desperation of six-and-thirty ; and then the insidious humility with which he seduces you to give a free opinion on any of his works, can be exceeded only by the petulant arrogance with which he is sure to reject your observations.

Dangle. Very true, egad—though he's my friend.

Sneer. Then his affected contempt of all newspaper strictures ; though, at the same time, he is the sorest man alive, and shrinks like scorched parchment from the fiery ordeal of true criticism : yet is he so covetous of popularity, that he had rather be abused than not mentioned at all.

Dangle. There's no denying it—though he is my friend.

Sneer. You have read the tragedy he has just finished, haven't you ?

Dangle. O yes ; he sent it to me yesterday.

Sneer. Well, and you think it execrable, don't you ?

Dangle. Why, between ourselves, egad, I must own—though he is my friend—that it is one of the most——He's here—(*aside*)—finished and most admirable perform——

Sir Fretful (*without*). Mr. Sneer with him, did you say ?

(*Enter Sir Fretful Plagiary.*)

Dangle. Ah, my dear friend !—Egad, we were just speaking of your tragedy.—Admirable, Sir Fretful, admirable !

Sneer. You never did anything beyond it, Sir Fretful—never in your life.

Sir Fretful. You make me extremely happy ; for without a compliment, my dear Sneer, there isn't a man in the whole world whose judgment I value as I do yours and Mr. Dangle's.

Mrs. Dangle. They are only laughing at you, Sir Fretful ; for it was but just now that——

Dangle. Mrs. Dangle !—Ah, Sir Fretful, you know Mrs. Dangle.—My friend Sneer was rallying just now :—he knows how she admires you, and——

Sir Fretful. O Lord, I am sure Mr. Sneer has more taste and sincerity than to—— (*Aside*) A damned double-faced fellow !

Dangle. Yes, yes—Sneer will jest—but a better-humoured——

Sir Fretful. Oh, I know——

Dangle. He has a ready turn for ridicule—his wit costs him nothing.

Sir Fretful. No, egad—(*aside*)—or I should wonder how he came by it.

Mrs. Dangle (*aside*). Because his jest is always at the expense of his friend.

Dangle. But, Sir Fretful, have you sent your play to the managers yet ?—or can I be of any service to you ?

Sir Fretful. No, no, I thank you : I believe the piece had sufficient recommendation with it.—I thank you though.—I sent it to the manager of Covent Garden Theatre this morning.

Sneer. I should have thought now, that it might have been cast (as the actors call it) better at Drury Lane.

Sir Fretful. O Lud ! no—never send a play there while I live—hark'ee ! (*Whispers Sneer.*)

Sneer. Writes himself !—I know he does.

Sir Fretful. I say nothing—I take away from no man's merit—am hurt at no man's good fortune—I say nothing.—But this I will say—through all my knowledge of life, I have observed—that there is not a passion so strongly rooted in the human heart as envy.

Sneer. I believe you have reason for what you say, indeed.

Rallying, Teasing.
Writes himself ! Referring to Sheridan, the manager.

Sir Fretful. Besides—I can tell you it is not always so safe to leave a play in the hands of those who write themselves.

Sneer. What, they may steal from them, hey, my dear Plagiary?

Sir Fretful. Steal!—to be sure they may; and, egad, serve your best thoughts as gypsies do stolen children, disfigure them to make 'em pass for their own.

Sneer. But your present work is a sacrifice to Melpomene, and he, you know, never——

Sir Fretful. That's no security: a dexterous plagiarist may do anything. Why, sir, for aught I know, he might take out some of the best things in my tragedy, and put them into his own comedy.

Sneer. That might be done, I dare be sworn.

Sir Fretful. And then, if such a person gives you the least hint or assistance, he is devilish apt to take the merit of the whole——

Dangle. If it succeeds.

Sir Fretful. Ay, but with regard to this piece, I think I can hit that gentleman, for I can safely swear he never read it.

Sneer. I'll tell you how you may hurt him more.

Sir Fretful. How?

Sneer. Swear he wrote it.

Sir Fretful. Plague on't now, Sneer, I shall take it ill!—I believe you want to take away my character as an author.

Sneer. Then I am sure you ought to be very much obliged to me.

Sir Fretful. Hey!—sir!——

Dangle. Oh, you know, he never means what he says.

Not always so safe, Sheridan had been accused of rejecting plays sent to him, and later using the ideas, or adapting passages to his own purpose, in plays of his own.
Melpomene, Muse of Tragedy; whereas Sheridan wrote comedy.

Sir Fretful. Sincerely then—you do like the piece ?

Sneer. Wonderfully !

Sir Fretful. But come now, there must be something that you think might be mended, hey ?—Mr. Dangle, has nothing struck you ?

Dangle. Why, faith, it is but an ungracious thing, for the most part, to——

Sir Fretful. With most authors it is just so indeed ; they are in general strangely tenacious ! But, for my part, I am never so well pleased as when a judicious critic points out any defect to me ; for what is the purpose of showing a work to a friend, if you don't mean to profit by his opinion ?

Sneer. Very true.—Why then, though I seriously admire the piece upon the whole, yet there is one small objection, which, if you will give me leave, I'll mention.

Sir Fretful. Sir, you can't oblige me more.

Sneer. I think it wants incident.

Sir Fretful. Good God ! you surprise me !—wants incident ?

Sneer. Yes ; I own I think the incidents are too few.

Sir Fretful. Good God ! Believe me, Mr. Sneer, there is no person for whose judgment I have a more implicit deference ; but I protest to you, Mr. Sneer, I am only apprehensive that the incidents are too crowded.—My dear Dangle, how does it strike you ?

Dangle. Really I can't agree with my friend Sneer. I think the plot quite sufficient ; and the four first acts by many degrees the best I ever read or saw in my life. If I might venture to suggest anything, it is that the interest rather falls off in the fifth.

Sir Fretful. Rises, I believe you mean, sir.

Dangle. No, I don't, upon my word.

Sir Fretful. Yes, yes, you do, upon my soul !—it certainly don't fall off, I assure you.—No, no ; it don't fall off.

Dangle. Now, Mrs. Dangle, didn't you say it struck you in the same light ?

Mrs. Dangle. No, indeed, I did not—I did not see a fault in any part of the play, from the beginning to the end.

Sir Fretful. Upon my soul, the women are the best judges after all !

Mrs. Dangle. Or, if I made any objection, I am sure it was to nothing in the piece, but that I was afraid it was, on the whole, a little too long.

Sir Fretful. Pray, madam, do you speak as to duration of time ; or do you mean that the story is tediously spun out ?

Mrs. Dangle. O lud ! no.—I speak only with reference to the usual length of acting plays.

Sir Fretful. Then I am very happy—very happy indeed—because the play is a short play, a remarkably short play. I should not venture to differ with a lady on a point of taste ; but, on these occasions, the watch, you know, is the critic.

Mrs. Dangle. Then I suppose it must have been Mr. Dangle's drawling manner of reading it to me.

Sir Fretful. Oh, if Mr. Dangle read it, that's quite another affair !—But I assure you, Mrs. Dangle, the first evening you can spare me three hours and a half, I'll undertake to read you the whole from beginning to end, with the prologue and epilogue, and allow time for the music between the acts.

Mrs. Dangle. I hope to see it on the stage next.

Dangle. Well, Sir Fretful, I wish you may be able to get rid as easily of the newspaper criticisms as you do of ours.

Sir Fretful. The newspapers ! Sir, they are the most villainous—licentious—abominable—infernal—— Not that I ever read them—no—I make it a rule never to look into a newspaper.

Dangle. You are quite right ; for it certainly must

hurt an author of delicate feelings to see the liberties they take.

Sir Fretful. No, quite the contrary! their abuse is, in fact, the best panegyric—I like it of all things. An author's reputation is only in danger from their support.

Sneer. Why, that's true—and that attack, now, on you the other day——

Sir Fretful. What? where?

Dangle. Ay, you mean in a paper of Thursday: it was completely ill-natured, to be sure.

Sir Fretful. Oh, so much the better.—Ha! ha! ha! I wouldn't have it otherwise.

Dangle. Certainly it is only to be laughed at; for——

Sir Fretful. You don't happen to recollect what the fellow said, do you?

Sneer. Pray, Dangle—Sir Fretful seems a little anxious——

Sir Fretful. O lud, no!—anxious!—not I,—not the least.—I—but one may as well hear, you know.

Dangle. Sneer, do you recollect?—(*Aside to Sneer.*) Make out something.

Sneer (*aside to Dangle*). I will.—(*Aloud.*) Yes, yes, I remember perfectly.

Sir Fretful. Well, and pray now—not that it signifies—what might the gentleman say?

Sneer. Why, he roundly asserts that you have not the slightest invention or original genius whatever; though you are the greatest traducer of all other authors living.

Sir Fretful. Ha! ha! ha!—very good!

Sneer. That as to comedy, you have not one idea of your own, he believes, even in your commonplace-book—where stray jokes and pilfered witticisms are kept with as much method as the ledger of the lost and stolen office.

Commonplace-book, A book in which one enters wise sayings for future reference.

Sir Fretful. Ha! ha! ha!—very pleasant!

Sneer. Nay, that you are so unlucky as not to have the skill even to steal with taste :—but that you glean from the refuse of obscure volumes, where more judicious plagiarists have been before you ; so that the body of your work is a composition of dregs and sediments—like a bad tavern's worst wine.

Sir Fretful. Ha! ha!

Sneer. In your more serious efforts, he says, your bombast would be less intolerable, if the thoughts were ever suited to the expression ; but the homeliness of the sentiment stares through the fantastic encumbrance of its fine language, like a clown in one of the new uniforms!

Sir Fretful. Ha! ha!

Sneer. That your occasional tropes and flowers suit the general coarseness of your style, as tambour sprigs would a ground of linsey-woolsey ; while your imitations of Shakespeare resemble the mimicry of Falstaff's page, and are about as near the standard of the original.

Sir Fretful. Ha!

Sneer. In short, that even the finest passages you steal are of no service to you ; for the poverty of your own language prevents their assimilating ; so that they lie on the surface like lumps of marl on a barren moor, encumbering what it is not in their power to fertilize!

Sir Fretful (*after great agitation*). Now, another person would be vexed at this.

Sneer. Oh! but I wouldn't have told you—only to divert you.

Sir Fretful. I know it—I am diverted.—Ha! ha! ha!—not the least invention!—Ha! ha! ha!—very good!—very good!

As tambour sprigs, etc., As fine embroidery would match a coarse material. (*Sprigs* of flowers worked in embroidery on a *tambour* frame.)   *Falstaff's page,* See 2 *Henry IV.*, II. ii.

Sneer. Yes—no genius ! ha ! ha ! ha !

Dangle. A severe rogue ! ha ! ha ! ha ! But you are quite right, Sir Fretful, never to read such nonsense.

Sir Fretful. To be sure—for if there is anything to one's praise, it is a foolish vanity to be gratified at it ; and if it is abuse,—why, one is always sure to hear of it from one damned good-natured friend or another !

(*Enter Servant.*)

Servant. Sir, there is an Italian gentleman, with a French interpreter, and three young ladies, and a dozen musicians, who say they are sent by Lady Rondeau and Mrs. Fugue.

Dangle. Gadso ! they come by appointment !— Dear Mrs. Dangle, do let them know I'll see them directly.

Mrs. Dangle. You know, Mr. Dangle, I shan't understand a word they say.

Dangle. But you hear there's an interpreter.

Mrs. Dangle. Well, I'll try to endure their complaisance till you come.   (*Exit.*)

Servant. And Mr. Puff, sir, has sent word that the last rehearsal is to be this morning, and that he'll call on you presently.

Dangle. That's true—I shall certainly be at home. —(*Exit Servant.*) Now, Sir Fretful, if you have a mind to have justice done you in the way of answer, egad, Mr. Puff's your man.

Sir Fretful. Pshaw ! Sir, why should I wish to have it answered, when I tell you I am pleased at it ?

Dangle. True, I had forgot that. But I hope you are not fretted at what Mr. Sneer——

Sir Fretful. Zounds ! no, Mr. Dangle ; don't I tell you these things never fret me in the least ?

Dangle. Nay, I only thought——

Complaisance, Fussy politeness.

253

Sir Fretful. And let me tell you, Mr. Dangle, 'tis damned affronting in you to suppose that I am hurt when I tell you I am not.

Sneer. But why so warm, Sir Fretful ?

Sir Fretful. Gad's life ! Mr. Sneer, you are as absurd as Dangle : how often must I repeat it to you, that nothing can vex me but your supposing it possible for me to mind the damned nonsense you have been repeating to me !—and let me tell you, if you continue to believe this, you must mean to insult me, gentlemen—and then, your disrespect will affect me no more than the newspaper criticisms—and I shall treat it with exactly the same calm indifference and philosophic contempt—and so your servant.   (*Exit.*)

Sneer. Ha ! ha ! ha ! poor Sir Fretful ! Now will he go and vent his philosophy in anonymous abuse of all modern critics and authors.—But, Dangle, you must get your friend Puff to take me to the rehearsal of his tragedy.

Dangle. I'll answer for't, he'll thank you for desiring it. But come and help me to judge of this musical family : they are recommended by people of consequence, I assure you.

Sneer. I am at your disposal the whole morning : —but I thought you had been a decided critic in music as well as in literature.

Dangle. So I am—but I have a bad ear. I'faith, Sneer, though, I am afraid we were a little too severe on Sir Fretful—though he is my friend.

Sneer. Why, 'tis certain, that unnecessarily to mortify the vanity of any writer is a cruelty which mere dullness never can deserve ; but where a base and personal malignity usurps the place of literary emulation, the aggressor deserves neither quarter nor pity.

Dangle. That's true, egad !—though he's my friend !

SCENE II.　*A drawing-room, harpsichord, etc.*

(*Italian family, French interpreter, Mrs. Dangle and
　　Servants discovered.*)

Interpreter. Je dis, madame, j'ai l'honneur to introduce et de vous demander votre protection pour le
signor Pasticcio Ritornello et pour sa charmante
famille.

Signor Pasticcio. Ah! vosignoria, noi vi preghiamo
di favoritevi colla vostra protezione.

First Signora. Vosignoria fatevi questi grazie.

Second Signora. Si, signora.

Interpreter. Madame—me interpret.—C'est à dire—
in English—qu'ils vous prient de leur faire l'honneur——

Mrs. Dangle. I say again, gentleman, I don't
understand a word you say.

Signor Pasticcio. Questo signore spiegherò——

Interpreter. Oui—me interpret.—Nous avons les
lettres de recommendation pour monsieur Dangle
de——

Mrs. Dangle. Upon my word, sir, I don't understand you.

Signor Pasticcio. La contessa Rondeau è nostra
padrona.

Third Signora. Si, padre, et miladi Fugue.

Interpreter. O!—me interpret.—Madame, ils disent

Pasticcio, An opera made up of a patchwork of several operas by
　　different composers.　A potpourri; pastiche.
Ritornello, A musical passage as a prelude or refrain.
Ah! vosignoria . . . protezione, Ah! my lady, we pray you to
　　favour us with your protection.
Vosignoria . . . grazie, My lady, do us these favours.
Si, signora, Yes, madam.
Questo, etc., This gentleman will explain.
La contessa, etc., Countess Rondeau is our patroness.
Si, padre, etc., Yes, father, and Lady Fugue.

—in English—qu'ils ont l'honneur d'être protégés de ces dames.—You understand ?

Mrs. Dangle. No, sir,—no understand !

              (*Enter Dangle and Sneer.*)

Interpreter. Ah, voici monsieur Dangle !

All Italians. Ah ! signor Dangle !

Mrs. Dangle. Mr. Dangle, here are two very civil gentlemen trying to make themselves understood, and I don't know which is the interpreter.

Dangle. Eh, bien !

(*The Interpreter and Signor Pasticcio here speak at the same time.*)

Interpreter. Monsieur Dangle, le grand bruit de vos talents pour la critique, et de votre intérêt avec messieurs les directeurs à tous les théâtres——

Signor Pasticcio. Vosignoria siete si famoso par la vostra conoscenza, e vostra interessa colla le direttore da——

Dangle. Egad, I think the interpreter is the hardest to be understood of the two !

Sneer. Why, I thought, Dangle, you had been an admirable linguist !

Dangle. So I am, if they would not talk so damned fast.

Sneer. Well, I'll explain that—the less time we lose in hearing them the better—for that, I suppose, is what they are brought here for.

(*Sneer speaks to Signor Pasticcio—they sing trios, etc., Dangle beating out of time.*)

        (*Enter Servant and whispers Dangle.*)

Dangle. Show him up.—(*Exit Servant.*)   Bravo ! admirable ! bravissimo ! admirablissimo !—Ah ! Sneer, where will you find voices such as these in England ?

Sneer. Not easily.

Dangle. But Puff is coming.—Signor and little

Vosignoria, etc., The Italian for the French that has just been spoken.

signoras obligatissimo !—Sposa signora Danglena.—
Mrs. Dangle, shall I beg you to offer them some
refreshments, and take their address in the next room.

*(Exit Mrs. Dangle with Signor Pasticcio, Signore
  Pasticcio, Musicians, and Interpreter, ceremoniously.)*

(Re-enter Servant.)

Servant. Mr. Puff, sir. *(Exit.)*

(Enter Puff.)

Dangle. My dear Puff.

Puff. My dear Dangle, how is it with you ?

Dangle. Mr. Sneer, give me leave to introduce Mr.
Puff to you.

Puff. Mr. Sneer is this ?—Sir, he is a gentleman
whom I have long panted for the honour of knowing
—a gentleman whose critical talents and transcendent
judgment——

Sneer. Dear sir——

Dangle. Nay, don't be modest, Sneer ; my friend
Puff only talks to you in the style of his profession.

Sneer. His profession !

Puff. Yes, sir ; I make no secret of the trade I
follow : among friends and brother authors, Dangle
knows I love to be frank on the subject, and to
advertise myself *viva voce.*—I am, sir, a practitioner
in panegyric, or, to speak more plainly, a professor of
the art of puffing, at your service—or anybody else's.

Sneer. Sir, you are very obliging !—I believe, Mr.
Puff, I have often admired your talents in the daily
prints.

Puff. Yes, sir, I flatter myself I do as much business
in that way as any six of the fraternity in town.—
Devilish hard work all the summer, friend Dangle,—
never worked harder ! But, hark'ee,—the winter
managers were a little sore, I believe.

Dangle. No ; I believe they took it all in good part.

Obligatissimo, Your very humble servant.
Sposa, My wife. *Prints,* Newspapers.

Puff. Ay! then that must have been affectation in them; for, egad, there were some of the attacks which there was no laughing at!

Sneer. Ay, the humorous ones.—But I should think, Mr. Puff, that authors would in general be able to do this sort of work for themselves.

Puff. Why, yes—but in a clumsy way. Besides, we look on that as an encroachment, and so take the opposite side. I dare say, now, you conceive half the very civil paragraphs and advertisements you see to be written by the parties concerned, or their friends? No such thing: nine out of ten manufacturered by me in the way of business.

Sneer. Indeed!

Puff. Even the auctioneers now—the auctioneers, I say—though the rogues have lately got some credit for their language—not an article of the merit theirs; take them out of their pulpits, and they are as dull as catalogues!—No, sir; 'twas I first enriched their style—'twas I first taught them to crowd their advertisements with panegyrical superlatives, each epithet rising above the other, like the bidders in their own auction-rooms! From me they learned to inlay their phraseology with variegated chips of exotic metaphor: by me too their inventive faculties were called forth:—yes, sir, by me they were instructed to clothe ideal walls with gratuitous fruits—to insinuate obsequious rivulets into visionary groves—to teach courteous shrubs to nod their approbation of the grateful soil; or on emergencies to raise upstart oaks, where there never had been an acorn: to create a delightful vicinage without the assistance of a neighbour; or fix the temple of Hygeia in the fens of Lincolnshire!

Gratuitous, Freely given (because non-existent).
Vicinage, Neighbourhood.
Fens, Then undrained, and notoriously unhealthy. Puff's whole
    speech is a skit on how house agents praise the property and land
    they have to sell.

Dangle. I am sure you have done them infinite service; for now, when a gentleman is ruined, he parts with his house with some credit.

Sneer. Service! if they had any gratitude, they would erect a statue to him; they would figure him as a presiding Mercury, the god of traffic and fiction, with a hammer in his hand instead of a caduceus.— But pray, Mr. Puff, what first put you on exercising your talents in this way?

Puff. Egad, sir, sheer necessity!—the proper parent of an art so nearly allied to invention. You must know, Mr. Sneer, that from the first time I tried my hand at an advertisement, my success was such, that for some time after I led a most extraordinary life indeed!

Sneer. How, pray?

Puff. Sir, I supported myself two years entirely by my misfortunes.

Sneer. By your misfortunes!

Puff. Yes, sir, assisted by long sickness, and other occasional disorders; and a very comfortable living I had of it.

Sneer. From sickness and misfortune! You practised as a doctor and an attorney at once?

Puff. No, egad; both maladies and miseries were my own.

Sneer. Hey! what the plague!

Dangle. 'Tis true, i'faith.

Puff. Hark'ee!—By advertisements—*To the charitable and humane!* and *To those whom Providence hath blessed with affluence.*

Sneer. Oh, I understand you.

Puff. And, in truth, I deserved what I got; for I suppose never man went through such a series of

---

Mercury, Latin god of commerce (*traffic*), and of eloquence (*fiction*).
Hammer, Auctioneer's hammer.
Caduceus, The staff of Mercury, as messenger of the gods, of olive wood, with twined serpents.

calamities in the same space of time. Sir, I was five times made a bankrupt, and reduced from a state of affluence, by a train of unavoidable misfortunes : then, sir, though a very industrious tradesman, I was twice burned out, and lost my little all both times : I lived upon those fires a month. I soon after was confined by a most excruciating disorder, and lost the use of my limbs : that told very well ; for I had the case strongly attested, and went about to collect the subscriptions myself.

Dangle. Egad, I believe that was when you first called on me.

Puff. In November last ?—O no ; I was at that time a close prisoner in the Marshalsea, for a debt benevolently contracted to serve a friend. I was afterwards twice tapped for a dropsy, which declined into a very profitable consumption. I was then reduced to—O no—then, I became a widow with six helpless children, after having had eleven husbands pressed, and without money to get me into an hospital !

Sneer. And you bore all with patience, I make no doubt ?

Puff. Why, yes ; though I made some occasional attempts at *felo de se* ; but as I did not find those rash actions answer, I left off killing myself very soon. Well, sir, at last, what with bankruptcies, fires, gouts, dropsies, imprisonments, and other valuable calamities, having got together a pretty handsome sum, I determined to quit a business which had always gone rather against my conscience, and in a more liberal way still to indulge my talents for fiction and embellishments, through my favourite channels of diurnal communication—and so, sir, you have my history.

Sneer. Most obligingly communicative indeed ! and your confession, if published, might certainly serve the

---

Marshalsea, Debtors' prison (in Southwark). Abolished, 1849.
Pressed, Forced to join the navy.　　　*Felo de se*, Suicide.

cause of true charity, by rescuing the most useful channels of appeal to benevolence from the cant of imposition. But surely, Mr. Puff, there is no great mystery in your present profession ?

Puff. Mystery, sir ! I will take upon me to say the matter was never scientifically treated nor reduced to rule before.

Sneer. Reduced to rule !

Puff. O lud, sir, you are very ignorant, I am afraid ! —Yes, sir, puffing is of various sorts ; the principal are, the puff direct, the puff preliminary, the puff collateral, and the puff collusive, and the puff oblique, or puff by implication. These all assume, as circumstances require, the various forms of Letter to the Editor, Occasional Anecdote, Impartial Critique, Observation from Correspondent, or Advertisement from the Party.

Sneer. The puff direct, I can conceive——

Puff. O yes, that's simple enough ! For instance, —a new comedy or farce is to be produced at one of the theatres (though, by-the-bye, they don't bring out half what they ought to do)—the author, suppose Mr. Smatter, or Mr. Dapper, or any particular friend of mine—very well ; the day before it is to be performed, I write an account of the manner in which it was received ; I have the plot from the author, and only add — " characters strongly drawn — highly coloured—hand of a master—fund of genuine humour —mine of invention—neat dialogue—Attic salt." Then for the performance—" Mr. Dodd was astonishingly great in the character of Sir Harry. That universal and judicious actor, Mr. Palmer, perhaps never appeared to more advantage than in the colonel ;— but it is not in the power of language to do justice

Attic salt, Pointed, neat wit.
Mr. Dodd, Creator of Sir Benjamin Backbite in *The School for Scandal*, is Dangle in this play. So, *Mr. Palmer* (Joseph Surface) is Sneer, and *Mr. King* (Sir Peter Teazle) is Puff himself. This adds to the fun.

to Mr. King : indeed he more than merited those repeated bursts of applause which he drew from a most brilliant and judicious audience. As to the scenery—the miraculous powers of Mr. De Loutherbourg's pencil are universally acknowledged. In short, we are at a loss which to admire most, the unrivalled genius of the author, the great attention and liberality of the managers, the wonderful abilities of the painter, or the incredible exertions of all the performers."

Sneer. That's pretty well indeed, sir.

Puff. Oh, cool !—quite cool !—to what I sometimes do !

Sneer. And do you think there are any who are influenced by this ?

Puff. O lud, yes, sir ! the number of those who undergo the fatigue of judging for themselves is very small indeed.

Sneer. Well, sir, the puff preliminary ?

Puff. O, that, sir, does well in the form of a caution. In a matter of gallantry now—Sir Flimsy Gossamer wishes to be well with Lady Fanny F te—he applies to me—I open trenches for him with a paragraph in the *Morning Post.*—" It is recommended to the beautiful and accomplished Lady F four stars F dash E to be on her guard against that dangerous character, Sir F dash G ; who, however pleasing and insinuating his manners may be, is certainly not remarkable for the *constancy of his attachments* ! " —in italics. Here, you see, Sir Flimsy Gossamer is introduced to the particular notice of Lady Fanny, who perhaps never thought of him before—she finds herself publicly cautioned to avoid him, which naturally makes her desirous of seeing him ; the observa-

Mr. de Loutherbourg, Theatrical scene designer (1740–1812), employed by Garrick at Drury Lane. Introduced first such stage effects as running water and the moon rising. As a painter his best work is *The Destruction of the Armada.*
Morning Post, Established 1772.

tion of their acquaintance causes a pretty kind of mutual embarrassment; this produces a sort of sympathy of interest, which if Sir Flimsy is unable to improve effectually, he at least gains the credit of having their names mentioned together by a particular set, and in a particular way—which nine times out of ten is the full accomplishment of modern gallantry.

Dangle. Egad, Sneer, you will be quite an adept in the business!

Puff. Now, sir, the puff collateral is much used as an appendage to advertisements, and may take the form of anecdote.—" Yesterday, as the celebrated George Bonmot was sauntering down St. James's Street, he met the lively Lady Mary Myrtle coming out of the park :—' Good God, Lady Mary, I'm surprised to meet you in a white jacket,—for I expected never to have seen you but in a full-trimmed uniform and a light horseman's cap!'—' Heavens, George, where could you have learned that?'—' Why,' replied the wit, ' I just saw a print of you, in a new publication called the *Camp Magazine*; which, by-the-bye, is a devilish clever thing, and is sold at No. 3, on the right hand of the way, two doors from the printing-office, the corner of Ivy Lane, Paternoster Row, price only one shilling.'"

Sneer. Very ingenious indeed!

Puff. But the puff collusive is the newest of any; for it acts in the disguise of determined hostility. It is much used by bold booksellers and enterprising poets.—" An indignant correspondent observes, that the new poem called *Beelzebub's Cotillon*, or *Proserpine's Fête Champêtre*, is one of the most unjustifiable performances he ever read. The severity with which certain characters are handled is quite shocking; and as there are many descriptions in it too warmly

Beelzebub, A Philistine deity; in the New Testament, synonymous with Satan, the Devil.

coloured for female delicacy, the shameful avidity with which this piece is bought by all people of fashion is a reproach on the taste of the times, and a disgrace to the delicacy of the age." Here you see the two strongest inducements are held forth ; first that nobody ought to read it ; and, secondly, that everybody buys it : on the strength of which the publisher boldly prints the tenth edition, before he had sold ten of the first ; and then establishes it by threatening himself with the pillory, or absolutely indicting himself for *scan. mag.*

Dangle. Ha ! ha ! ha ;—'gad, I know it is so.

Puff. As to the puff oblique, or puff by implication, it is too various and extensive to be illustrated by an instance: it attracts in titles and presumes in patents; it lurks in the limitation of a subscription, and invites in the assurance of crowd and incommodation at public places ; it delights to draw forth concealed merit, with a most disinterested assiduity ; and sometimes wears a countenance of smiling censure and tender reproach. It has a wonderful memory for parliamentary debates, and will often give the whole speech of a favoured member with the most flattering accuracy. But, above all, it is a great dealer in reports and suppositions. It has the earliest intelligence of intended preferments that will reflect honour on the patrons ; and embryo promotions of modest gentlemen, who know nothing of the matter themselves. It can hint a ribbon for implied services in the air of a common report ; and with the carelessness of a casual paragraph, suggest officers into commands, to which they have no pretension but their wishes. This, sir, is the last principal class of the art of puffing—an art which I hope you will now agree with me is of the highest dignity, yielding a tablature

Scan. mag., Slander of important people. (Mediæval Latin, *scanda-lum magnatum.*)   *Patents*, Special privileges, monopolies.
Tablature, Record, picture.

of benevolence and public spirit ; befriending equally trade, gallantry, criticism, and politics : the applause of genius—the register of charity—the triumph of heroism—the self-defence of contractors—the fame of orators—and the gazette of ministers.

Sneer. Sir, I am completely a convert both to the importance and ingenuity of your profession ; and now, sir, there is but one thing which can possibly increase my respect for you, and that is, your permitting me to be present this morning at the rehearsal of your new trage——

Puff. Hush, for heaven's sake !—*My* tragedy !—Egad, Dangle, I take this very ill : you know how apprehensive I am of being known to be the author.

Dangle. I'faith I would not have told—but it's in the papers, and your name at length in the *Morning Chronicle.*

Puff. Ah ! those damned editors never can keep a secret !—Well, Mr. Sneer, no doubt you will do me great honour—I shall be infinitely happy—highly flattered——

Dangle. I believe it must be near the time—shall we go together ?

Puff. No ; it will not be yet this hour, for they are always late at that theatre ; besides, I must meet you there, for I have some little matters here to send to the papers, and a few paragraphs to scribble before I go.—(*Looking at memorandums.*) Here is *A Conscientious Baker, on the subject of the Army Bread ;* and *A Detester of visible Brickwork, in favour of the new-invented Stucco ;* both in the style of Junius, and promised for to-morrow. The Thames navigation, too, is at a stand. Misomud or Anti-shoal must go to work again directly.—Here, too, are some political

Gazette, News-provider.
The Thames navigation, etc., The correspondence relating to Thames navigation, by Misomud (" Hater-of-mud ") and Anti-shoal (" Opposer-of-sandbanks "), is held up.

memorandums—I see; ay—*To take Paul Jones, and get the Indiamen out of the Shannon—reinforce Byron—compel the Dutch to*—so!—I must do that in the evening papers, or reserve it for the *Morning Herald*; for I know that I have undertaken to-morrow, besides, to establish the unanimity of the fleet in the *Public Advertiser*, and to shoot Charles Fox in the *Morning Post.*—So, egad, I ha'n't a moment to lose!

    Dangle. Well, we'll meet in the Green Room.

                        (Exeunt severally.)

Paul Jones, etc., During the War of American Independence, Captain Paul Jones, an American commander, took some converted East India Company ships from the Shannon and sailed towards Scotland, 1778. The following year he captured two British men-of-war off Flamborough Head.

Byron, Vice-admiral ("Foul-weather Jack"), and grandfather of the poet. In this year, 1779, he fought the French indecisively off Grenada, Windward Islands.

Compel the Dutch to, The English Government demanded that the Dutch should not receive Paul Jones and his prizes. Jones was sent away, and sold his captures to the French.

Evening papers, Then only additional issues of the morning papers.

Morning Herald, A Tory paper.

Public Advertiser, In which the Letters of Junius had appeared.

Charles Fox, The Whig statesman (1749–1806), who sympathized with the American colonists, and was anathema to the Tories.

Green Room, Common-room for actors at Drury Lane.

ACT II

SCENE I. *The Theatre.*

(*Enter Dangle, Puff, and Sneer, as before the Curtain.*)

Puff. No, no, sir ; what Shakespeare says of actors may be better applied to the purpose of plays ; they ought to be " the abstract and brief chronicles of the time." Therefore when history, and particularly the history of our own country, furnishes anything like a case in point, to the time in which an author writes, if he knows his own interest, he will take advantage of it ; so, sir, I call my tragedy *The Spanish Armada,* and have laid the scene before Tilbury Fort.

Sneer. A most happy thought, certainly !

Dangle. Egad it was—I told you so. But pray now, I don't understand how you have contrived to introduce any love into it.

Puff. Love ! oh, nothing so easy ! for it is a received point among poets, that where history gives you a good heroic outline for a play, you may fill up with a little love at your own discretion : in doing which, nine times out of ten, you only make up a deficiency in the private history of the times. Now I rather think I have done this with some success.

Sneer. No scandal about Queen Elizabeth, I hope ?

Puff. O lud ! no, no ;—I only suppose the governor of Tilbury Fort's daughter to be in love with the son of the Spanish admiral.

Sneer. Oh, is that all !

Dangle. Excellent, i'faith ! I see at once. But won't this appear rather improbable ?

Puff. To be sure it will—but what the plague ! a play is not to show occurrences that happen every day, but things just so strange, that though they never did, they might happen.

Sneer. Certainly nothing is unnatural, that is not physically impossible.

Puff. Very true—and for that matter Don Ferolo Whiskerandos, for that's the lover's name, might have been over here in the train of the Spanish Ambassador ; or Tilburina, for that is the lady's name, might have been in love with him, from having heard his character, or seen his picture ; or from knowing that he was the last man in the world she ought to be in love with—or for any other good female reason.—However, sir, the fact is, that though she is but a knight's daughter, egad ! she is in love like any princess !

Dangle. Poor young lady ! I feel for her already ! for I can conceive how great the conflict must be between her passion and her duty ; her love for her country, and her love for Don Ferolo Whiskerandos !

Puff. Oh, amazing !—her poor susceptible heart is swayed to and fro by contending passions like——
(*Enter Under Prompter.*)

Under Prompter. Sir, the scene is set, and everything is ready to begin, if you please.

Puff. Egad, then we'll lose no time.

Under Prompter. Though I believe, sir, you will find it very short, for all the performers have profited by the kind permission you granted them.

Puff. Hey ! what ?

Under Prompter. You know, sir, you gave them leave to cut out or omit whatever they found heavy or unnecessary to the plot, and I must own they have taken very liberal advantage of your indulgence.

Puff. Well, well.—They are in general very good

Don Ferolo Whiskerandos, " Lord Fierce Whiskers."

judges, and I know I am luxuriant.—Now, Mr. Hopkins, as soon as you please.

Under Prompter (to the Orchestra). Gentlemen, will you play a few bars of something, just to——

Puff. Ay, that's right ; for as we have the scenes and dresses, egad, we'll go to 't, as if it was the first night's performance ;—but you need not mind stopping between the acts.

(*Exit Under Prompter. Orchestra play. Then the bell rings.*)

Puff. So ! stand clear, gentlemen. Now you know there will be a cry of Down ! down !—Hats off !— Silence !—Then up curtain, and let us see what our painters have done for us.

SCENE II.

(*The curtain rises, and discovers Tilbury Fort. Two Sentinels asleep.*)

Dangle. Tilbury Fort !—very fine indeed !

Puff. Now, what do you think I open with ?

Sneer. Faith, I can't guess——

Puff. A clock.—Hark !—(*Clock strikes.*) I open with a clock striking, to beget an awful attention in the audience : it also marks the time, which is four o'clock in the morning, and saves a description of the rising sun, and a great deal about gilding the eastern hemisphere.

Dangle. But, pray, are the sentinels to be asleep ?

Puff. Fast as watchmen.

Sneer. Isn't that odd, though, at such an alarming crisis ?

Puff. To be sure it is,—but smaller things must give way to a striking scene at the opening ; that's a rule. And the case is, that two great men are coming to this very spot to begin the piece ; now, it is not to be supposed they would open their lips, if these fellows were watching them ; so, egad, I must either have sent them off their posts, or set them asleep.

Sneer. Oh, that accounts for it.—But tell us, who are these coming ?

Puff. These are they—Sir Walter Raleigh and Sir Christopher Hatton. You'll know Sir Christopher by his turning out his toes—famous, you know, for his dancing. I like to preserve all the little traits of character.—Now attend.

(*Enter Sir Walter Raleigh and Sir Christopher Hatton.*)
Hatton. True, gallant Raleigh !——

Dangle. What, they had been talking before ?

Puff. O yes ; all the way as they came along.—
(*To the Actors.*) I beg pardon, gentlemen, but these are particular friends of mine, whose remarks may be of great service to us.—(*To Sneer and Dangle.*) Don't mind interrupting them whenever anything strikes you.

Hatton. True, gallant Raleigh !
But oh, thou champion of thy country's fame,
There is a question which I yet must ask :
A question which I never asked before—
What mean these mighty armaments ?
This general muster ? and this throng of chiefs ?

Sneer. Pray, Mr. Puff, how came Sir Christopher Hatton never to ask that question before ?

Puff. What, before the play began ?—how the plague could he ?

Dangle. That's true, i'faith !

Puff. But you will hear what he thinks of the matter.

Raleigh, Actually in Ireland when the Armada appeared. But hurried to the south of England, and organized coast defences.
Hatton, Lord Chancellor, and a favourite of Queen Elizabeth. In 1584 he led a united prayer in the House of Commons for the Queen's safety, after the assassination of the Prince of Orange.

Hatton. Alas ! my noble friend, when I behold
Yon tented plains in martial symmetry
Arrayed ; when I count o'er yon glittering lines
Of crested warriors, where the proud steeds' neigh
And valour-breathing trumpet's shrill appeal,
Responsive vibrate on my listening ear ;
When virgin majesty herself I view,
Like her protecting Pallas, veiled in steel,
With graceful confidence exhort to arms !
When, briefly, all I hear or see bears stamp
Of martial vigilance and stern defence,
I cannot but surmise—forgive, my friend,
If the conjecture's rash—I cannot but
Surmise the state some danger apprehends !

Sneer. A very cautious conjecture that.

Puff. Yes, that's his character ; not to give an opinion but on secure grounds.—Now then.

Raleigh. O most accomplished Christopher !——

Puff. He calls him by his Christian name, to show that they are on the most familiar terms.

Raleigh. O most accomplished Christopher ! I find
Thy staunch sagacity still tracks the future,
In the fresh print of the o'ertaken past.

Puff. Figurative !

Raleigh. Thy fears are just.
Hatton. But where ? whence ? when ? and what
The danger is,—methinks I fain would learn.
Raleigh. You know, my friend, scarce two revolving
    suns,
And three revolving moons, have closed their course,
Since haughty Philip, in despite of peace,
With hostile hand hath struck at England's trade.
Hatton. I know it well.
Raleigh. Philip, you know, is proud Iberia's king !
Hatton. He is.
Raleigh. His subjects in base bigotry
And Catholic oppression held :—while we,
You know, the Protestant persuasion hold.

Hatton. We do.

Raleigh. You know, beside, his boasted armament,
The famed Armada, by the Pope baptized,
With purpose to invade these realms—

  Hatton.   Is sailed,
Our last advices so report.

Raleigh. While the Iberian admiral's chief hope,
His darling son——

  Hatton.   Ferolo Whiskerandos hight—

Raleigh. The same—by chance a prisoner hath been
  ta'en,
And in this fort of Tilbury—

  Hatton.   Is now
Confined—'tis true, and oft from yon tall turret's top
I've marked the youthful Spaniard's haughty mien—
Unconquered, though in chains.

  Raleigh.   You also know——

Dangle. **Mr.** Puff, as he knows all this, why does Sir Walter go on telling him?

Puff. But the audience are not supposed to know anything of the matter, are they?

Sneer. True; but I think you manage ill: for there certainly appears no reason why Sir Walter should be so communicative.

Puff. 'Fore Gad, now, that is one of the most ungrateful observations I ever heard!—for the less inducement he has to tell all this, the more, I think, you ought to be obliged to him; for I am sure you'd know nothing of the matter without it.

Dangle. That's very true, upon my word.

Puff. But you will find he was not going on.

Hatton. Enough, enough—'tis plain—and I no more
Am in amazement lost!

Puff. Here, now you see, Sir Christopher did not in fact ask any one question for his own information.

Sneer. No, indeed: his has been a most disinterested curiosity!

Hight, Called (archaic).

Dangle. Really, I find, we are very much obliged to them both.

Puff. To be sure you are. Now then for the commander-in-chief, the Earl of Leicester, who, you know, was no favourite but of the queen's.—We left off—*in amazement lost!*

Hatton.   Am in amazement lost.
But see where noble Leicester comes ! supreme
In honours and command.
    Raleigh.   And yet, methinks,
At such a time, so perilous, so feared,
That staff might well become an abler grasp.
    Hatton. And so, by Heaven ! think I ; but soft, he's
        here !

Puff. Ay, they envy him !

Sneer. But who are these with him ?

Puff. Oh ! very valiant knights : one is the governor of the fort, the other the master of the horse. And now, I think, you shall hear some better language : I was obliged to be plain and intelligible in the first scene, because there was so much matter of fact in it ; but now, i'faith, you have trope, figure, and metaphor, as plenty as noun-substantives.

(*Enter Earl of Leicester, Governor, Master of the Horse, Knights, etc.*)
    Leicester. How's this, my friends ! is't thus your
        new-fledged zeal
And plumed valour moulds in roosted sloth ?
Why dimly glimmers that heroic flame,
Whose reddening blaze, by patriot spirit fed,
Should be the beacon of a kindling realm ?
Can the quick current of a patriot heart
Thus stagnate in a cold and weedy converse,
Or freeze in tideless inactivity ?
No ! rather let the fountain of your valour

Leicester, A favourite of Queen Elizabeth. In 1585, his unsuccessful campaign in the Low Countries resulted in the death of his nephew, Sir Philip Sidney, at Zutphen. He was unpopular.
Trope, figure, metaphor, All mean the same thing, namely, metaphor.

Spring through each stream of enterprise,
Each petty channel of conducive daring,
Till the full torrent of your foaming wrath
O'erwhelm the flats of sunk hostility !

Puff. There it is—followed up !

Raleigh. No more !—the freshening breath of thy
　　　rebuke
Hath filled the swelling canvas of our souls !
And thus, though fate should cut the cable of
　　　　　　　　　　　　　　(All take hands.)
Our topmost hopes, in friendship's closing line
We'll grapple with despair, and if we fall,
We'll fall in glory's wake !
Leicester. There spoke old England's genius !
Then, are we all resolved ?
All. We are—all resolved.
Leicester. To conquer—or be free ?
All. To conquer, or be free.
Leicester. All ?
All. All.

Dangle. Nem. con. egad !
Puff. O yes !—where they do agree on the stage,
their unanimity is wonderful !

Leicester. Then let's embrace—and now——　*(Kneels.)*

Sneer. What the plague : is he going to pray ?
Puff. Yes ; hush !—in great emergencies, there is
nothing like a prayer.

Leicester. O mighty Mars !

Dangle. But why should he pray to Mars ?
Puff. Hush !

Leicester.　　　　　　　　If in thy homage bred,
Each point of discipline I've still observed ;
Nor but by due promotion, and the right

Nem. con., Carried without opposition. (Not the same as unani-
mous—all voting for.)　L. Nemine contradicente.

Of service, to the rank of major-general
Have risen ; assist thy votary now !

Governor. Yet do not rise—hear me !	*(Kneels.)*
Master. And me !	*(Kneels.)*
Knight. And me !	*(Kneels.)*
Raleigh. And me !	*(Kneels.)*
Hatton. And me !	**(Kneels.)**

Puff. Now pray altogether.

All. Behold thy votaries submissive beg,
That thou wilt deign to grant them all they ask ;
Assist them to accomplish all their ends,
And sanctify whatever means they use
To gain them !

Sneer. A very orthodox quintetto !

Puff. Vastly well, gentlemen !—Is that well managed or not ? Have you such a prayer as that on the stage ?

Sneer. Not exactly.

Leicester (*to Puff*). But, sir, you haven't settled how we are to get off here.

Puff. You could not go off kneeling, could you ?

Raleigh (*to Puff*). O no, sir ; impossible !

Puff. It would have a good effect, i'faith, if you could exeunt praying !—Yes, and would vary the established mode of springing off with a glance at the pit.

Sneer. Oh, never mind, so as you get them off !—I'll answer for it, the audience won't care how.

Puff. Well, then, repeat the last line standing, and go off the old way.

All. And sanctify whatever means we use
To gain them.   (*Exeunt.*)

Dangle. Bravo ! a fine exit.

Sneer. Well, really, Mr. Puff——

Puff. Stay a moment.

(*The Sentinels get up.*)

First Sentinel. All this shall to Lord Burleigh's ear.
Second Sentinel. 'Tis meet it should.   (*Exeunt.*)

Dangle. Hey!—why, I thought those fellows had been asleep?

Puff. Only a pretence; there's the art of it: they were spies of Lord Burleigh's.

Sneer. But isn't it odd they never were taken notice of, not even by the commander-in-chief?

Puff. O lud, sir! if people, who want to listen or overhear, were not always connived at in a tragedy, there would be no carrying on any plot in the world.

Dangle. That's certain!

Puff. But take care, my dear Dangle! the morning-gun is going to fire.   (*Cannon fires.*)

Dangle. Well, that will have a fine effect!

Puff. I think so, and helps to realize the scene.—(*Cannon twice.*) What the plague! three morning guns! there never is but one!—Ay, this is always the way at the theatre: give these fellows a good thing, and they never know when to have done with it.—You have no more cannon to fire?

Under Prompter (*within*). No, sir.

Puff. Now, then, for soft music.

Sneer. Pray what's that for?

Puff. It shows that Tilburina is coming;—nothing introduces you a heroine like soft music. Here she comes!

Dangle. And her confidant, I suppose?

Puff. To be sure! Here they are—inconsolable to the minuet in Ariadne!   (*Soft music.*)

(*Enter Tilburina and Confidant.*)

Tilburina. Now has the whispering breath of gentle morn
Bid Nature's voice and Nature's beauty rise;

Lord Burleigh, Elizabeth's Chief Secretary of State. An able administrator who employed many spies.
Ariadne, Opera by Handel, produced in 1733.

While orient Phœbus, with unborrowed hues,
Clothed the waked loveliness which all night slept
In heavenly drapery ! Darkness is fled.
Now flowers unfold their beauties to the sun,
And, blushing, kiss the beam he sends to wake them—
The striped carnation, and the guarded rose,
The vulgar wallflower, and smart gillyflower,
The polyanthus mean—the dapper daisy,
Sweet-william, and sweet marjoram—and all
The tribe of single and of double pinks !
Now, too, the feathered warblers tune their notes
Around, and charm the listening grove. The lark !
The linnet ! chaffinch ! bullfinch ! goldfinch ! green-
    finch !
But O, to me no joy can they afford !
Nor rose, nor wallflower, nor smart gillyflower,
Nor polyanthus mean, nor dapper daisy,
Nor William sweet, nor marjoram—nor lark,
Linnet, nor all the finches of the grove !

Puff. Your white handkerchief, madam !——
Tilburina. I thought, sir, I wasn't to use that till
heart-rending woe.
Puff. O yes, madam, at *the finches of the grove*, if
you please.

Tilburina.   Nor lark,
Linnet, nor all the finches of the grove !   (*Weeps.*)

Puff. Vastly well, madam !
Dangle. Vastly well, indeed !

Tilburina. For, O, too sure, heart-rending woe is now
The lot of wretched Tilburina !

Dangle. Oh !—'tis too much !
Sneer. Oh !—it is indeed !

Confidant. Be comforted, sweet lady, for who knows,
But Heaven has yet some milk-white day in store ?

The striped carnation, etc., Cf. Winter's Tale, IV. iv. 116-27, Perdita's
flower speech.

Tilburina. Alas ! my gentle Nora,
Thy tender youth as yet hath never mourned
Love's fatal dart.   Else wouldst thou know, that when
The soul is sunk in comfortless despair,
It cannot taste of merriment.

Dangle. That's certain !

Confidant. But see where your stern father comes :
It is not meet that he should find you thus.

Puff. Hey, what the plague !—what a cut is here !
Why, what is become of the description of her first
meeting with Don Whiskerandos—his gallant behaviour in the sea-fight—and the simile of the canary-
bird ?
Tilburina. Indeed, sir, you'll find they will not be
missed.
Puff. Very well, very well !
Tilburina (*to Confidant*). The cue, ma'am, if you
please.

Confidant. It is not meet that he should find you thus.
Tilburina. Thou counsel'st right ; but 'tis no easy
    task
For barefaced grief to wear a mask of joy.
                    (*Enter Governor.*)
Governor. How's this ! in tears ?—O Tilburina, shame !
Is this a time for maudlin tenderness,
And Cupid's baby woes ?—Hast thou not heard
That haughty Spain's pope-consecrated fleet
Advances to our shores, while England's fate,
Like a clipped guinea, trembles in the scale ?
Tilburina. Then is the crisis of my fate at hand !
I see the fleets approach—I see——

Puff. Now pray, gentlemen, mind.   This is one of
the most useful figures we tragedy writers have, by
which a hero or heroine, in consideration of their

Clipped guinea, Guinea piece reduced in value by having chips cut
    from the edges.   (Here : when weighed, it does not quite tip the
    scale.)

being often obliged to overlook things that are on the
stage, is allowed to hear and see a number of things
that are not.

Sneer. Yes ; a kind of poetical second-sight !

Puff. Yes.—Now then, madam.

Tilburina.   I see their decks
Are cleared !—I see the signal made !
The line is formed !—a cable's length asunder !
I see the frigates stationed in the rear ;
And now, I hear the thunder of the guns !
I hear the victor's shouts !—I also hear
The vanquished groan !—and now 'tis smoke—and now
I see the loose sails shiver in the wind !
I see—I see—what soon you'll see——
    Governor. Hold, daughter ! peace ! this love hath
        turned thy brain :
The Spanish fleet thou canst not see—because—
It is not yet in sight !

Dangle. Egad, though, the governor seems to make
no allowance for this poetical figure you talk of.

Puff. No, a plain matter-of-fact man ;—that's his
character.

Tilburina. But will you then refuse his offer ?
Governor. I must—I will—I can—I ought—I do.
Tilburina. Think what a noble price.
Governor. No more—you urge in vain.
Tilburina. His liberty is all he asks.

Sneer. All *who* asks, Mr. Puff ? Who is——

Puff. Egad, sir, I can't tell ! Here has been such
cutting and slashing, I don't know where they have
got to myself.

Tilburina. Indeed, sir, you will find it will connect
very well.

—And your reward secure.

Puff. Oh, if they hadn't been so devilish free with
their cutting here, you would have found that Don

Whiskerandos has been tampering for his liberty, and has persuaded Tilburina to make this proposal to her father. And now, pray observe the conciseness with which the argument is conducted. Egad, the *pro* and *con* goes as smart as hits in a fencing-match. It is indeed a sort of small-sword logic, which we have borrowed from the French.

> *Tilburina.* A retreat in Spain !
> *Governor.* Outlawry here !
> *Tilburina.* Your daughter's prayer ?
> *Governor.* Your father's oath.
> *Tilburina.* My lover !
> *Governor.* My country !
> *Tilburina.* Tilburina !
> *Governor.* England !
> *Tilburina.* A title !
> *Governor.* Honour !
> *Tilburina.* A pension !
> *Governor.* Conscience !
> *Tilburina.* A thousand pounds !
> *Governor.* Ha ! thou hast touched me nearly !

Puff. There you see—she threw in *Tilburina.* Quick, parry quarte with *England !*—Ha ! thrust in tierce *a title !*—parried by *honour.* Ha ! *a pension* over the arm !—put by by *conscience.* Then flankonade with *a thousand pounds*—and a palpable hit, egad !

> *Tilburina.* Canst thou—
> Reject the suppliant, and the daughter too ?
> *Governor.* No more ; I would not hear thee plead in
>   vain :
> The father softens—but the governor
> Is fixed !   (*Exit.*)

Dangle. Ay, that antithesis of persons is a most established figure.

Tampering, Using bribery, making secret proposals.
Parry quarte, Fourth defence position in fencing.
In tierce, With the wrist dropped, and sword on the eye level.
Flankonade, A thrust in the side.

Tilburina. 'Tis well,—hence then, fond hopes,—fond passion, hence ;
Duty, behold I am all over thine——
Whiskerandos (*without*). Where is my love—my——
Tilburina. Ha !

> (*Enter Don Ferolo Whiskerandos.*)

Whiskerandos. My beauteous enemy !——

Puff. O dear, ma'am, you must start a great deal more than that ! Consider, you had just determined in favour of duty—when, in a moment, the sound of his voice revives your passion—overthrows your resolution—destroys your obedience. If you don't express all that in your start, you do nothing at all.

Tilburina. Well, we'll try again !

Dangle. Speaking from within has always a fine effect.

Sneer. Very.

Whiskerandos. My conquering Tilburina ! How ! is't thus
We meet ? why are thy looks averse ? what means
That falling tear—that frown of boding woe ?
Ha ! now indeed I am a prisoner !
Yes, now I feel the galling weight of these
Disgraceful chains—which, cruel Tilburina !
Thy doting captive gloried in before.—
But thou art false, and Whiskerandos is undone !

Tilburina. O no ! how little dost thou know thy Tilburina !

Whiskerandos. Art thou then true ?——Begone cares, doubts, and fears,
I make you all a present to the winds ;
And if the winds reject you—try the waves.

Puff. The wind, you know, is the established receiver of all stolen sighs and cast-off griefs and apprehensions.

Tilburina. Yet must we part !—stern duty seals our doom :
Though here I call yon conscious clouds to witness,

Could I pursue the bias of my soul,
All friends, all right of parents, I'd disclaim,
And thou, my Whiskerandos, shouldst be father
And mother, brother, cousin, uncle, aunt,
And friend to me!

    Whiskerandos. O, matchless excellence! and must we
      part?
Well, if we must—we must—and in that case
The less is said the better.

    Puff. Heyday! here's a cut!—What, are all the
mutual protestations out?

    Tilburina. Now, pray, sir, don't interrupt us just
here! you ruin our feelings.

    Puff. Your feelings!—but zounds, my feelings,
ma'am!

    Sneer. No; pray don't interrupt them.

    Whiskerandos. One last embrace.
    Tilburina. Now,—farewell, for ever.
    Whiskerandos. For ever!
    Tilburina. Ay, for ever!   *[Going.)*

    Puff. 'Sdeath and fury!—Gad's life!—sir! ma-
dam! if you go out without the parting look, you
might as well dance out. Here, here!

    Confidant. But pray, sir, how am I to get off here?

    Puff. You! pshaw! what the devil signifies how
you get off! edge away at the top, or where you will
—(*Pushes the Confidant off.*) Now, ma'am, you
see——

    Tilburina. We understand you, sir.

    Tilburina. Ay, for ever.
    Both. Oh! (*Turning back, and exeunt.—Scene closes.*)

    Dangle. Oh, charming!

    Puff. Hey!—'tis pretty well, I believe; you see I
don't attempt to strike out anything new—but I
take it I improve on the established modes.

Sneer. You do, indeed! But, pray, is not Queen Elizabeth to appear?

Puff. No, not once—but she is to be talked of for ever; so that, egad, you'll think a hundred times that she is on the point of coming in.

Sneer. Hang it, I think it's a pity to keep her in the green room all the night.

Puff. O no, that always has a fine effect—it keeps up expectation.

Dangle. But are we not to have a battle?

Puff. Yes, yes, you will have a battle at last; but, egad, it's not to be by land, but by sea—and that is the only quite new thing in the piece.

Dangle. What, Drake at the Armada, hey?

Puff. Yes, i'faith—fire-ships and all; then we shall end with the procession. Hey, that will do, I think?

Sneer. No doubt on't.

Puff. Come, we must not lose time; so now for the under-plot.

Sneer. What the plague! have you another plot?

Puff. O Lord, yes; ever while you live have two plots to your tragedy. The grand point in managing them is only to let your under-plot have as little connection with your main-plot as possible.—I flatter myself nothing can be more distinct than mine; for as in my chief plot the characters are all great people, I have laid my under-plot in low life; and as the former is to end in deep distress, I make the other end as happy as a farce.—Now, Mr. Hopkins, as soon as you please.

(*Enter Under Prompter.*)

Under Prompter. Sir, the carpenter says it is impossible you can go to the park scene yet.

Puff. The park scene! No! I mean the description scene here, in the wood.

Under Prompter. Sir, the performers have cut it out.

Puff. Cut it out !

Under Prompter. Yes, sir.

Puff. What ! the whole account of Queen Elizabeth ?

Under Prompter. Yes, sir.

Puff. And the description of her horse and side-saddle ?

Under Prompter. Yes, sir.

Puff. So, so ; this is very fine indeed !—Mr. Hopkins, how the plague could you suffer this ?

Mr. Hopkins (within). Sir, indeed the pruning-knife——

Puff. The pruning-knife—zounds !—the axe ! Why, here has been such lopping and topping, I shan't have the bare trunk of my play left presently !—Very well, sir—the performers must do as they please ; but, upon my soul, I'll print it every word.

Sneer. That I would, indeed.

Puff. Very well, sir ; then we must go on. —Zounds ! I would not have parted with the description of the horse !—Well, sir, go on.—Sir, it was one of the finest and most laboured things.— Very well, sir ; let them go on.—There you had him and his accoutrements, from the bit to the crupper.— Very well, sir ; we must go to the park scene.

Under Prompter. Sir, there is the point : the carpenters say, that unless there is some business put in here before the drop, they shan't have time to clear away the fort, or sink Gravesend and the river.

Puff. So ! this is a pretty dilemma, truly !—Gentlemen, you must excuse me—these fellows will never be ready, unless I go and look after them myself.

Sneer. O dear, sir, these little things will happen.

Puff. To cut out this scene !—but I'll print it— egad, I'll print it every word !   *(Exeunt.)*

Before the drop, On the front-stage, before a drop-curtain.

ACT III

Before the Curtain.

(Enter Puff, Sneer, and Dangle.)

Puff. Well, we are ready ; now then for the justices.   *(Curtain rises.)*

(Justices, Constables, etc., discovered.)

Sneer. This, I suppose, is a sort of senate scene.

Puff. To be sure ; there has not been one yet.

Dangle. It is the under-plot, isn't it ?

Puff. Yes.—What, gentlemen, do you mean to go at once to the discovery scene ?

Justice. If you please, sir.

Puff. Oh, very well !—Hark'ee, I don't choose to say anything more ; but, i'faith, they have mangled my play in a most shocking manner.

Dangle. It's a great pity !

Puff. Now then, Mr. Justice, if you please.

Justice. Are all the volunteers without ?
Constable.   They are.
Some ten in fetters, and some twenty drunk.

Justice. Attends the youth, whose most opprobrious fame
And clear convicted crimes have stamped him soldier ?

Constable. He waits your pleasure ; eager to repay
The blest reprieve that sends him to the fields
Of glory, there to raise his branded hand
In honour's cause.

Discovery, In a play, when people who think themselves strangers discover they are related. *Cf.* " long-lost brother," " recognition."

285

Justice.   'Tis well—'tis justice arms him !
Oh ! may he now defend his country's laws
With half the spirit he has broke them all !
If 'tis your worship's pleasure, bid him enter.
    Constable. I fly, the herald of your will.   (*Exit.*)

Puff. Quick, sir.

Sneer. But, Mr. Puff, I think not only the Justice, but the clown seems to talk in as high a style as the first hero among them.

Puff. Heaven forbid they should not in a free country !—Sir, I am not for making slavish distinctions, and giving all the fine language to the upper sort of people.

Dangle. That's very noble in you, indeed.

(*Enter Justice's Lady.*)

Puff. Now, pray mark this scene.

Lady. Forgive this interruption, good my love ;
But as I just now passed a prisoner youth,
Whom rude hands hither lead, strange bodings seized
My fluttering heart, and to myself I said,
An if our Tom had lived, he'd surely been
This stripling's height !
Justice. Ha ! sure some powerful sympathy directs
Us both——
            (*Re-enter Constable with Son.*)
                    What is thy name ?
Son. My name is Tom Jenkins—*alias* have I none—
Though orphaned, and without a friend !
Justice.   Thy parents !
Son. My father dwelt in Rochester—and was,
As I have heard—a fishmonger—no more.

Puff. What, sir, do you leave out the account of your birth, parentage, and education ?

Son. They have settled it so, sir, here.

Puff. Oh ! oh !

Lady. How loudly nature whispers to my heart !
Had he no other name ?

Son.   I've seen a bill
Of his signed Tomkins, creditor.
Justice. This does indeed confirm each circumstance
The gipsy told !—Prepare !
Son.   I do.
Justice. No orphan, nor without a friend art thou—
I am thy father ; here's thy mother ; there
Thy uncle—this thy first cousin, and those
Are all your near relations !
Lady. O ecstasy of bliss !
Son. O most unlooked-for happiness !
Justice. O wonderful event !
                    (*They faint alternately in each other's arms.*)

Puff. There, you see relationship, like murder, will
out.

Justice. Now let's revive—else were this joy too much !
But come—and we'll unfold the rest within ;
And thou, my boy, must needs want rest and food.
Hence may each orphan hope, as chance directs,
To find a father—where he least expects !   (*Exeunt.*)

Puff. What do you think of that ?
Dangle. One of the finest discovery-scenes I ever
saw !—Why, this under-plot would have made a
tragedy itself.
Sneer. Ay, or a comedy either.
Puff. And keeps quite clear, you see, of the other.
        (*Enter Scenemen, taking away the seats.*)
Puff. The scene remains, does it ?
Sceneman. Yes, sir.
Puff. You are to leave one chair, you know.—But
it is always awkward in a tragedy, to have you
fellows coming in in your playhouse liveries to remove
things.—I wish that could be managed better.—So
now for my mysterious yeoman.

                (*Enter Beefeater.*)
Beefeater. Perdition catch my soul, but I do love thee.

Perdition, etc., *Cf. Othello,* III. iii. 87–88, Othello speaking to Desde-
mona.

Sneer. Haven't I heard that line before ?

Puff. No, I fancy not.—Where, pray ?

Dangle. Yes, I think there is something like it in *Othello.*

Puff. Gad ! now you put me in mind on't, I believe there is—but that's of no consequence ; all that can be said is, that two people happened to hit on the same thought—and Shakespeare made use of it first, that's all.

Sneer. Very true.

Puff. Now, sir, your soliloquy—but speak more to the pit, if you please—the soliloquy always to the pit, that's a rule.

Beefeater. Though hopeless love finds comfort in despair,
It never can endure a rival's bliss !
But soft—I am observed.   (*Exit.*)

Dangle. That's a very short soliloquy.

Puff. Yes—but it would have been a great deal longer if he had not been observed.

Sneer. A most sentimental Beefeater that, Mr. Puff !

Puff. Hark'ee—I would not have you be too sure that he is a Beefeater.

Sneer. What ! a hero in disguise ?

Puff. No matter—I only give you a hint. But now for my principal character. Here he comes—Lord Burleigh in person ! Pray, gentlemen, step this way —softly—I only hope the Lord High Treasurer is perfect—if he is but perfect !

(*Enter Lord Burleigh, goes slowly to a chair, and sits.*)

Sneer. Mr. Puff !

Puff. Hush !—Vastly well, sir ! vastly well ! a most interesting gravity !

Dangle. What ! isn't he to speak at all ?

Puff. Egad, I thought you'd ask me that !—Yes,

it is a very likely thing—that a minister in his situation, with the whole affairs of the nation on his head, should have time to talk !—But hush ! or you'll put him out.

Sneer. Put him out ! how the plague can that be, if he's not going to say anything !

Puff. There's the reason ! why, his part is to think ; and how the plague do you imagine he can think if you keep talking ?

Dangle. That's very true, upon my word !

(*Lord Burleigh comes forward, shakes his head, and exit.*)

Sneer. He is very perfect indeed ! Now, pray what did he mean by that ?

Puff. You don't take it ?

Sneer. No, I don't, upon my soul.

Puff. Why, by that shake of the head, he gave you to understand that even though they had more justice in their cause, and wisdom in their measures— yet, if there was not a greater spirit shown on the part of the people, the country would at last fall a sacrifice to the hostile ambition of the Spanish monarchy.

Sneer. The devil ! did he mean all that by shaking his head ?

Puff. Every word of it—if he shook his head as I taught him.

Dangle. Ah ! there certainly is a vast deal to be done on the stage by dumb show and expression of face ; and a judicious author knows how much he may trust to it.

Sneer. Oh, here are some of our old acquaintance.

(*Enter Sir Christopher Hatton and Sir Walter Raleigh.*)

Hatton. My niece and your niece too !
By Heaven ! there's witchcraft in 't.—He could not else
Have gained their hearts.—But see where they
    approach :

(4,535)

19

Some horrid purpose lowering on their brows !
   Raleigh. Let us withdraw and mark them.

                          (They withdraw.)

   Sneer. What is all this ?
   Puff. Ah ! here has been more pruning !—but the
fact is, these two young ladies are also in love with
Don Whiskerandos.—Now, gentlemen, this scene goes
entirely for what we call situation and stage effect,
by which the greatest applause may be obtained,
without the assistance of language, sentiment, or
character : pray mark !

              (Enter the two Nieces.)
   First Niece. Ellena here !
She is his scorn as much as I—that is
Some comfort still !

   Puff. O dear, madam, you are not to say that to
her face !—aside, ma'am, aside.—The whole scene is
to be aside.

   First Niece (*aside*). She is his scorn as much as I—
    that is
Some comfort still.
   Second Niece (*aside*). I know he prizes not Pollina's
    love ;
But Tilburina lords it o'er his heart.
   First Niece (*aside*). But see the proud destroyer of my
    peace.
Revenge is all the good I've left.
   Second Niece (*aside*). He comes, the false disturber of
    my quiet.
Now, vengeance, do thy worst,
         (Enter Don Ferolo Whiskerandos.)
   Whiskerandos. O hateful liberty—if thus in vain
I seek my Tilburina !
   Both Nieces. And ever shalt !
   (*Sir Christopher Hatton and Sir Walter Raleigh come
    forward.*)
   Hatton and Raleigh. Hold ! we will avenge you.
   Whiskerandos. Hold *you*—or see your nieces bleed !
   (*The two Nieces draw their two daggers to strike Whisker-*

*andos, the two Uncles at the instant, with their two
swords drawn, catch their two Nieces' arms, and
turn the points of their swords to Whiskerandos,
who immediately draws two daggers, and holds them
to the two Nieces' bosoms.)*

Puff. There's situation for you! there's an heroic
group!—You see the ladies can't stab Whiskerandos
—he durst not strike them, for fear of their uncles—
the uncles durst not kill him, because of their nieces
—I have them all at a deadlock!—for every one of
them is afraid to let go first.

Sneer. Why, then they must stand there for ever!

Puff. So they would, if I hadn't a very fine contrivance for't.—Now mind——

(*Enter Beefeater, with his halberd.*)

Beefeater. In the queen's name I charge you all to drop
Your swords and daggers!

(*They drop their swords and daggers.*)

Sneer. That is a contrivance indeed!

Puff. Ay,—in the queen's name.

Hatton. Come, niece!

Raleigh. Come, niece!   (*Exeunt with the two Nieces.*)

Whiskerandos. What's he, who bids us thus renounce
     our guard?

Beefeater. Thou must do more—renounce thy love!

Whiskerandos. Thou liest—base Beefeater!

Beefeater.   Ha! hell! the lie!
By Heaven thou'st roused the lion in my heart!
Off, yeoman's habit!—base disguise! off! off!

(*Discovers himself, by throwing off his upper dress, and
     appearing in a very fine waistcoat.*)

Am I a Beefeater now?
Or beams my crest as terrible as when
In Biscay's Bay I took thy captive sloop?

Puff. There, egad! he comes out to be the very
captain of the privateer who had taken Whiskerandos
prisoner—and was himself an old lover of Tilburina's.

Dangle. Admirably managed, indeed !

Puff. Now, stand out of their way.

Whiskerandos. I thank thee, Fortune, that hast thus bestowed

A weapon to chastise this insolent.

(Takes up one of the swords.)

Beefeater. I take thy challenge, Spaniard, and I thank thee,

Fortune, too !   *(Takes up the other sword.)*

Dangle. That's excellently contrived !—It seems as if the two uncles had left their swords on purpose for them.

Puff. No, egad, they could not help leaving them.

Whiskerandos. Vengeance and Tilburina !

Beefeater.   Exactly so——

(They fight—and after the usual number of wounds given, Whiskerandos falls.)

Whiskerandos. O cursèd parry !—that last thrust in tierce

Was fatal.—Captain, thou hast fencèd well !

And Whiskerandos quits this bustling scene

For all eter——

Beefeater.   ——nity—he would have added, but stern death

Cut short his being, and the noun at once !

Puff. Oh, my dear sir, you are too slow : now mind me.—Sir, shall I trouble you to die again ?

Whiskerandos. And Whiskerandos quits this bustling scene

For all eter——

Beefeater.   ——nity—he would have added.——

Puff. No, sir—that's not it—once more, if you please.

Whiskerandos. I wish, sir, you would practise this without me—I can't stay dying here all night.

Puff. Very well; we'll go over it by-and-by.—
(*Exit Whiskerandos.*) I must humour these gentlemen!

Beefeater. Farewell, brave Spaniard! and when
next——

Puff. Dear sir, you needn't speak that speech, as
the body has walked off.

Beefeater. That's true, sir—then I'll join the fleet.

Puff. If you please.—(*Exit Beefeater.*) Now, who
comes on?

(*Enter Governor, with his hair properly disordered.*)

Governor. A hemisphere of evil planets reign!
And every planet sheds contagious frenzy!
My Spanish prisoner is slain! my daughter,
Meeting the dead corse borne along, has gone
Distract!   (*A loud flourish of trumpets.*)
          But hark! I am summoned to the fort:
Perhaps the fleets have met! amazing crisis!
O Tilburina! from thy aged father's beard
Thou'st plucked the few brown hairs which time had
     left!   (*Exit.*)

Sneer. Poor gentleman!

Puff. Yes—and no one to blame but his daughter!

Dangle. And the planets——

Puff. True.—Now enter Tilburina!

Sneer. Egad, the business comes on quick here.

Puff. Yes, sir—now she comes in stark mad in
white satin.

Sneer. Why in white satin?

Puff. O Lord, sir—when a heroine goes mad, she
always goes into white satin.—Don't she, Dangle?

Dangle. Always—it's a rule.

Puff. Yes—here it is—(*Looking at the book.*)
" Enter Tilburina stark mad in white satin, and her
Confidant stark mad in white linen."

Stark mad, A burlesque of Ophelia's madness, *Hamlet*, IV.

(*Enter Tilburina and Confidant mad, according to custom.*)

Sneer. But, what the deuce, is the Confidant to be mad too ?

Puff. To be sure she is : the Confidant is always to do whatever her mistress does ; weep when she weeps, smile when she smiles, go mad when she goes mad.—Now, madam Confidant—but keep your madness in the background, if you please.

Tilburina. The wind whistles—the moon rises—see,
They have killed my squirrel in his cage !
Is this a grasshopper ?—Ha ! no ; it is my
Whiskerandos—you shall not keep him—
I know you have him in your pocket—
An oyster may be crossed in love !—Who says
A whale's a bird ?—Ha ! did you call, my love ?—
He's here ! he's there !—He's everywhere !
Ah me ! he's nowhere !   (*Exit.*)

Puff. There, do you ever desire to see anybody madder than that ?

Sneer. Never, while I live !

Puff. You observed how she mangled the metre ?

Dangle. Yes—egad, it was the first thing made me suspect she was out of her senses !

Sneer. And pray what becomes of her ?

Puff. She is gone to throw herself into the sea, to be sure—and that brings us at once to the scene of action, and so to my catastrophe—my sea fight, I mean.

Sneer. What, you bring that in at last ?

Puff. Yes, yes—you know my play is called *The Spanish Armada ;* otherwise, egad, I have no occasion for the battle at all.—Now then for my magnificence ! —my battle !—my noise !—and my procession !— You are all ready ?

Under Prompter (*within*). Yes, sir.

Puff. Is the Thames dressed ?

(Enter Thames with two attendants.)

Thames. Here I am, sir.

Puff. Very well, indeed !—see, gentlemen, there's a river for you !—This is blending a little of the masque with my tragedy—a new fancy, you know—and very useful in my case ; for as there must be a procession, I suppose Thames, and all his tributary rivers, to compliment Britannia with a fête in honour of the victory.

Sneer. But pray, who are these gentlemen in green with him ?

Puff. Those ?—those are his banks.

Sneer. His banks ?

Puff. Yes, one crowned with alders, and the other with a villa !—you take the allusions ?—But hey ! what the plague ! you have got both your banks on one side.—Here, sir, come round.—Ever while you live, Thames, go between your banks.—*(Bell rings.)* There, so ! now for't !—Stand aside, my dear friends ! —Away, Thames !   *(Exit Thames between his banks.)*

(Flourish of drums, trumpets, cannon, etc., etc. Scene changes to the sea—the fleets engage—the music plays " Britons, strike home."—Spanish fleet destroyed by fire-ships, etc.—English fleet advances— music plays " Rule Britannia."—The procession of all the English rivers, and their tributaries, with their emblems, etc., begins with Handel's water music, ends with a chorus, to the march in " Judas Maccabæus."—During this scene Puff directs and applauds everything—then)

Puff. Well, pretty well—but not quite perfect.— So, ladies and gentlemen, if you please, we'll rehearse this piece again to-morrow.   *(Curtain drops.)*

Water music, Because played on a boat following King George I.'s barge on the Thames.
Judas Maccabæus, Oratorio (1747) by Handel ; with the march, " See, the conquering hero comes."

QUESTIONS ON "THE CRITIC"

PERSONS OF THE PLAY

1. What is Mr. Dangle's foible ? Why does it irritate his wife ?

2. (a) What do we gather about Sir Fretful before he appears ? (b) How does he fulfil our expectations ?

3. Sir Fretful Plagiary was Sheridan's caricature of Richard Cumberland, the chief sentimental playwright of the time. When Cumberland and his children saw the play the latter laughed and laughed till their father muttered, " Keep still, you little dunces ! " Said Sheridan, " It was ungrateful of Cumberland to have been displeased with his children for laughing at my comedy, for when I went to see his tragedy I laughed from beginning to end." Explain the point of all this.

4. Describe the personality and manner of Mr. Puff.

5. Certain persons in the play either (a) use a characteristic phrase frequently, or (b) in one memorable remark crystallize their point of view. Give examples of both (a) and (b).

PLOT AND PRODUCTION

1. How does Act I. differ from the two other acts ? Is it comedy or farce ?

2. Briefly analyse the plot scene by scene ; and the play within the plot. Is there any unity (or pattern) about it ?

3. Sketch a set for the battle scene in *The Spanish Armada*, and say how the spectacle and the effects could be produced ; or suggest a method of simplifying it for production on a school stage.

QUESTIONS ON "THE CRITIC"

4. Make drawings of exaggerated figures and costumes for the characters in *The Spanish Armada*.

5. What effects in *The Critic* are abnormal in plays ?

WIT, SATIRE, TYPE OF PLAY

1. Comment on and illustrate the brilliance of phrase in this play. (*E.g.* "A mock Mæcenas to second-hand authors.")

2. What are the charges Sneer and Dangle pretend (Act I.) have been brought by a newspaper critic against Sir Fretful Plagiary ?

3. Put into simpler words, with modern illustrations, the five forms of *puffing*.

4. Compare eighteenth-century advertisement with that practised by radio advertisers to-day.

5. In some typical passages replace the period references to actors, theatres, newspapers, etc., by modern ones.

6. Illustrate the wit of the *aside* in this play.

7. Make your own comments on the actions and speeches in *The Spanish Armada*.

8. How does Sheridan mockingly exemplify the following points in a tragic play : (*a*) striking opening, (*b*) historical traits in the chief figures, (*c*) exposition, (*d*) exciting development, (*e*) variety by contrast in the under-plot, (*f*) "poetical second sight," (*g*) heated argument pro and con, (*h*) suspense, (*i*) dramatic silences, (*j*) madness of the heroine, (*k*) recognition (of long-lost son), (*l*) grand finale, (*m*) musical effects ?

9. How does *The Spanish Armada* represent " the true sentimental " ?

10. How does the play teach a lesson in how a play should *not* be written, acted, and produced ?

11. The usual ingredients of a farce are (*a*) impossible situations, (*b*) wildly exaggerated characters, (*c*) laughable stage " business," (*d*) broadly comic dialogue, often topical. Are they to be found in *The Critic* ?

12. The play has been called an *extravaganza*. Why ?

Printed in Great Britain by
Thomas Nelson (Printers) Ltd, London and Edinburgh